The
# PUMA
Story

Rolf-Herbert Peters

# The
# PUMA
# Story

**The remarkable turnaround of an endangered species into one of the world's hottest sportlifestyle brands**

CYAN

Authorized translation from the original German language edition published by Carl Hanser Verlag, Munich/FRG

English translation copyright © 2007 Helen E. Robertson Translations Limited

First published in English in 2007 by:

Cyan Communications Limited
5th Floor (Marshall Cavendish)
32–38 Saffron Hill
London EC1N 8FH
United Kingdom
T: +44 (0)20 7421 8145
E: sales@cyanbooks.com
www.cyanbooks.com

A CIP record for this book is available from the British Library.

ISBN-13: 978-1-905736-40-9
ISBN-10: 1-905736-40-1

Printed and bound in Great Britain by
Mackays of Chatham Limited, Chatham, Kent

# Contents

# Foreword

I first came across Puma as a sports product at the end of the 1970s in my home town of Warburg. At that time, the uniform of the nonconformist youth, which we considered ourselves to be, consisted of a parka, jeans and trainers. Although we were not as brand-aware as adolescents today, we did not buy just any old product. Coolness was important. I had treated myself to some low-priced Pumas bearing an ochre-coloured curved stripe, the "Formstrip". Trainers like these were not exactly in vogue, but were accepted as politically correct within our group. None of us associated an image with the Puma brand. We did not consider it either innovative or rebellious – attributes that today's consumers associate with Puma, after many years of power marketing. When we were at school, it is unlikely that we could have named even three teams off the top of our heads whose shirts and football boots were sponsored by Puma, even though we were dyed-in-the-wool football fans and hardly ever missed an episode of the Saturday night TV sports show *Sportschau*. Borussia Mönchengladbach perhaps: during that decade they became league champions five times sporting the Puma strip.

When I was a student in the 1980s Nike and Reebok were occupying an increasing amount of space on the sports shoe shelves. Puma had declined into insignificance. It was not until 7 July 1985, when a young Boris Becker overpowered his South-African-born opponent Kevin Curren to win Wimbledon, that the big cat started to roar again: Becker raised his racket bearing the company logo to the sky. I had followed the match on television in my halls of residence. "Puma? Are they still around?" a student friend had asked when he saw the logo on the strings. In spite of all the euphoria surrounding Becker, the brand soon disappeared off my radar again.

In the mid-1990s – I was a business journalist by that time – Puma came to my attention once more: suddenly, the wounded big cat, under its new tamer, a young Hotspur by the name of Jochen Zeitz, was getting set to leap up the stock market rankings. One of the most astonishing corporate stories of the post-war era, which saw breathtaking rises in sales and share prices, got under-way. For many managers, it became a lesson in how to be success-ful using the power of the brand alone, even in an oversaturated market. During a family holiday on the Turkish Riviera in 2006, I was surprised by how the tourist markets were overflowing with fake Puma products and how these imitations were often more popular than those of Prada or Gucci. I wondered what made Puma so desirable. The time was ripe to delve into the background of Puma's business history, which spanned a period of almost 60 years, and make it into a book: the story of the company that began with the dispute between brothers Rudolf and Adolf Dassler, and all the dramatic ups and downs that followed.

Looking back into the group's past proved to be a genuinely thrilling task. Its story is as multifaceted as a crime novel set in the business world: guerrilla marketing, back-room diplomacy, nego-tiations over big names, hostile takeovers, stock market games – everything is there. And surrounding it all was always an aura of glamour, as many stars of the sports, film and music industries have contributed to the company's prestige. Without tennis ace Serena Williams, fashion designer Jil Sander, pop diva Madonna, Formula 1 hero Michael Schumacher or Italy's World Cup-winning football team, the idea of Puma would probably not still capture our imaginations.

I would like to express my thanks to everyone at Puma and all those close to the company who spoke to me. They devoted many hours of their time for interviews. I particularly appreciated the cooperation of Puma's management, who granted me free access to all sources. Finally, I would like to thank my wife Claudia Reis-chauer, who supported my work intensively over the months as first reader and critic.

Stommeln, June 2007

# 1

## The Dassler Brothers: Rise and Fall of a Dynasty

# 1.0 In the Beginning

Tuesday, 30 June 1981, marked the dawning of a new era for German television. At 9.45 that evening, the German TV channel ARD showed the opening episode of the US TV series *Dallas*. This was German television's first soap opera. *Dallas* followed the daily lives of members of an obscenely wealthy business family which would go to any lengths to exert power over those around them. The soap had taken the US by storm three years earlier and Germany was no different – audiences were smitten and streets emptied when *Dallas* was aired. Up to 40 million viewers were glued to the set week after week, torn between fascination and disgust, as they watched an electrifying drama unfold which ran the whole gamut of big business, family feuds, hate, jealousy, intrigue, sex ... and Scotch on tap, it seemed.

The story revolved round two brothers and the ongoing battle between them. The ruthless John Ross, or "JR", would stop at nothing to get his way; Bobby, on the other hand, was the athletic but slightly naive all-American male. The brothers fought each other tooth and nail to claim their share of power and the oil market and the affairs within the family only served to exacerbate the bitter rivalry between them.

*Dallas* was the brainchild of a man called David Jacobs. But in creating the story, Jacobs could have saved himself a great deal of mental effort if he had known about Herzogenaurach. This little town in Germany's Franconia – a region in northern Bavaria – would have provided him with the perfect template for his drama, right down to a bitter feud between two brothers, Rudolf and Adolf

*The birthplace of the
Dassler brothers, ca. 1925*

Dassler. The pair opened a shoe factory together in the 1920s, swept the global market with their products and, some 25 years later, went on to become the heads of Puma and Adidas respectively – at which stage they fought each other for all they were worth. In many respects, the rise and fall of the Dassler brothers bears an uncanny resemblance to the dramatic twists and turns in *Dallas*. The story from Franconia also bore all the hallmarks of hate, envy and intrigue, but this time the setting was a glitzy sportswear business.

The spirit of enterprise and the inexhaustible energy of the two very different brothers during the founding phases of their empire are truly awe-inspiring. The Dasslers were among the very few manufacturers who managed to steer their business through the turbulent waters of the Weimar Republic and the Third Reich, and stay afloat in the postwar era. Their sports equipment companies, Adidas and Puma, reigned virtually unchallenged throughout the 1970s. Fuelled by their unstoppable drive, theirs was ultimately a business legend which spread to the distant corners of the earth, far beyond its humble beginnings in the shoemakers' town of Herzogenaurach. However, what many people didn't know or hear about were the smear campaigns that the brothers launched against each other after the feud started. Yet written records and accounts by contemporaries reveal that, through the generations, the members of the Puma and Adidas clans were quite prepared to resort to undisguised foul play and underhanded tactics to score the points they needed to reach the top of their industry's league. Each company was fixated on outdoing the other, having better sales than the other and getting a yet more famous sports personality than the other to promote their products. Psychologists would have a field day with this part of the story.

Before going on, though, we should take a step back in time to the beginning of the story of the Dassler sportswear empire. At the end of the 19th century, a boy was born in a modest little brick-built house. As a man, he would drive the development of the entire sports shoe market with unbridled ambition, breathtaking chutzpah and a healthy dose of spite. And yet his spiritual legacy was to bring his company to the brink of ruin. This was Rudolf Dassler. They called him the "puma".

## 1.1 Brothers

### *The early years: snow-white sheets, feet red with blood, a black bullet and a dark era in history*

Rudolf Dassler was born on Friday, 29 April 1898, to 29-year-old Pauline and her husband, Christoph Dassler, a weaver by trade. The couple had two older children, Maria, who was twelve, and Fritz, who was just two years old. Two years later, Pauline produced a fourth child, who was christened Adolf. The Dasslers were happy with their lot. Although the family was poor, the children were strong and healthy and that was all that really mattered. There was plenty of work available at the local B Berneis shoe factory, where Christoph Dassler earned a hard and meagre living stitching shoes. Four days before Rudolf's birth, the Spanish-American War over Cuba had broken out. Though it shook the political world, its effects left this far-flung corner of Franconia virtually untouched. All the signs suggested this would be a story of a harmonious family, with a happy ending.

The family led a simple life in their little brick-built house with its small back yard. The house was just north of the River Aurach, on a street called "Hirtengraben", and there it remains to this day, not much more than half a mile away from Puma's headquarters. It was in this house that Pauline ran a small laundry business, making this rather rotund woman the first Dassler to own a business. In the summertime, the yard was always full of dozens of white linen sheets, all fluttering in the wind. Herzogenaurach gave the children the nickname "laundry lads", because they used to help their mother deliver the washing in return for some small change. Rudolf always saved his money.

Christoph, the father, was sturdily built and sported a dark beard. He worked from morning to night in the shoe factory, starting work early when it was still dark and not returning home until late. His keenness and the interest he showed in the running of the business did not go unnoticed among his bosses. In his spare time, he busied himself with the little local history museum that he had built up in his own house and locals dubbed him "Christoph the history man".

Nowadays, the name Herzogenaurach is known to most of the world's sports professionals, but in those days, hardly a soul knew or cared about the little Franconian town. People there were contented. A few textile producers and shoemakers had set up shop around the River Aurach, continuing the local tradition of manufacturing which had started as far back as the Middle Ages and was the town's economic mainstay. In fact, Rudolf Dassler's great grandfather had started out in the textile industry at the beginning of the 19th century. The textile factories expanded to become shoe manufacturers as well, specializing in carpet slippers, and Herzogenaurach came to be known as "the Pirmasens of Franconia", Pirmasens being the capital of Germany's shoe industry at the time. The town enjoyed prosperity and culture on a provincial scale. Locals formed clubs and societies for everything imaginable. One example was a dining club called "The Bottomless Pit" ("*Der Fressclub Nimmersatt*"), another was "The Bavaria Smokers' Circle" ("*Der Rauchclub Bavaria*") and yet another "The Women's Society for the Promotion of Intellectual Pursuits" ("*Verein für die geistigen Interessen der Frau*"). The gym club came along in 1864 and the first football club followed in 1916. Indeed, it was the local sports clubs more than anything else that provided the market driver for Rudolf's future factory.

A job in the shoe trade was the obvious course for Rudolf and, at the age of 15, he began an apprenticeship with the shoe factory Vereinigte Fränkische Schuhfabriken. With his new combed-back hairstyle, young Rudolf (or Rudi, as he was known) was a handsome young man. People liked him for his winning charm, open manner and occasional brashness. He was popular and was a welcome visitor wherever he went. Some friends nicknamed him "puma" because of his natural grace and ease. He was a head-turner for Herzogenaurach's young female population and he had an eye for the girls, too, particularly the blondes. But his carefree life was short-lived. In 1914, when Rudolf was just 16, Archduke Franz Ferdinand of Austria, heir to the Austro-Hungarian throne, was assassinated in Sarajevo, and the First World War broke out. Rudolf had to don a uniform and went off to Flanders to fight. He had to wait until the war ended in 1918 before he could come home again and he came back to a very different Herzogenaurach. Nearly half of the town's shoe factories had gone bankrupt in the intervening period. But Rudolf had changed, too. The war had marked him and left its indelible imprint on his character. The idea of making shoes no longer attracted him. He wanted to branch out on his own, do his own thing and try something new. He had decided on a business career and, through a friend, he landed a job as the manager of a china factory at the age of 20. Then, when he was 22, he moved to a leather wholesale company in Nuremberg. Leather ... shoes ... sport – it all fell into place somehow. He met people here he had known from his time in the shoe business and, moreover, rediscovered his passion for footwear.

### The first shared venture

In his spare time Rudolf pursued his love of football and skiing to keep fit. His brother Adolf (or Adi) was short but athletic. Like his older brother, he was a keen footballer, and loved boxing and running. However, he was at odds with his fate. In 1914, he became an apprentice baker in a Herzogenaurach firm (Weiss, on Bamberger

*Throwing the javelin –*
*Rudolf Dassler, 1930*

Strasse). He had no enthusiasm whatsoever for his job and had to literally drag himself to work every morning. Bread left him cold – sports and sports equipment was his all-consuming passion. Nevertheless, he did manage to complete a three-year apprenticeship. Shortly afterwards, he, too, was conscripted to the Imperial German Army and went to war in 1917. His wartime service, like Rudolf's, was spent in Belgium. Returning home after two years, at the age of 19, he persuaded his mother to let him go on experimenting with his ideas for footwear in the space formerly occupied by her little laundry, which she had now given up. His father gave him the practical tips of the trade. Adolf invented a piece of footwear that was a cross between a carpet slipper and a running shoe, which he tested extensively on woodland runs. With his experience as a successful sales professional in the leather company, Rudolf took on distribution and general management. A shared venture was begun and weekends found the brothers selling their handmade products at the market in Nuremberg. The cramped laundry, with its abandoned troughs and washtubs, thus housed the nucleus of a future global company which would revolutionize the sports and fashion worlds in the years to come.

*(left to right) Adolf Dassler, Josef Waitzer, Rudolf Dassler*

The post-war period was not the best of times for entrepreneurially minded athletic spirits like the Dasslers. The first Olympic Games after the First World War were held in Antwerp in 1920, but the Germans were banned from taking part – they were seen throughout the world as responsible for the bloodbath that had been the First World War. For the Dassler brothers, this was a bitter disappointment. Like many other young people at the time, they lived, ate, slept and breathed sport, especially Adi. And in the years that followed, the mood only grew worse. The reparation payments demanded by the Allies were crippling the economy and by 1923 hyperinflation had reached Herzogenaurach and was taking its toll there. On 19 October of that year, the US dollar was worth 12 billion German marks. Just three days later it stood at 50 billion marks. For a simple loaf of bread from the bakery where Adolf had done his apprenticeship, customers now had to fork out 1.7 billion marks. Not long afterwards the first shoe factories declared bankruptcy and unemployment soared.

With morale at rock bottom, something was awoken in Rudolf Dassler that heightened his determination just as the going got worse. In the summer of 1923, he sat down with his father and Adolf round the kitchen table and the three made a momentous decision – they were going to set up their own factory. They shared a dream – to work for themselves, to prosper and to enjoy life. With no seed money available, they relied heavily on their own skills and their contacts in the initial phase. Adolf declared himself willing to turn his experimental shoemaking into professional production, while Rudolf took on the task of sorting out the financial and sales side of things. That same year, the Dassler company was officially registered. The company's founding capital? A typewriter, or so the family chronicles say.

The first year of business could not have been called a resounding success by any stretch of the imagination. At the end of it, the company showed a profit of 3,357 reichsmarks, Germany's new, post-inflation currency. However, it was a respectable sum, considering that this factory was just one among many shoe producers in this community of only 3,500 people.

There was no stopping Adi's creativity. He played football all summer long and took part in track and field events, effectively making the world of his customers his own training ground. It was no wonder he constantly came up with new ideas for sports shoes. Meanwhile, physical exercise was becoming increasingly popular in Herzogenaurach. Although there could be no mention of German athletes, newspaper coverage of the Olympic Games stimulated the locals' enthusiasm for exercise and the teams from the neighbouring towns of Nuremberg and Fürth regularly made it into the finals of the German football championship.

The summer of 1924 marked the eighth modern Olympic Games, with Paris as the host city. It was then that Rudolf and Adolf decided to take a further innovative step: they would concentrate on developing and manufacturing functional sports footwear. On 1 July, the brothers opened their sports shoe factory, Gebrüder Dassler Sportschuhfabrik Herzogenaurach. Perhaps they were inspired by the mood that has made people look back on the 1920s as a golden era. A new age was dawning. The world seemed to be spinning round faster and faster. The grim political and economic climate that people had become used to was alleviated by rapid developments in the arts, culture and science. Traditional Franconian life was being shaken to its very foundations by avant-garde ideas and liberal thinking. The good people of Herzogenaurach were horrified, for example, that British law now allowed women to divorce adulterous husbands. The barflies of nearby Nuremberg just grinned about it as they cheerily downed a few Kir Royals and puffed away at their cigarettes.

A sense of pride stole over Rudolf and Adolf Dassler when they began their first official fiscal year as directors of their new company. Rudolf, the commercial director, now wore a white shirt to the office, while Adolf, the wiry powerhouse, stuck with his favoured sportswear. Although the new venture had little capital and even fewer orders, none of those involved doubted that hard work and dedication would eventually get them where they wanted to be.

All business is local, so the saying goes, and through some hefty exploitation of connections Rudolf secured a substantial commission from the local gym club. This was the company's first major order, and Rudolf's success in obtaining it bears testimony to his skill at building networks and making the most of them, even to the point of opportunistic self-detriment. The contract stated that the company was to produce several tens of thousands of pairs of gym shoes within four months. The price of each pair would be 2.39 reichsmarks. The fantastic prices of hyperinflation were a thing of the past; the new currency had been introduced at the end of August 1924. When the old 1923 mark went out of circulation, the exchange rate was one to one trillion. Meanwhile, state gold reserves had gradually risen enough to guarantee a reasonable level of economic stability for the country.

The books show that the Dassler business now had 6,000 reichsmarks of assets. These comprised small capital goods such as second-hand typewriters, office furniture, spare parts and the warehouse stock of undelivered shoes. Just four employees appeared on the payroll. Business-minded Rudolf, always careful with money since his days as a laundry lad, now put 380 reichsmarks into expanding production capacity and hired new staff. To date, the company's range had been confined to gym shoes and running shoes, but now they added football boots to their repertoire: there were already indications by 1926–7 that football was destined to become Germany's national sport.

It soon became evident that the Dassler brothers had hit the nail on the head with their ideas for sports shoes. They knew exactly what runners on slippery tracks and footballers on wet grass needed, and started nailing studs on the soles of their footwear. They nailed them through from the outer sole and simply bent the tops over on the inner sole to keep the studs in place. Only a fakir could have come through with undamaged feet. Despite the blood, though, the shoes were a hit and just three years after the company had opened, Rudolf Dassler, accountant-in-chief, recorded a profit of 17,287.75 reichsmarks in the company accounts. The Dasslers now had a staff of twelve, and to cope with bulging order books, they had to move premises. They moved to a former shoe factory near Herzogenaurach's railway station, just at a time when the country was looking forward to the ninth summer

**Deutschlands billigster Fußballstiefel!**

ist unser Artikel 153, aus braun oder schwarz **Rindlederkern, (kein Spalt)** mit **Spannband und Streifenbeschlag,** zum Preise von

RM **5.95** für die Größe 31/34

„ **6.45** „ „ „ 35/38 Diese Preise sind **rein netto,** freibleibend, ab Fabrik, bei Kasse sofort mit 3% Skonto,

„ **6.95** „ „ „ 39/46 30 Tage 2% oder 60 Tage netto bar.

Bei Bestellungen unter 12 Paar kommt ein Kleinmengenzuschlag von 5% in Anrechnung ● Wir leisten, trotz dieses unerreicht niedrigen Preises, Garantie für Haltbarkeit der Vorderkappen ● Wollen Sie Ihren Umsatz in diesem Artikel heben, dann empfehlen wir Ihnen wenigstens einen Versuch mit diesem Fußballstiefel zu machen.

**Sportschuhfabrik Gebr. Dassler**

Herzogenaurach b/Nbg.
Alleinhersteller der bewährten Olympia-Rennschuhe „Modell Waitzer"

*The first advertisement, 1932. The Dasslers' leather football boots are described as the cheapest in Germany, though the firm is still prepared to guarantee their durability. The advertisement is aimed at retailers*

Olympic Games, due to take place in Amsterdam in 1928. Athletes from 46 different countries would be taking part in a total of 109 events and it was expected that this would appeal to Germany's sporting spirit – and deliver rocketing sales growth for the Dasslers.

Through it all, though, Rudolf managed the company's finances and business strategies in his characteristic cool manner, quashing any signs of euphoria. His diary repeatedly features sober entries of good business maxims, as if he was having trouble keeping his feet on the ground: "Work hard, and never be satisfied with anything. Businessmen who are too satisfied make no progress – a true businessman never rests on his laurels." Some people may have guessed that this veiled pessimism was not without good reason. In 1927, the mood of the country began to swing back again. The first warning signs of the imminent world economic crisis became evident, a crisis which was to culminate in 1929 in an economic crash in the industrialized world, with one business after another collapsing, leaving many families in abject poverty. In Germany, people increasingly reacted as they had always done in times of uncertainty – they hoarded their money. The very idea of buying sports shoes swiftly became sheer indulgence.

### Making connections

Still, though, the running shoes were going amazingly well. Adolf had invented cushioning to protect the ball of the foot, elasticated straps and the crepe-rubber heel. Athletes were grateful to him, there was no doubt, but Rudolf was only too aware that gratitude alone was not enough to guarantee a successful business. He needed to expand his career-building network of contacts, both business and personal. In 1928, the brothers approached Germany's national sports trainers, having identified football and track and field sports as the most promising future business areas. The national track and field trainer was a man with a crew-cut called Josef Waitzer. He was tough but kind, and had enormous influence over his athletes. They worked with Waitzer to track down the latest trends and had developed the first running shoes with him. Friends in high places had paid off, it seemed, and despite the impending economic crisis, the brothers succeeded in selling 8,000 pairs of Dassler sports shoes. Over half of all the Olympic athletes in Amsterdam put their faith in Herzogenaurach's output and this included competitors from Germany, which was now allowed to take part in the Olympics for the first time since the First World War. In a matter of weeks, a brand was born: Dassler shoes – the shoes of champions. From then on, they were considered state of the art in sports stadia. The Dasslers could not have hoped for a better advertisement to address the recreational sports sector.

The Olympic Games were a major coup for the Gebrüder Dassler Sportschuhfabrik. Business boomed and even Christoph Dassler, who had left the business, would be sitting at his sewing machine at the crack of dawn to help resolve production bottlenecks. But success also attracted imitators and it was not long before a company called Brüttig started producing football boots a mere 13 miles or so away from the Dassler factory. Rudolf Dassler, that native of self-sufficient Herzogenaurach, quickly came to realize that Germany was not the centre of the world. He decided it was time to expand and set his sights on international markets. He had his eye on the footballing nations of Hungary, Switzerland and Austria in particular, and before long, Dassler sales representatives were knocking on the doors of their sports associations, showing off the latest in Dassler sports shoe design.

It was a newspaper article that alerted Rudolf to a true megamarket – the USA. There, many millions of retail dollars were already being spent on sports shoes. What caught his attention in particular was the fact that Converse (taken over by Nike in 2003) had established its brand throughout the New World. Marquis Mills Converse was the man who had founded the Converse Rubber Shoe Company and, in 1908, had produced winterized boots, followed by canvas shoes. Converse was to produce the most successful sports shoes of all time – the "All Stars" basketball shoes. These ankle-high canvas shoes were promoted and endorsed by the American basketball player and shoe salesman Chuck Taylor, with total sales topping 600 million pairs. The cult shoes are still worn today throughout the world and are known as "Chucks".

Meanwhile, back in Herzogenaurach, the mood was increasingly one of doom and gloom. The community was once again severely affected by the new economic crisis and textile factories were closing down. By the end of 1928, there was 70 percent unemployment in the town. The townspeople went in droves to the USA or Brazil in search of a new life. A state of emergency was declared in the town, but the Dasslers held out. On 6 May that year, Rudolf married his girlfriend, Friedl, who came from the neighbouring town of Fürth, and some six months later, on 15 September 1929, they had their first son. They christened him Armin Adolf, and his Uncle Adi was godfather. Rudolf was delighted to have an heir for the family – and for the business. He continued to work hard as always, as did his brother. They defied the bad times almost like men possessed, steadfastly placing their faith in their contacts and connections as the key to their company's survival. That year, they sold 10,500 pairs of running shoes and 18,500 pairs of football boots. While the economy fell apart around him, Rudolf kept investing. Adolf developed a pristine white tennis shoe. Tennis was currently the thing among the moneyed classes. It was a burgeoning market and Rudolf was quick to recognize the trend. The leading light of the sport at the time was the Frenchwoman Suzanne Lenglen. She was much in demand by Hollywood photographers and soon became an international star. By this time, 25 people were earning their living as employees of the Gebrüder Dassler Sportschuhfabrik and Rudolf's accounts showed a healthy company turnover of 245,649 reichsmarks for 1931.

The tenth summer Olympic Games in Los Angeles in 1932, however, were not the success for the company that the Amsterdam Olympics had been four years earlier. Many German athletes simply couldn't afford the fare to take them to the Pacific Coast of the USA, but most of those who could go wore Dassler shoes. The world economic crisis meant that only about half the athletes that had participated in Amsterdam could take part in LA. Nevertheless, there were plenty of great moments in LA's Coliseum Stadium: 18 world records were set or bettered and nearly all the gold medallists were wearing shoes from Herzogenaurach. But although sales had

*Adi Dassler in uniform (right) at Josef Waitzer's wedding, 1934*

increased, Rudolf could do nothing to prevent a virtually profitless year: the costs had consumed the revenues.

## Nazi material?

When Hitler became Chancellor on 30 January 1933, business conditions once again only worsened for the Dasslers' company. Most young men joined the Storm Troopers – the "brownshirts" – and paramilitary training took over from sporting events as their main preoccupation. When the Hitler Youth needed special shoes for training purposes, the Dasslers were not immediately considered as suppliers. In addition, production of football boots plummeted by two thirds. International trade also came to a standstill. The new government of the German Reich took charge of Customs, a move which inhibited trade with Switzerland in particular. Managing Director Rudolf Dassler had planned ahead. In 1932, the Dasslers had granted the Swiss company Graf a licence to produce Dassler shoes. The deal was that they would pay the Dasslers a royalty of 9 percent of the selling price: not a lot, but it was a steady stream of income. The Dassler brothers were now expanding into children's footwear, ski boots and canvas outdoor shoes. More was to come.

While Rudolf managed the business with a steady hand, and also directed the now 70-strong staff, the self-made shoemaker Adolf found he had exhausted his creativity and was eventually forced to acknowledge that enthusiasm alone was no substitute for professional know-how in the long run. At the age of 32, he decided to go to training college in Pirmasens and train under expert craftsmen to hone his skills. The course usually took two years, but Adolf worked round the clock to accomplish it in just half the time. Nevertheless, he managed to find the time to fall head-over-heels in love with the daughter of his trainer. Her name was Katharina Maria Martz, just 15 and consequently 17 years younger than her husband-to-be. Käthe, as he called her, followed him back to Herzogenaurach, and they married two years later, in March 1934.

Another two years later, their first son, Horst Rudolf, was born, and his Uncle Rudolf was godfather. Adolf and his wife moved into the ground floor of the new, turreted family home which the brothers had built next to the company premises. Locals nicknamed it simply "the villa". Rudi and Friedl took the first floor, together with their son Armin. The grandparents, Christoph and Pauline, took the second floor.

The Dasslers were hopeful that things were finally improving, and, indeed, many others thought the same. Hitler's preparations for war, together with the expansion of industry and the infrastructure of the country, were bringing the long-awaited economic upturn. Unemployment gradually dropped from seven million to two million. National Socialist (Nazi) ideals looked upon sport as a tried and tested means of instilling discipline into the masses and this, in turn, held the promise of good business for the future. Hitler, meanwhile, wrote in *Mein Kampf*: "If our nation is blessed with six million superbly fit athletes all suffused with a supreme love of the Fatherland and trained to be ready to fight for it, a national state will create an army out of them, if necessary, in less than two years." The Nazis were bursting with confidence and their winning the bid for the 1936 Olympics led an ever increasing number of Germans to fall for their propaganda. Hitler used huge amounts of tax money to support sport and Herzogenaurach regained confidence. The Dasslers' sales shot up and in 1935 their turnover was almost 400,000 reichsmarks – 35 percent more than in the previous year. Adi took a new initiative and created his first ever poster campaign to advertise Dassler products. He also commissioned a hand-painted logo for the company. The first company slogan, though, was not particularly inspiring: "Dassler sports shoes: praised by all who try them."

The Berlin Olympic Games of 1936 became a summer's fairy-tale for many Germans, with the nation gripped by medal fever. Rudolf and Adolf Dassler, both fundamentally apolitical people, sat silent among the VIPs on the grandstand in the Berlin Olympic Stadium as the games were opened by Hitler. Adi once went on record as saying, "Sport is my politics. As for the rest, I've really got no interest in it at all." He was a salt-of-the-earth type and was on the naive side, politically speaking. Despite such assertions, however, he followed the lead of his brother Rudi, who willingly went with the spirit of the times and became a member of the NSDAP (Nazi Party) in 1933. In 1935, he also joined the Hitler Youth, acting as trainer and supplier, and wore a Nazi uniform in

*Rudolf and Adolf's father, Christoph, with grandsons Armin and Horst*

public. Rudolf was later to admit that he had voted National Socialist as a calculated bid to help his business in 1932, when over two-thirds of Herzogenaurach's conservative population were still staunch supporters of von Hindenburg, President of the Reich.

Prior to the Games, the Führer's inflammatory propaganda newspaper the *Völkischer Beobachter* (*People's Observer*) had proclaimed that "negroes" had no place in what was an "Aryan event". In 1935, the Führer had written racial segregation into the Nuremberg Laws. But Adi Dassler took no notice. With the help of Josef Waitzer, he equipped the USA's greatest black sports talent to wear running shoes of his design. This was JC or "Jesse" Owens, the "buckeye bullet" son of an Alabama share-cropper. The shoes had spikes set at an angle, cushioned heels and were super-light at just 169 grams (or approximately 6 ounces) each. Owens won three races and the long jump, on each occasion wearing Dassler shoes. But after the events, there was an uproar when Owens snubbed Hitler, refusing to salute him. Nevertheless, the Dassler brothers still returned home triumphant. Competitors wearing Dassler shoes had, between them, won seven gold, five silver and five bronze medals. Not only that, but they had broken two world records and three Olympic records. Annual sales for the Dassler shoe factory in 1936 were up by 20 percent on the previous year, bringing in 484,000 reichsmarks. For the first time, "advertising" was included as an item in the annual report, at 1.7 percent of sales. At the end of that same year, the Dassler brothers bought two spanking new vehicles for company use. And they continued to invest. The future looked secure and, in 1938, they spent 25,000 reichsmarks to expand the factory building and added a new warehouse area.

The renowned historian Joachim Fest maintained in his famous biography of Hitler that if the German leader had been assassinated at the end of 1938, hardly a soul would have hesitated to call him one of Germany's greatest statesmen, perhaps even the consummation of its history. The Dassler brothers clearly felt quite comfortable in this environment and took a "go-with-the-flow" attitude towards Nazism so that their business could continue to flourish. Rudolf clearly enjoyed the good life and this became more and more noticeable. He wore only the best, drove a huge Mercedes and used all his charismatic charm to get ahead. Adi, pale-faced, just beavered away non-stop in the background to come up with ever new technical improvements to the Dassler range. Despite the various worries for the political future, the Dassler factory gave every indication of going from strength to strength. This was particularly so after the Munich Agreement, which was signed by Hitler and the heads of government of Britain, France and Italy on the night of 29 September 1938. The deal was an attempt by the major European powers to appease the aggressor Hitler by allowing him to annexe Czechoslovakia's Sudetenland. This, in turn, opened up a new sales territory for the Dasslers, but although Rudolf seemed outwardly delighted by the idea, privately – as he revealed in his diary – he was sceptical about whether the accord would work.

Poster advertisement, 1935
The slogan reads "Dassler sports shoes: praised by all who try them"

## 1.2 No Small Affair

### *The rift: friends in high places, marital infidelity, witnesses for the prosecution and the splitting of the assets*

The brotherly relationship was harmonious for the best part of 25 years, and Rudolf and Adolf marched happily in the same direction. Together, they had withstood the ravages of inflation and brought the Gebrüder Dassler Sportschuhfabrik successfully through the most serious global economic crisis ever. Together, they had outfitted the black superstar of athletics, Jesse Owens, with their products, and at the same time exploited Hitler's system to their own business ends.

But suddenly it was all over. Contemporaries were astonished, the change seemed to come right out of the blue. The finality of the brothers' parting surprised even those closest to them. So wide was the rift that they only managed to cross it again a very few times in their lives, and then only with superhuman effort. The most that was ever achieved between the families was a temporary ceasefire. The actual cause of the schism was one of Franconia's best-kept secrets for many years. Those who knew the truth in the Catholic stronghold of Herzogenaurach did not want to talk about it.

Initially, everything seemed to be running smoothly. The year 1939, which marked the beginning of the Second World War, was initially an uneventful one in Herzogenaurach. Rudolf invested in additional company premises for 54,000 reichsmarks, and his wife gave birth to their second son, Gerd, on 11 July. Meanwhile, Adolf was happiest burying himself away in the factory and working on refining the spikes for his running shoes. The suspiciously peaceful period came to an end that summer, however, shortly before Hitler gave orders for the invasion of Poland on 1 September. Rationing was extended to shoes, which meant the Dassler's products could no longer be bought without vouchers. The brothers had to cut their production by half. Now, the Nazi troops needed boots. The Dasslers' staff levels had dropped from 110 to 55. From 1 January 1940 onwards, the production of sports shoes was banned completely. The Dasslers used their connections – including Josef Waitzer – to protest to the government. It worked, and the Reich's Ministry of Economic Affairs allowed them to produce 6,000 pairs of non-military shoes per month. Ultimately, despite a lack of raw materials, the Bavarian Ministry of the Interior and Economic Affairs got the stringent measures relaxed still further, and they were permitted to produce 10,000 pairs per month. In return, the

*The shoe factory, 1940*

Nazis demanded help with the production of "equipment to support the war effort", such as rucksacks, belts and parts for tanks, as well as an anti-tank device known as the Panzerschreck or "Tank Terrorizer". Elisabeth Cofor was a Dassler employee at the time, and she remembers how she and her female colleagues were sent off to learn soldering at a special course for women, and were then listed on the company records as "armaments workers".

Adolf was called up for military service in December 1940, but was released from duty after only three months as essential to his factory's manufacturing output. He went back to producing shoes, which he was now calling "Kampf" ("Battle") and "Blitz" ("Lightning"). In October, he requisitioned Russian prisoners-of-war to come and work in the factory because of the staff shortage.

The military authorities called up Rudolf, who had to report for duty on 1 March 1943 to Glachau in Saxony, because of the newly introduced "Total Mobilization" (a provision which allowed for the deployment of people, both military and civilian, to wherever they were needed, in the interests of the war effort). A month later, they moved him to Litzmannstadt, today's Lód, to serve in the offices of the Reich's Ministry of Finance. Contemporary accounts say that he had pretended to suffer from night blindness. On 18 January 1945, he fled from Litzmannstadt as the Russians approached. It took him a whole week to make his weary way back to Herzogenaurach, and, en route, he suffered severe frostbite, the effects of which were to handicap him for the rest of his life.

Rudolf was only half way to recovery when fate dealt him two further cruel blows. On 2 April that year, his father, Christoph, died. And three days later, the Gestapo (the Secret State Police) arrested him on the grounds of desertion because he had failed to comply with his call-up to the notorious SD (an intelligence and espionage arm of the SS) – the Nazis had not yet surrendered by that time. He was one of 27 prisoners being marched to the Dachau concentration camp, near Munich, when they were freed by American soldiers near Pappenheim, in middle Bavaria. After a short spell back at home, he fell into American hands once again. This time, they arrested him. He was taken to the American internment camp in Hammelburg (also in Bavaria) and held there for a year on account of his alleged Nazi past. During this time, he was neither formally charged nor tried, but stood accused of counter-espionage and working for the SD and the censorship authorities. Rudolf suspected that Adolf had informed on him. Thanks to the intervention of an American friend in the shoe trade, he was released again on 31 July 1946.

He evidently never got over the fact that his brother had managed to avoid wartime service and therefore been able to gain the upper hand in the running of their factory. Käthe Dassler later revealed that Rudolf had sent Adolf an angry letter from Litzmannstadt, threatening to get the government of the Reich to close down the Dassler factory. In turn, Adolf had not lifted a finger to help Rudolf during his internment in Hammelburg. In fact, it seemed that Adolf had actually been quite relieved to have his brother safely out of the way behind barbed wire.

But when prisoner 2597, Rudolf Dassler, returned home after his internment in the summer of 1946, it appeared that Adolf, too, had come under suspicion. Some two weeks earlier, the American Denazification Committee had officially classified him as a "Belasteter", someone who had actively supported the Nazi regime and benefited from it. However, intervention with the help of local politicians eventually succeeded in getting the Americans to put him into a lower category of suspect. Rudolf later openly told the Denazification Committee that Adolf, and Adolf alone, had been in support of the production of weapons at Dassler, while he had always been utterly against it, and had said so. Käthe, his sister-in-law, vehemently denied this statement and managed to get her husband reclassified as a so-called "Mitläufer", or follower, someone who had never been actively involved in Nazi activities. In the months which followed, the discord between the brothers escalated to a point where Käthe and Adolf announced that they wanted nothing further to do with Rudolf. It was only after Christmas 1947 that rumours of the rift between the two brothers began to circulate in the factory itself.

### Love moves in mysterious ways

The brothers' mutual mistrust following the end of the Nazi period was definitely not the only thing that kept the families apart, however. In fact, the split probably had its roots in something that had happened much earlier and which gave rise to the deep mistrust in the first place. Stories from their few descendants and their friends are illuminating, and if they are to be believed, the heart of the problem lay some five years back. It appears certain that Rudolf was having an affair with Adolf's wife, Käthe, at the beginning of the 1940s. It is possible that the affair began while Adolf was away from home doing

*Käthe and Friedl Dassler, 1940*

his three-month stint of military service in 1940–1. There is no written evidence of this, of course, only hearsay. However, there is now little reason to doubt that it is true. For example, the company's first bookkeeper and a prop and stay of the organization, the late Mrs Welker, knew about the affair. Indeed, she revealed as much at a private family celebration.

It is not as if Käthe was the kind of person to be averse to the idea of spontaneous flirtations, and more. She was an attractive and articulate woman. In fact, she showed that she was inclined towards impetuous amours in 1978, after her husband had died, and she fell in love with the married head of a Brazilian shoe factory. Despite her determined advances, however, the Swiss-born object of her affections rejected her. Not long after, she turned her attention to yet another shoe manufacturer. Much to the disapproval of her daughters, this man was not only considerably younger than their mother, but was also the head of Adidas Austria.

Family writings also make veiled references to the adulterous affair and the damage it caused. In the chronicle written to mark Rudolf's 70th birthday, his sons talk of the period from 1940 (sic!)

*Puma running shoes, 1948*

to 1948 as a time of bitter disappointment in the family's personal life. And when Rudolf died in 1974 and Adolf was asked to put together something in appreciation of his brother's life, Adolf's family responded with an arrogance that bordered on the cynical: "For reasons of propriety, the family of Adolf Dassler does not wish to comment on the death of Rudolf Dassler." One thing is certain, though – then, as now, a dalliance with one's sister-in-law was the worst possible thing that could happen between brothers. It would have been practically impossible to keep the affair quiet, since all the members of the Dassler family, including Käthe, worked in the family firm. All the administration and bookkeeping activities took place in one single room.

It was quite striking that the wives of the Dassler brothers, both clearly deeply wounded, energetically furthered the family split. Not even the universally respected local clergyman, Siegbert Keiling, was able to restore harmony, despite his earnest prayers for divine aid. Käthe in particular, who was known for her ruthlessness when it came to gaining an advantage, now really stirred things up, and her four daughters followed in her footsteps. A former Adidas manager, Horst Widmann, who knew Adolf's side of the family better than most, is convinced that what started out as a quarrel between the brothers turned into a quarrel between their wives in the years that followed. He maintains that the brothers themselves did return to a better understanding with each other. Time evidently healed their wounds. They called each other more and more often. Widmann also personally witnessed two meetings between them. One was in the early 1970s, when "birthday boy" Adolf Dassler was waiting for a flight with the German national football team at Frankfurt Airport, and Rudolf unexpectedly joined them. The brothers went off to the lounge of the Adidas shop in what is now Terminal A. They spent 20 minutes together, deep in conversation. On another occasion, Widmann had to drive his boss, Adolf, to the Grand Hotel – now Le Meridien

– by Nuremberg's main station. Rudolf was waiting for him, and they spent half an hour together. Adi was always insistent that his wife should know nothing of these meetings. But in the company of those close to him, Adolf would sometimes refer to Rudolf affectionately as "my dear Rudi", just as Rudolf repeatedly talked of "my dear Adi".

Throughout the whole period and even to this day, the families and their descendants have rarely referred to the story of the rift, and any mention was and is carefully couched in politically correct language. In today's officialese, a press release announcing the split might read something like: " ... because of irreconcilable differences regarding the strategic direction of the company ...". But this is only part of the truth, and, according to sources, the lesser part. Love can so easily turn to hate when it fades, a piece of wisdom as old as humanity itself. It should come as no surprise, then, to hear that Käthe is said to have later decried her former lover as "one of the *Herrenvolk*". She is supposed to have stopped using his first name, sneeringly referring to him as "the Puma". She defended her husband with fierce rage against his brother's accusations – as though she had a lot to make up for. As far as Rudolf was concerned, though, she was malice personified.

### Schism in Franconia

What happened next was what always happens when there's bad blood in a family: a vicious battle over money and possessions. After months of wrangling, the parties concerned decided at the beginning of 1948 to divide the company into two separate entities. Adolf approached matters with an almost cocky self-confidence. He got the original building and the lion's share of the manufacturing facilities. Rudi was convinced that the Gebrüder Dassler Sportschuhfabrik had no chance of survival without him. He moved into the additional factory building overlooking the River Aurach which had been acquired in 1939. His mother, Pauline, took his side. Franziska Geinzer, one-time factory worker with the Dasslers, recalls that even the most insignificant objects were divided up to the last scruple. Employees were free to choose where they wanted to work in future, and while 47 production workers remained with Adolf, 13 employees and a few freelance sales representatives went with Rudolf. The final official split of the company assets came on 21 June 1948, the day of the German currency reform.

*Standard football boots,
1952*

Adi soon started looking for a new name – there were too many negative associations with the name Gebrüder Dassler Sportschuhfabrik. He created it from "Adi", the familiar abbreviation of his first name, and the first syllable of his last name, making "Adidas". Rudolf thought his creative brother's idea was not bad, and tried out "Ru-Da" for his company. However, he couldn't convince either his family or his employees, and so, in the same year, he renamed his company Puma Rudolf Dassler Schuhfabrik. His own old nickname was a very good fit with the company's promotional message: any athlete wearing Puma shoes would acquire the qualities of the big cat itself – stamina, power, litheness and elegance.

The split between the brothers represented, for Herzogenaurach, a fate similar to that suffered by Berlin 15 years later, albeit on a smaller scale: the little town was suddenly divided. Locals began to refer to it as "the town of downcast eyes" because people only ever looked at each other's shoes. The question asked by the inhabitants of Herzogenaurach even today, is "What's your religion – Puma or Adidas?" The wall along the Aurach, dividing Rudolf's realm from Adolf's, may have only existed in the minds of the townspeople. However, the consequences of the split reverberate to this day, since Puma and Adidas control the town more than ever. And this despite the fact that not a single shoe or garment is made in Herzogenaurach any more – only the administrative headquarters remain.

## 1.3 Germany: A Summer's Fairytale

### Puma – the early years: cake and block ice, Sepp repulsed and the football studs war

Rudolf was 50 when he began his second entrepreneurial life at Puma-Schuhfabrik Rudolf Dassler. Now he had to prove himself as a researcher and developer. If the life expectancy of the time were anything to go by, he was long past the peak of his powers. He set to work once more like a man possessed. His trusty followers sometimes put in 14-hour days – even on Sundays – in the two-storey building on Würzburger Strasse. The stitching work was done on the top floor, which was also the location of the leather store, and on the ground floor were the lasting room and the accounts department, where Rudolf's wife Friedl worked. His mother Pauline continued to run the household well into old age, until her death in 1955. "We are one family," was Rudolf's rallying cry, and his staff would call out: "Father's here!" when he marched through the production room. His son Armin had to work in the company after successfully completing a shoemaker's apprenticeship in Pirmasens – he would much rather have studied electrical engineering but was not allowed to. Rudolf enjoyed a good relationship with his brother Fritz, who still lived in the family home Am Hirschgraben, making *Lederhosen* there under the "Kraxler" brand name.

Keeping the workers on the go was one of the boss's most important daily tasks. Every afternoon at about 3pm there was coffee and cake, and in summer Rudolf would have block ice placed on the window sills to cool the rooms. And when the monthly sales figures were high, he would give the team "Puma juice" – a mixture of bock beer and sparkling wine. At the same time, he also kept down the costs. Pay was modest and the boss was tight-fisted to the extreme in small things. At the end of the working day the members of the leather union would assemble in the stitching room in order to prepare for the next pay round. Laster and machinist Fritz Malke recalls an appearance by the boss: "On one occasion he stormed into the meeting room during tough wage negotiations, tossed his tail coat over the coat hook and thundered so all could hear: 'Would you like the coat off my back as well?'"

At first, the market dictated production and there were few changes to the existing customer base. Running shoes left the production hall in the first instance, followed by the one-price, sturdy leather, metal-clad "Jedermannschuhe", ordered by economic director Ludwig Erhard. And there were also the "Burschenschuhe" – simple, affordable pump-type shoes in black for youths. The leather sourced by Puma from the small town of Backnang in Baden-Württemberg was hard and the footwear not very comfortable.

In order to build business, Rudolf made an effort to build up contacts with the representatives of sports equipment companies. It was clear to him that Puma would only make progress if he managed to get them on his side against Adidas. Once a year, he convened a conference in Herzogenaurach in order to develop his network. The meeting would take place in Café Mauser (a *café*

*Company outing, 1955*

*dansant*, famous far beyond the region), for example, and the manager would give explanations and presentations and very patiently charm his audience. Moments like these, demanding the reverence and respect of the employees for their patriarch, became increasingly rare. Rudolf became more cranky and stubborn with each passing year. Whereas previously he would simply enjoy the pleasure of fishing for hours on end followed by a game of cards with his friends and business partners, now the quiet periods he spent by the water increasingly became therapeutic necessity: Rudolf had to recover from the stresses of the day. Gone were the holidays in the sunshine of Italy; Langenargen on the shores of Lake Constance was now his holiday base.

It soon became apparent that Adi, on the other side of the Aurach river, looked set to rocket ahead of him: not only did he have more technical and creative skills, he also had better relationships with public officials and athletes. The amount of time spent in the arenas was now starting to pay off doubly for him and Adidas. As early as 1950, he was selling his goods abroad. In Switzerland, the USA and Scandinavia, retailers were selling the products with the three stripes on their own account. At Puma too, however, all the signs pointed to growth. In 1950, the factory on Würzburger Strasse already had over 50 employees. The company took on its first apprentice on the commercial side. She was 16 years old and her name was Elfriede Wagner. In the first year, she was paid 45 marks a month and the wage increased by ten marks in the second year. The factory was remodelled and the accounts department moved from the ground floor to the first floor, which was also the location of the company boss's private suite. Rudolf had had a vast picture hung on the wall in the reception room: "Here the customer is king!" read the caption. Adorning the other wall was the Puma emblem: a fierce-looking predator jumping through a letter D.

## A missed opportunity

Rudolf's increasing moroseness and miserliness obscured the company leader's view of some good opportunities. In 1951, at the sports equipment trade fair in Wiesbaden, a good old friend of the firm visited the Puma stand: Josef "Sepp" Herberger. This son of a working-class family from Mannheim had formerly played football for the national side, had been training the German team since 1949 and had excellent connections right to the very top of the German football league (DFB). For reasons of long-standing allegiance – he went in and out at Puma like a member of the family – he had also ensured that some of his players ran out onto the pitch wearing his mate Rudi's Puma boots – while others, however, wore Adidas boots made by his other pal, Adi. Now he wanted to be rewarded for his commitment: he wanted 1,000 marks per month for his agency services and his development work. Rudolf Dassler looked at him – and shook his head. Payment is for goods, not for favours, was his philosophy. "I am deeply disappointed in you," he snapped, and extended his hand to bid Herberger goodbye. Herberger turned on his heel. It was the parting of the ways. The legendary trainer turned his back on Puma and went straight to Adidas. In 1954, when the German national team pulled off the "Miracle of Bern" to win the World Cup in Switzerland, not one of the players wore Puma. Just one year earlier, around half of them had opted for Puma shoes, notably the Kaiserslautern team players Horst Eckel and Werner Liebrich.

Rudolf had his first misgivings about the effects of his decision before he ever left Wiesbaden. A prisoner of his own principles, he missed the opportunity of his life when he said "No". His brother Adolf agreed to Herberger's request for a fee. It was the start of a relationship that remained intact for decades, not just between Adi Dassler and Sepp Herberger, but also between Adidas and the German national football team. Rudolf's misgivings reached their peak when Germany had beaten Hungary 3–2 in the final of the

*Billboard advertisement for Puma as outfitter of the US Olympic team*

Swiss World Cup and the nation fell down and worshipped the heroes with the three stripes on their shoes, Puma's leader started to fear that the 1,000 marks he had saved might well cost him millions of times that amount in sales in the years to come. It was not until 2006 that the near-marriage between the DFB and Adidas became shaky, thanks to a breathtaking offer from Nike: the Americans offered a sponsorship deal worth half a billion euros for eight years from 2011 onwards.

Adi Dassler later spread the popular tale that he was the inventor of the screw-in studs which had made the "Miracle of Bern" on the waterlogged pitch a possibility ("Adi, stoll' auf!") – a true publicity coup. Puma had in actual fact been experimenting with the new technology since 1948 – supported by Sepp Herberger, who at the time taught football as a lecturer at the Cologne college of physical education. In the same year, just after the company was set up, the first shoe using this system came onto the market: the "Atom". At the start of the 1952–3 football season, the first prominent players were kitted out with the "Super Atom". A billboard advertisement dating from 1954 with the headline "Germany's Football Elite" proudly displays a specialist retailer's letter, showering praise on the removable studs. And pictures from the time reveal that eight Hannover 96 players were kitted out during the German championship final on 23 May 1954, in other words, some weeks before the World Cup in July, in "Brasil" boots with screw-in studs.

The Adidas managers take a different view, of course: according to them, Adidas also tried out exchangeable stud systems in 1948 and in 1949 trialled the first patented screw-in studs for football boots on the market. It is not really important to know the whole truth of the matter. It has since emerged that developers had worked on replaceable sole grips for field sports decades earlier in England and in the USA. John T. Riddell, for example, founder of sports equipment firm Riddell Sports, already considered this possibility at Evanston High School in 1913 and used it in the 1920s without much success. It seems likely that Rudolf and Adolf Dassler jointly acquired a patent in the 1930s for their own factory and subsequently used it separately.

Puma entered the international stage once more at the Olympic Games in Helsinki in 1952, where Germany was taking part for the first time after 16 years of enforced absence. The young brand caused no sensation, even though athletes wearing Puma shoes picked up several medals. Of much greater significance for Rudolf Dassler were the new contacts he was able to form with foreign teams and associations, helping him to ensure that his limping export trade could slowly gather momentum.

Thanks to a sizeable piece of luck, Puma even acquired its first superstar in 1954: the sprinter Heinz Fütterer. Two weeks after the football World Cup, the young athlete from the south German village of Elchesheim-Illingen won the 100-metre and 200-metre sprints at the European Championships, which were also being held in Bern. Puma's commercial director, a former fellow prisoner of Rudolf's in the Hammelburg internment camp, had established contact with Fütterer. Dassler believed in the young athlete's talent and sent Fütterer a brand new pair of spikes made of smooth, dark kangaroo leather. In Paris in 1953, when he won a 60-metre sprint against four black rivals, the French sports paper *L'Equipe* wrote: "The German shot down the hall like a bolt of white lightning." And so Fütterer's nickname of "White Lightning" was born. He later made a career at Puma in sales and as chief lobbyist for track and field.

*Puma star Heinz Fütterer, 1959*

## The War of the Roses

Successes like these were never an unalloyed pleasure for Rudolf Dassler. The cold war was still very much on. As long as his brother basked in more limelight than he did, he could know no peace. Adolf was no different. More and more often, their lawyers squared up in court because one feuding brother could not bear to see the other launch an innovation, and laid claim to it himself. Adi later maintained that his brother had copied his products with cool effrontery. "If I had made a hole in Rudolf every time I had to prod him and say: 'Hey, that was my invention', he would look like a piece of Swiss cheese by now." Rudolf could probably have said the same thing.

The wives also made their contribution to the disagreements. Käthe in particular lost no opportunity to make snide remarks about the unbeloved relatives on the other side of the Aurach river. Business partners who dared to get too close to the rival company or came to appointments in the wrong clothing were "excommunicated". Fear of espionage from the other camp reached neurotic proportions. At trade fairs in Wiesbaden or Cologne, the directors would have someone check their rooms for bugging devices before they went in. Managers were much more delighted by a downfall in the rival camp than they were by their own company's achievements.

The Dassler brothers honed their underhandedness to perfection solely as a way of getting at each other. In 1956, at a track and field event, just as "White Lightning" Heinz Fütterer was tying his shoelaces, Adi Dassler suddenly turned up at his bench wearing a brown trench coat. Fütterer, who was under contract to Puma, appeared honoured. Dassler squinted at him through his horn-rimmed glasses and held a pair of shoes under the sprinter's nose. Would he be interested in trying out the latest development from the House of Adidas? Only in an unimportant qualifying round. Fütterer agreed, slipped into the Adidas shoes and promptly won. In the final, he ran in his Puma shoes again. However, the newspapers on the following day only printed photos of Fütterer wearing

*Rudi's birthday, 1959 –
joking about the Herberger
disaster*

the three stripes in the qualifying race. Adi Dassler – whatever means of persuasion he had brought to bear – had got the photographers to hand in these pictures and these alone. Rudi was livid.

Two years later, Puma needed a new leather press. Rudolf Dassler called in person on a supplier friend of his who ran his business on Adidas land. The machine was delivered in just two weeks. Two days later, however, it emerged that an engineer had made a miscalculation and the press was unsuitable for football boots. Rudolf exchanged the machine at great expense. Two days later, however, it emerged that Adidas was about to replace a machine, too. A spy had passed on information about the Puma contract – and Adi Dassler had ordered the same piece of equipment. Rudolf soon forgot his pain over the money he had lost, and revelled happily in his brother's misfortune.

The brothers' battles were reflected in the town's daily life too, just like in the soap opera *Dallas*. In the 1960s and 1970s, in particular, fights between Puma and Adidas employees were not uncommon. Some bars refused to serve beer to guests if they were on the wrong side, and some bakers would not serve customers from the other faction. The gulf was evident in the two football clubs FC and ASV Herzogenaurach. Even now, no player would get changed in the other team's dressing room when they are about to play against one another.

The defeat inflicted on Rudolf Dassler by his brother in the battle of the sportswear manufacturers at the 1954 football World

Cup stuck in his craw for a long time. Four years later, at the World Cup in Sweden, he wanted to do everything better. For the first time, the players were to display on their boots the Formstrip that remains the Puma trade mark to this day. The three Adidas stripes were already firmly imprinted on the minds of the athletes and fans – this could not continue. In the final, in which Brazil played Sweden, Puma was worn by most of the players in a team that also included the 17-year-old Pelé. The PR success was based on an audacious trick: because the South Americans never played in anything but their own, handmade boots, the Puma strategists had simply painted the Formstrip onto them. In return, the players received a fee of a few hundred dollars. The commercialization of the beautiful game had reached another dimension.

## 1.4 Passport to Europe

*Expansion: love in Austria, leather from the mountain horses, flying shoes and French contracts*

Although Rudolf's son Armin was a success in the company as a marketing specialist, his father's discontent with him was increasing. They had never really got along and the relationship cooled further as the years went on. Armin wrote in his diary that he could not explain it himself, as there had practically never really been any violent quarrels. But business is business: because the tariff regulations for exports to Austria were complicated and made trade difficult, Rudolf sent his son to Salzburg in 1962 to set up Puma's first foreign subsidiary. He sent him on his way with 50,000 marks in cash, a Mercedes and a second-hand typewriter. On the other side of the scales, the value of Puma Austria was deducted from Armin's share in the German limited partnership. He could not rely on any further support from his father, who declined all requests for loans. Just why the boss was so strict with his son, who was now 32 years old, remains a mystery to this day.

Armin Dassler was accompanied to Austria by an attractive and self-assured female colleague from the International Correspondence department. Her name was Irene Braun, and she came from Nuremberg. Rudolf had appointed her in 1956 as an expert in foreign correspondence, even though, at her interview, she asked for 380 marks, which was 100 marks more than she earned at her then employer, the toy manufacturer Schuco. She soon realized that she had not been too bold, however: she was the only person in the company who spoke English and French. Rudolf liked the lady and one evening in a fit of fatherly kindness he even confided to her that she was the right woman for his son Armin. In so doing, he was theoretically breaching his own principle that love affairs were banned in the company – he was all too well aware of the damage they could cause. Secretaries who turned into lovers had to leave on his orders. Romance did indeed soon blossom between Armin and Irene. On 10 September 1964, they married in the marble hall of Mirabell Castle in Salzburg. His father issued a curt response to their wedding invitation: "I shall not be interrupting my holiday for your wedding. Regards, Rudolf."

On 25 February 1962, production started at Puma Austria. Five hundred pairs of shoes, mainly for footballers, went onto the marketplace every week. Armin rubbed his hands together. Business had

*Sports equipment trade fair, Wiesbaden, 1961*

got off to a brisk start. Six months later, however, the orders suddenly stopped, right out of the blue. He frantically rang round the dealers and discovered that they were clearing the shelves to make way for the ski boots – it was the start of the winter season. Armin and Irene were stunned. Puma's first foreign subsidiary was on the verge of insolvency. With a huge effort, they managed to squeeze a loan out of banker Georg Berger-Sandhofer of Bankhaus Berger in the elegant surrounds of the "Goldener Hirsch" Hotel. Puma Austria was given a lifeline. Armin allowed himself a wage of 450 marks a month and Irene got half this amount. He drove a light green Mercedes 280 while she rattled around the idyllic Alpine landscape in a pale green VW beetle. Perhaps they already had a premonition that they would be at the helm of the Puma Group in a few years' time.

Gradually, the young Dassler gained the confidence to step further away from his father. He designed his own shoes in-house: the Condor-Dassler shoes. He registered the Puma Austria brand and gave the branch office its own logo. His aim was to be better than his father and uncle in Herzogenaurach.

Instead of kangaroo leather he used horse leather for his creations, and they were advertised as being "Made from specially tanned Austrian Mountain Horse Leather". When he discovered that no such animals existed, he quickly posed for a photo alongside a Haflinger dray-horse. He altered the advertising slogan: "These shoes were made in Mozart's home city of Salzburg. Please come and see us when you visit Austria." Two months later, an American couple turned up at the reception of Puma Austria and asked for a free city tour. Irene Dassler put on her coat and acted as tourist guide.

The USA became an important market for the young Mr and Mrs Dassler. The Americans came to love the shoes made from the leather of the mountain horses. In 1964, Puma Austria recorded overseas sales of 1.3 million marks with the Condor-Dassler shoes. With such figures, Armin managed to secure a little respect from his father. When he and Irene travelled to Herzogenaurach at the end of 1964, they were received with an unusual degree of warmth. There was, however, no real change in the underlying hostility. "The shoes continue to fly around in the boss's office," reported Armin in his diary, in reference to his difficult father. On one occasion when Irene wanted to mediate between the two, her father-in-law had her ejected from the room.

### French encounters

Armin's brother Gerd did not yet have to concern himself with such feuds. Admittedly, he was a tall man, but ten years younger than Armin and therefore always the "little brother". He was very evidently his father's favourite son. Gerd had felt little of the stress of the early years. Between 1950 and 1957 he lived in a school boarding house at Hohenschwangau near Füssen in southern Bavaria, which cost 80 marks per month (a lot of money in those days), and he only came home in the holidays. Then, the Dassler family would often travel together to Langenargen on Lake Constance to spend ten days' summer holiday there. When Gerd started becoming too estranged, his mother Friedl brought him home and enrolled him at the secondary school in Nuremberg. He gained average marks in his final school leaving exams, then went on to carry out his military service. After that he returned to Nuremberg and began a business management degree. At the age of 27, he entered the firm in which his father and his brother were already rivals for power. He was very grateful when one evening his

*Friedl and Rudolf Dassler
with sons Armin (left) and
Gerd and daughters-in-law*

father took him to one side and said: "You are going to France for Puma, and you'll be in charge there."

Puma France in Soufflenheim, a village of 1,500 inhabitants in the Alsace region, was not exactly spectacular in the beginning. Rudolf Dassler had bought the small local firm Ott & Cie. and turned it into a subsidiary. With 6,000 marks monthly salary and nearly 80 employees, Gerd started his job as a managing director and a short time later – like his brother in Austria – developed his own models. He appears to have had talent: his range of leisure footwear "Puma Hobby" and "Puma Weekend", for example, show some traces of the modern lifestyle footwear of Vienna designer Helmut Lang. They were, however, unable to find their way to the trendy boutiques and department stores – Puma lacked the distribution channels.

With sportswear, the situation was better: after a period of six years Gerd already had three football teams from the French First Division under contract. And this despite the fact that he was facing a turf war against an extremely tough opponent: his cousin Horst, son of Adi Dassler, who was doing business for Adidas in nearby Landersheim, close to Strasbourg. The two men share very similar histories and some contemporaries maintain they could have been brothers. One thing was clear. each one suffered under his father's omnipotence. Unlike their fathers, however, they treated one another with respect. Once, during the 1956 Olympics, they even ignored the ban on contact between the families and met officially in a hotel room in Melbourne, Australia.

Horst was a highly ambitious man. He was soon playing a global role in the industry and Landersheim was rivalling the Adidas headquarters in Herzogenaurach. The leading figures of the sporting world were soon regular visitors to Landersheim, enjoying the expensive wine and the free services of the *filles de joie*. The plant became the primordial cell of the network with which he later mercilessly dominated the market for sports equipment and sponsorship as Adidas boss. Former companions said that no one was better at attempting to get honorary officials on side with money and consultancy contracts. He always carried an A4 pad of squared paper with him to record the names of the supporters and opponents of his preferred candidates ahead of important selection procedures. At the end of the year there were so-called special payments on the Adidas balance sheet, which Horst Dassler had used to persuade the opponents to join his camp. His "billion-dollar game", as journalists Thomas Kistner and Jens Weinreich describe it in the book of the same name, became public in 1989 when access was gained to the records of the Stasi sports informer IM Möwe, whom the DDR had installed in the western sports associations. Horst did not have to justify himself: he had died two years earlier aged just 51.

Gerd acted for Puma in relatively dutiful fashion, although he managed to land a major coup for the company and as such go down in its history. Along with his school friend, the then football caricaturist Lutz Backes, he designed the new company logo which is still used today: the leaping cat. Backes charged the company 600 marks for his work. In addition, he also got a pair of shoes and a sports bag.

## 1.5 Other People's Money

*The start of sports marketing: dubious change of shoes, undone bootlaces, dealings in the catacombs and a black fist*

In the 1950s, Puma grew very nicely – albeit at a much slower pace than Adidas. In the final year of the decade, the company posted turnover of three million marks – 25 percent up on the previous year. Puma and Adidas dominated the global market for football boots and track and field footwear, which were increasingly being made of synthetic materials such as polyamide and nylon. Both brothers were highly innovative: in 1956, for example, Puma launched a range of boots featuring an antibacterial effect which

The Dassler family feud in
the press (1970)

was meant to control the horrible odour of sweat which usually arose from the players' boots following 90 minutes on the pitch. Another innovation was the "Lastic" sole that was vulcanized onto the football boot to form one inseparable unit. In 1958, at the World Cup in Sweden, Puma introduced the conspicuous strip – the Formstrip – on the side of its shoes: it forms part of the brand image to this day.

In the same year, Rudolf's wife Friedl and his two sons Armin and Gerd took limited partnerships in the firm – now called Puma-Sportschuhfabriken Rudolf Dassler KG. While Gerd did not take on a managerial role initially, Friedl entered service as a senior manager with power of attorney to act for the firm in commercial matters. Armin became a junior manager and took over all Public Relations, and was consequently responsible for contacts with athletes. The relationship between father and sons grew even more complicated. Rudolf saw himself as being in sole command of the family, and increasingly viewed Armin as the young rebel. Armin and Gerd did not get along at all either: their father stoked this rivalry and on repeated occasions, didn't mind being unfair to one of them to set him against the other.

In Germany, Rudolf occupied an excellent position in the

football leagues, for example with brilliant performers Frankfurter Eintracht, who wore Puma boots in all their matches. But Adi was already one step ahead; he was rolling up the international market with Adidas. Since the mid 1950s his son Horst had roamed the catacombs of sports arenas, bearing charm and overflowing cases, generously handing out the firm's goods and securing the allegiance of the athletes. In comparison, Puma PR man Armin Dassler was rarely seen at the major events.

It was not until the Rome Olympics in 1960 that Rudi, too, appeared to realize that the world was changing and that the world of sport would increasingly be ruled by money. His son Armin was now more often in evidence in the stadia. At the world games in the holy city, German sprinter Armin Hary caused the first great stir in sports sponsorship. As a member of the German track and field team, he should really have been wearing Adidas spikes. However, this exceptional athlete, who was the first person to run the 100-metre sprint in 10.0 seconds, crossed the finish line at the Olympic event in Puma shoes. On the winners' podium, however, he appeared again in footwear displaying the three stripes. Both Dassler brothers were incensed. According to a report in the Adidas chronicle *Make a Difference*, Hary had made an upfront demand for a loyalty bonus or, alternatively, rights of sole representation of Adidas in the USA plus 10,000 pairs of shoes, interest-free on commission. Adidas officially denied that cash was the glue in the relationship. Later, the two sports goods manufacturers both accused each other of paying bribes to the great sprinter. It was a dubious business; of that there is no doubt. It is probably impossible to reconstruct the actual events. Hary himself insists that he remembers nothing extraordinary about Rome apart from the fact that he left the stadium a winner.

Doing deals with amateurs was still one of the big taboos in those days. The myth of purity continued to be fostered long after officials and athletes had started filling their pockets behind the scenes. Companies would stop at nothing to get top stars to wear their ranges of footwear, especially innocent-looking athletes such as the Ethiopian Abebe Bikila. In Rome in 1960, the bodyguard of sovereign Haile Selassie won the marathon in 2 hours 15 minutes and 16 seconds – barefoot. Immediately, Puma employees went hunting for him, tracked him down and gave him three boxes containing new running shoes. At the Olympic Games in Tokyo in 1964 the African again won the marathon – this time wearing Puma. Rudolf Dassler sent his congratulations by telegram.

## A panther for Puma

There was another African happy to receive a donation of shoes from Franconia: Eusébio da Silva Ferreira, born in Mozambique in 1942, the star striker for SL Benfica and European Footballer of the Year 1965. In the following year, as a national player for Portugal, he went on to become the absolute superhero of the football World Cup in England when he scored nine goals. During the quarter-final against the unexpectedly successful North Korean team, his play took him to the heights of football legend: Portugal were in a seemingly hopeless position, trailing 0–3, before finally going on to win 5–3. "The black panther", as fans called him, scored four goals himself and set up the fifth. And all in Puma boots.

Right after the tournament Eusébio travelled to Herzogenaurach in order to secure a better contract to reward his skills and ability. Rudolf Dassler offered him his own collection and a fee of 10,000 marks. Eusébio accepted the deal and became involved in the development of the "Eusébio King" football boot. The "King" proved a money-spinner. Customers were no longer just buying sports gear – they were buying

*Advert from France*

an image. For the first time, a product was positioned to exercise a fascination over consumers so that they were willing to pay more for that reason alone. They no longer idolized the football studs and leather – in some way it was Eusébio they were now wearing. It was the start of cult marketing in the House of Puma. Rudolf Dassler took part because he recognized the spirit of the times, but underneath he had an aversion to the practice. He wanted to have no other gods beside him. He also did not want to keep on paying money for athletes' agents or association officials who promised him the moon. He preferred to pursue the customary method and increase prices for models that flew off the shelves, while removing products that did not sell. But he could not prevent more and more athletes from realizing their market value and wanting to convert this into hard cash.

The true heroes of the sports fans – Dassler quickly realized – had started right at the bottom and fought their way to the very top. They were street players who had matured into fine men whose exemplary characters shone through. Among them was a man called Edson Arantes do Nascimento, who was born in 1940 in Três Corações in the Brazilian state of Minas Gerais, and raised as the son of a poor washerwoman. As a young boy, he worshipped the goalkeeper of the team his father played for. The keeper's name was Bilé – Edson pronounced it Pelé – and so his nickname was born. Today, the Brazilians prefer to call Pelé "O Rei" – "the King". His reputation as the best player of all time is virtually unchallenged. In 2006, when Puma brought him to Germany to the World Cup, the audience took him to their hearts straight away in whichever stadium or studio he appeared.

Puma had certainly backed the right horse in 1962 in supporting Pelé: at the World Cup in Chile, he won the tournament in Puma boots and revealed his great talent for the first time. He rose to the ranks of a football god eight years later at the World Cup in Mexico. Once again, Pelé was wearing Puma, for the whole world to see. Ahead of the kick-off in the final against Italy, the Brazilian kneeled down and leisurely tied his laces. For several seconds, the Puma Formstrip in all its glory was broadcast to millions of television screens across the globe. When Brazil went on to win the match 4–1, Puma's triumph was complete.

The undone bootlace was no accident. What happened behind the scenes before the tournament was pure Hollywood. Armin Dassler had enlisted the services of sports journalist Hans Henningsen, who lived in Rio and had wonderful contacts, to do discreet PR work for the House of Puma. It was his responsibility, using financial arguments, to get as many players as possible to wear Puma footwear in Mexico. However, he was to keep his hands off Pelé. There was said to be a secret pact between Armin Dassler and his Adidas cousin Horst to prevent fees for the top players from becoming exorbitant. Henningsen nevertheless made Pelé an offer on his own initiative: 25,000 dollars for the World Cup and a further 100,000 dollars for the next four years. In addition, he granted him a ten percent royalty on boots to be sold under his name. Pelé agreed and Armin Dassler consented – family pact or no.

When Armin told his father about the deal after the tournament, the atmosphere over the next two weeks was rather frosty. The company leader had never changed his stance on the

Herberger principle, i.e., not setting up any long-term contracts for sportsmen and officials. With difficulty, Armin managed to persuade him that this was a critical step in the battle to block Adidas' dominance. In the end, he actually agreed to hand over the money in person to world star Pelé. They flew to Rio de Janeiro with Air France via Paris. Henningsen met them at the airport and accompanied them to the Hotel Savoy. The next day they travelled on to São Paulo. A taxi took them to Santos, where Pelé was a player at the time. The Brazilian took the two men to his luxurious estate. They chatted a little and then Rudolf opened the money coffer. Pelé did not bother to count it, but just threw the notes into a suitcase. Rudolf was horrified: the case already contained stacks of cash. Had he paid too much?

*Friedl Dassler with Pelé, 1970*

Nevertheless, the move paid off. The "King Pelé" boot later became a real winner in the sports stores. There was one boot imprinted with his monogram costing 95 marks and one – of the same design – without the imprint for 79 marks. Virtually every customer went for the expensive design. Over the course of the next few years, as well as Eusébio and Pelé, Puma took on board many of the most creative and unconventional stars of world football, including German Günter Netzer, the Dutchman Johan Cruyff and the Argentinians Mario Kempes and Diego Armando Maradona. But well-behaved German stalwarts like Lothar Matthäus and Rudi Völler received nice contracts, too.

## Te deum in France

Everything seemed to be going well when Rudolf Dassler celebrated his 70th birthday in Herzogenaurach on 29 April 1968. That year, sales at the order trade fairs in Cologne and Wiesbaden rose by over 50 percent on the previous year. There were even more reasons to celebrate. Toasts were being drunk to Rudi and Friedl's 40th wedding anniversary and his 55th year in business, as well as two decades of Puma. Miser Rudolf splashed out on this day. He had invited 600 employees from all five German and foreign operations, and addressed them from the balcony like a king while a man in a black double-breasted suit held an umbrella over him to protect him from the rain. In the morning, a congratulatory group attended the offices and Armin gave a welcome speech. In the afternoon, this was followed by a celebration featuring musical accompaniment by the Nuremberg Symphony orchestra. Representatives of banks, public authorities and associations as well as customers and suppliers shook hands with the host. Mayor Hans Maier praised Rudolf Dassler to the hilt, telling him he had created "a small economic miracle" in Herzogenaurach. And even the chairman of the Works Council had some warm words to say about the pension that the manager granted to his workers after ten years of service with the firm. It was an enjoyable day – even though Armin was forced to realize time and again that his father was not making any plans for his retirement.

Despite all the adulation, Adi Dassler and his Adidas factory 400 metres away had become quite a long way removed from his brother both in terms of sales and public presence. Major sporting events, broadcast across the globe, were increasingly the domain of the three stripes. They were on screen with ever increasing frequency as victorious athletes listened to their national anthems with tears in their eyes. Adi was always trying to make things as difficult as possible for his brother, to get new sports stars under contract or even join them on the winner's podium. In the summer of 1968, at the Olympic Games in Mexico, the Puma envoys found to their horror that all boxes containing the new shoes for the athletes had been confiscated by customs. The authorities told them that they had no import licence from the chamber of trade and commerce therefore the delivery had been put in storage. Rudolf Dassler and his son Armin immediately realized that only Adidas could be behind this. Not long before, Brother Adi had induced the International Track and Field Association to ban brilliant new spikes designed by his brother – the "Bürstenschuh" – at a track and field competition. The American Vincent Matthew had run a new world record over 400 metres in this shoe. Puma's top man in South America tried to get the officials to release the packages by the "usual local method" – and languished in jail for five days. Armin Dassler bought his freedom. The English Puma delegation came on a terrific idea, albeit too late: just write a large letter A on the next consignment – A for Adidas. Indeed, the Puma packages labelled A went unchecked through customs – although not until the Games were over.

Puma was to be granted another emotional high in Mexico,

*Mr and Mrs Dassler with*
*FC Herzogenaurach, 1970*

which, however, proved no unmixed pleasure for Rudolf Dassler: black US sprinter Tommie Smith won the 200 metres gold medal with a new world record of 19.83 seconds. Third was black fellow countryman John Carlos. Both took to the winners' podium in socks and placed their Puma boots next to their feet in photogenic fashion. Then they raised their black gloved fists in the air – the symbol of the Black Power movement, which opposed discrimination against the Afro-American population. Before the ceremony was over, they had been fired by the American Olympic Committee for this supposed affront and were shortly afterwards requested to leave the Olympic Village. This signalled the end of their careers as superstars.

Two years later the Central American country was once again the focus of attention: On 30 May, the football World Cup opened in Mexico City. To the sports goods manufacturers, the event was a true spectacle: for the very first time audiences got to see the players on the pitch live and in colour. The new PAL system presented the shoes and shirts in all their glory. There were even more innovations on view: for the first time, with "Telstar", a football was specially designed for a World Cup and for television broadcast. Unlike other balls, it was made of twelve black pentagons and 20 white hexagons so that viewers could see it more easily. Telstar was short for "television star" and provided the original design for all modern footballs, developing into an important market segment for Puma, too.

### Puma sees red

Puma's results were dealt a severe blow that year. With 23 million marks' turnover, there remained a loss of 700,000 marks. Cash payments alone to the World Cup athletes and the first-class flights of the employees amounted to 350,000 marks. PR managers handed over between 500 and 5,000 dollars per game to the leading players. Track and field athletes, who – unrealistically – were still governed by stringent amateur regulations, had to dispose of the unlawful sponsorship fees discreetly in back rooms. Armin Dassler knew the prices: a 100-metre sprinter likely to be among the title contenders could no longer be secured for less than 5,000 dollars. Against this background a new profession arose: agents. Two years later, at the Olympic Games in Munich, the clamour for sponsorship money had matured into a professional market whose middlemen charged a small fortune. Adidas put sponsorship in the hands of its top management: Adi's wife Käthe travelled in person to the Bavarian capital and went after new business partners in the catacombs of the Olympic Stadium, armed with a leather bag full of notes.

The red figures in 1970 made clear to Rudolf Dassler for the very first time the thin line he was treading with his unconditional growth strategy. Admittedly, he continued to keep a tight rein on the pfennigs, though when he was trying to keep close on his brother's heels or even get ahead in terms of sales, he would turn a blind eye to this policy. Observers commented that he lacked one major quality to move into the lead in this commercialized sporting era: the effrontery with which Adi and Käthe Dassler went about their business. Of course, Rudolf also had his fair share of ruthlessness, but this was counteracted by his rampant stubbornness and self-satisfaction.

## 1.6 Sneakers

### Rudolf Dassler's final years: protest shoes, Helanca-clad marksmen, the first imitators and the end of a legend

On 2 June 1967, West Germany took on a new face. This was the day the Shah of Iran, together with his wife, visited the Deutsche Oper in Berlin as a state guest. He was received by a group of demonstrators, organized by the German Socialist Student Association (Sozialistische Deutsche Studentenbund). Paint bombs, tomatoes and bags of flour rained down on the representative of the tyrannical state, whilst choruses of "Shah, Shah, Charlatan" filled the air. The police had positioned paid supporters of the Shah, so-called "Jubelperser" ("cheering Persians"), between the opera house and the demonstrators. They hit out at the demonstrators with roof battens and iron bars. Panic set in and the street battle spread. A shot then rang out in the back yard of the house at Krumme Strasse 66/67. A policeman had killed Benno Ohnesorg, a student of Romance and German literature and culture. The precise circumstances surrounding this act remain unexplained to this day.

The incident in Berlin radicalized the student movement and triggered a nationwide groundswell towards liberation. Its aim was to bring to an end the social system that had been handed down from the post-war period. As students went out onto the street, so too did sneakers. Jeans and cheap unbranded sneakers became a non-conformist uniform in the fight against the establishment. With the young people of '68, the sneakers generation was born. Suddenly, it was cool to break social conventions and demonstrate your independence by your shoes. This development reached its peak over 15 years later on 12 December 1985, when Joschka Fischer, Green Party member of the Hessian state parliament and new Environment Minister for the federal state of Hesse, attended his oath of office ceremony in a pair of white Nike sneakers. There was, however, a second circumstance that boosted the sale of sports shoes and sports clothing for leisure-time wear: the children of West Germany's economic miracle had put on weight. At the end of 1969, West German health insurers were warning that a third of men and 40 percent of women were overweight by an average of seven pounds. On 16 March 1970, the West German Sports Association launched the "Trimm dich – durch Sport!" ("Keep fit with sport!") advertising campaign. A cheerful little fellow by the name of Trimmy gave sport as a recreational activity the thumbs-up. Right across the country, mayors had keep-fit courses covering distances of several kilometres installed in their local forests, with areas for jogging, keep fit, gymnastics and strength-based sports. In the years that followed, sport developed into a mass phenomenon. It was no longer about medals, but about exercise. Aerobics, stretching, nordic walking and mountain bikes had not yet been invented. Nevertheless, manufacturers of sports equipment responded to the trend: they put clothing and footwear suitable for recreational sport onto the shelves, and labelled them with fitness-related names. Puma manufactured its clothing from a highly elastic polyamide filament yarn: the "Helanca" tracksuit was born.

*Puma rebel Günter Netzer*

In the USA jogging had already become established in the mid-1960s. In the morning and evening, hordes of affluent young urbanites lined the promenades of America's east and west coasts, naturally in stylish gear (this was important even then). New Zealand athletics coach Arthur Lydiard had brought the idea of jogging to America with him from his homeland, and in the home of fast food it was greeted with great enthusiasm. In West Germany it took another decade for jogging to sweep the nation. Suddenly, keeping fit was no longer boring: in July 1979 Sony launched the first Walkman, the TPS-L2, onto the market.

At the beginning of the 1970s, Puma was once again operating more profitably. The company achieved sales of 80 million marks in 1972. Adidas, however, was already generating more than two and a half times this amount. This was mainly thanks to a major event that saw the whole of West Germany and a substantial proportion of the world's population catch the sporting bug: the Olympic Games, held in Munich between 26 August and 11 September 1972.

### Macabre advertising

Six days before the end of the Games, on 5 September, one of the most terrible events in sporting history occurred in the Olympic Village. Between 4.30 and 5am eight members of the Palestinian terrorist organization "Black September" scaled the fence of the Olympic Village and forced their way into the apartment of the Israeli Olympic team at Connollystrasse 31. They killed two Israeli athletes and took nine others hostage. Their demands to the Israeli and West German governments were that 232 Palestinians who were serving prison sentences in Israel be released, alongside West German terrorists Andreas Baader and Ulrike Meinhof. The police response was amateurish. All nine hostages died in the rescue attempt. "The games must go on!" declared IOC President Avery

Brundage. For Puma, this tragedy unintentionally developed into a tragicomic PR event.

Among the troops of the Federal Border Guard was a senior sergeant and sports fanatic by the name of Helmut Fischer. A native of Herzogenaurach, he had volunteered to serve in the Olympic Village. His good relations with Puma and Adidas had helped him secure the assignment. For two weeks he provided personal security for IOC chief Brundage and top athletes such as high-flyer Mark Spitz, who won seven gold medals in the swimming pool. When the attack took place he was assigned to the role of a reconnaissance scout. At the heart of the Olympic Village, directly opposite the Israeli camp, was a Puma shop. Rudolf Dassler had had it set up as a service centre and to allow equipment to be handed over discreetly, as officially the Olympic athletes were not allowed to receive any money or merchandise due to the amateur status of the Games. Shop manager Irmgard Hacker was just preparing for business when Fischer stormed in: "We need tracksuits!" he announced, out of breath. The police marksmen were to be disguised as athletes, to prevent them from being immediately identified by the hostage-takers. Irmgard Hacker handed him around 20 Helanca tracksuits. Police marksmen dressed in Puma gear – the images spread right across the globe on television and in the newspapers. Helmut Fischer went on to make a career with Puma and is now head of advertising for Puma Germany.

In sporting terms, the 1972 Olympics were a triumph for many West German athletes. With 40 medals, West Germany came fourth in the medals table behind the Soviet Union, the USA and East Germany. The real winner, however, was the Franconian sports equipment industry. At the time, Puma claimed to be supplying equipment to around a third of all participants, whilst Adidas proudly announced a figure of 75 percent. It is likely that both were exaggerating. Adi Dassler, however, found himself in pole position: as official supplier to the West German Olympic team he

*Advertisement for the 1972 Olympics in Munich in which Puma extols the virtues of its new running shoe, designed to protect both the athlete and the running track*

provided competition and leisure clothing, together with training shoes, while his nephew Armin Dassler attempted to lure top athletes and journalists over to his side at the specially rented "Puma Country Club" recreation centre on Lake Starnberg, just outside Munich.

Puma's 2,000 employees were producing 18,000 pairs of shoes a day. Somehow these had to get to the man and woman in the street. By now the company was exporting its products to 128 countries, with foreign trade accounting for 60 percent of its business. Besides Austria and France, Rudolf Dassler had founded his own subsidiaries in Yugoslavia, Australia and Nigeria, and there were factories producing under licence in the UK and the Netherlands.

The sports equipment business was not getting any easier. At the annual conference of the Association of Bavarian Shoe Factories (*Vereinigung der bayerischen Schuhfabriken*) in 1973, Armin Dassler complained about the increase in copies and the ruinous prices through which competitors in foreign markets were attempting to capture a piece of "the global prestige of the West German shoe industry". "The West German sports shoe industry is tending to become more and more of an international sports shoe industry under West German control," he observed with impressive foresight. However, in his view the lead that West Germany enjoyed was founded on a "very fragile base". Two years previously, US entrepreneurs Bill Bowerman and Phil Knight had renamed their sports shoe factory Blue Ribbon Sports, founded in 1962, after a Greek goddess: Nike. Although the Americans from Beaverton, Oregon, did not offer their products for sale in Europe until 1978, Armin Dassler appeared to have a premonition of what lay in store for the big guns from Franconia. In line with the spirit of the times, Puma expanded its product range that year to include football shirts. Business continued to increase in 1974, with high, double-digit growth rates, although profitability suffered.

### The death of the patriarch

It was a time of mourning in Herzogenaurach. The life of Rudolf Dassler, the egocentric shoe manufacturer born in the previous century, was drawing to a close. On 26 October, four months after West Germany's magnificent 2–1 victory over the Netherlands in the 1974 football World Cup, he lay on his deathbed. Armin and Gerd had arrived and sat with their mother at his bedside, as the

Rudolf Dassler on his 75th birthday

doctor did his best for his patient. The Catholic priest pressed for a reconciliation and called the Adidas household: Adi should come and offer Rudolf his hand before he passed away. Käthe turned down the request. Adi whispered down the phone that he forgave his brother. It is not known for certain whether Rudolf heard these conciliatory words. He died during the night.

His son Armin was plagued by a guilty conscience. He had often argued with his father but had never really talked to him. The funeral in Herzogenaurach became the last great tribute to the company's tireless founder. Four hundred mourners attended, although hardly anyone from the Adidas clan was to be seen. At the funeral meal whispers about the identity of his successor at Würzburger Strasse did the rounds. Everything seemed clear; Armin would take over as boss. He was already mentally preparing himself for his new leadership role.

On the day the will was read his dreams were shattered: his father had rewritten his will by hand four times in the weeks leading up to his death – and had disinherited Armin in favour of his unloved brother Gerd. Armin had in fact been disinherited entirely by his father, who used his last will and testament to give his rebellious son a final stab in the back. Over the weeks that followed, Armin and Irene attempted to ensure that at least the inheritance of the company shares was legally safeguarded. According to the partners' agreement, he was entitled to 60 percent and his brother Gerd to 40 percent. A new episode in the unspeakable soap

*Armin Dassler in the factory*

opera and a new fraternal feud began. On the feast of Epiphany in 1975, Armin achieved his aim. A Düsseldorf lawyer informed him of a precedent in a case ruled upon by the Federal Court of Justice. According to this ruling, agreements setting up a limited partnership take precedence over wills. Armin shoved this ruling under his brother's nose. Gerd had no option but to give way. A few days later, 45-year-old Armin was managing partner of Puma-Sportschuhfabriken Rudolf Dassler KG, with 60 percent of the shares. Gerd took up the position of second-in-command.

## 1.7 Ransom

### *The Armin Dassler era: the power of Mammon, delight at Borussia Mönchengladbach and a silent valet*

Armin Dassler made a confident first appearance before the press as the new head of the company. For 1975 he announced that sales would take a leap to more than 160 million marks, and he explained to the sceptical journalists that the company needed to take this expansion into account. The management team would therefore be increased by four members and employee numbers by around 50 percent to 3,500. He was oblivious to the danger that one day the price/cost trap would snap shut, wiping out all revenue. On 19 February 1975 the *Handelsblatt* financial newspaper ran with the headline "Puma setzt zum Sprung an" ("Puma prepares to leap").

There was one area in which Armin blindly followed his late father's path: getting on Adidas's nerves was one of the company's main objectives. The world was unable to fathom why the dispute between the clans could not be settled after Rudolf Dassler's death and why the companies did not join forces to increase their power. US magazine *Time* wrote that a merger between the two giants appeared to be a logical step, but that it would be impossible for as long as the Dassler family refused to talk to each other. Armin said that he would not object to meeting with his cousin Horst, but added that it was not down to him to bury the hatchet.

When it came to managing his staff, Armin employed new methods. In the mornings he would wander through the plant, talking to the workforce, and they appreciated his sociable nature. When employees had a birthday, he would hand them ten marks. A note here, a note there: Armin honed his ability to buy people's favour or, you could say, to train them with the help of his money. If he was running late for a flight from Nuremberg Airport, he would ask his secretary to promise the person in charge 100 marks and a pair of new Puma shoes if the departure time was put back for him. He impressed upon his managerial staff that they should always pay tips in advance: "How does it benefit you afterwards if you'll never see the people again?" he asked them rhetorically. He increasingly enjoyed playing the role of the patronizing sole commander, pushing his brother Gerd into the background as much as possible. Once he even tried to buy his number two out of the company. He offered him 13 million marks for his shares. Gerd turned him down – to him it seemed an immorally lousy offer. Years later, when Puma was faced with imminent insolvency, he would live to regret this decision.

In 1976, with the Olympic Games set to take place in Montreal, the value of the global market for sports shoes had grown to more than five billion dollars. Although it was clearly dominated by Adidas, with Puma also in a leading position, the two West German companies, with total combined sales of around half a billion dollars, accounted for only ten percent of the total market. Competition was fierce, especially in the USA. In second place among the sports shoe companies was Keds, a subsidiary of Uniroyal, with Converse Rubber Co. in third position. Puma, which generated total sales of over 200 million marks that year, was ranked only fourth. Adi Dassler was increasingly trying to kit out entire teams, and succeeded in the case of the American Basketball Association, for example. To take full advantage of the publicity opportunities that television broadcasting at the Olympics would offer, he also concluded a 250,000 dollar contract with COJO, the Olympic Games' senior organizing committee, as a result of which all 7,000 doormen, ushers, timekeepers and other employees were required to wear shoes and tracksuits bearing the three stripes. Armin Dassler was astonished, but focused, almost with restraint, on individual stars and football teams. He was far from matching his uncle's financial clout. To increase his company's margins, he sent his purchasers to East Asia to track down cheap production locations.

On 13 July 1976 the *Hamburger Morgenpost* headlined with: "Schuhkrieg!" ("Shoe war!"). The Montreal correspondent reported that contracts had fallen into the hands of the IOC under which Puma had given 50,000 dollars in sponsorship money to American athletes in return for their use of its products. Allegedly, American trainers or coaches had found the contracts somewhere. The whole thing had the whiff of a gangster movie: why would members of the US team hand the documents over to the Olympic Committee, of all organizations? The *Morgenpost*'s reporter speculated that it seemed reasonable to suspect that the aim was to get rid of athletes who were feared as favourites by informing on them. Armin Dassler assumed that his uncle lay behind this attack. Nevertheless, it was quite common for Puma, along with its competitors, to set aside 3 to 5 percent of sales as a "promotional budget", out of which generous favours were paid.

### Thin air

The air became thinner for Puma and huge efforts were needed to keep returns within tolerable limits. This was due in no small part to recreational sport: the new mass market was attracting an increasing number of competitors. Price increases were now virtually impossible. On the contrary, shoes and tracksuits were becoming cheaper and cheaper. In March 1977 Armin Dassler announced that substantial portions of production would be transferred abroad in order to benefit from the lower production and wage costs.

For Puma's managers, however, not all was doom and gloom that year – there was also plenty of reason to celebrate. The source of this delight had a name: Borussia Mönchengladbach. For years the team had been dominating the Bundesliga, together with FC Bayern Munich. And for years every pfennig that Puma had invested in the players from the Lower Rhine region had paid off two or three times over. Borussia Mönchengladbach became West German champions for the first time in 1970, successfully defended their title in 1971, and in 1973 won the West German Football Federation Cup as well as reaching the final of the UEFA Cup, where they narrowly lost out to Liverpool. In 1975 they carried off the West German title for the third time and won the UEFA Cup, beating FC Twente Enschede in the final. They won the championship again in 1976 and even achieved a hat trick of titles in 1977. Players such as Berti Vogts, Rainer Bonhof, Uli Stielike, Wolfgang Kneib and Jupp Heynckes had been elevated to the status of national footballing heroes. On 25 May 1977 the team reached for the stars again: in the final of the European Cup they lined up once more against Liverpool. Armin Dassler had had a special boot developed for "his lads" (who were being trained at the time by Udo Lattek) with a heel nine millimetres higher than before. The idea was that the centre of gravity would be shifted to the ball of the foot, thereby improving the ability to be quick off the mark. "The new wonder boot is our performance-enhancing drug," enthused Jupp Heynckes prior to the match. "It allows you to shoot harder and more accurately, as you get under the ball better," Berti Vogts proclaimed. Unfortunately, it did not do them any good: Borussia lost 3–1. Armin Dassler, however, could handle it: his "wonder boot" had been sufficiently celebrated in the press.

Over subsequent years sales at Puma grew at a dizzying pace. In 1978 the Herzogenaurach firm almost achieved the 500 million mark level. Every day, 50,000 pairs of shoes were being manufactured at the four West German and three French factories. These contributed 85 percent of total sales. According to its own figures, the company with the leaping cat logo had acquired a global market share of more than 30 percent, and even as much as 45 percent of the West German market. These high growth rates, however, concealed an acute danger of the company gradually running out of control. Five thousand employees had to be paid and huge quantities of materials bought. The gross margin, that is the percentage share of sales after the deduction of the cost of goods sold, was less than 30 percent – nowhere near enough to earn money in the sector. Earnings therefore only fluctuated around the zero mark.

Without its foreign business, Puma would have recorded figures well into the red. Only the inflows of funds from the licensing business prevented this. Anyone who wished to sell Puma products as a retailer or manufacturer had no problems obtaining

*Armin Dassler with Udo Jürgens*

permission from Herzogenaurach. Brand management was not Armin Dassler's thing: partners pretty much had free rein to do what they wanted with the logo as long as they paid handsome fees for the privilege.

Nevertheless, Dassler was proud of what he had achieved. His unloved father had been dead for five years when he celebrated his 50th birthday. The plan was for the entire workforce to come and celebrate him and join in the party. Armin wanted to have a marquee erected in Herzogenaurach. His wife Irene and his assistant Elfriede tried to get Austrian-born singer and composer Udo Jürgens to attend as a surprise guest. Dassler loved his songs "Aber bitte mit Sahne" and "Ehrenwertes Haus", for example. After a Jürgens concert, the two women crept backstage and approached the singer's Swiss manager, Freddy Burger, directly. "OK," he said, "that'll be 50,000 marks plus a transparent or white Schimmel grand piano and professional stage technology." The women gulped – but agreed. The birthday evening was a resounding success, with Armin and Udo arm in arm. Manager Freddy Burger took the opportunity to snap up the right to represent Puma in Switzerland. A few years later Armin even had an Udo Jürgens lifestyle collection designed. This odd 1980s outfit well and truly flopped. Puma and fashion were not yet meant for each other.

### Silent valet

How much does the world cost? Tying people to him by offering them a bit of cash became the Puma chief's great passion. On some occasions it assumed crazy proportions. In 1979 he travelled with his wife on Concorde to São Paulo, via Paris. A business meeting awaited them and they had booked a room at the Grand Hotel. The hotel manager received them and offered them the presidential suite. Armin and Irene looked at each other in astonishment. "I'm a friend of Puma," the hotel manager declared with a friendly smile. During their stay they were looked after by a young valet called Vivaldo. He spoke neither German nor English and went about his duties in a silent but friendly manner. Armin doted on him and asked him whether he would like to come back to West

Germany with them. Vivaldo did not take the offer particularly seriously.

A year later Armin checked into the Grand Hotel again. On this occasion his CFO Robert Wenzel had travelled with him. Once again Vivaldo was at their service all day long. This time Armin wanted to do the job properly. He called his wife and said he would be bringing the valet back home with him. Three weeks later the Brazilian arrived at Nuremberg Airport. Irene was horrified. She did not want to put him up in their own house and rented a room for him in the neighbouring Auracher Hof hotel. Vivaldo showed little talent for housework, so he took care of shining the shoes and walking the family dachshund, Florian. Gradually the valet started to enjoy his stay in Herzogenaurach. When his master and mistress were away on holiday he had his teeth fixed and bought himself a completely new wardrobe. He passed on bills of more than 1,200 marks to Armin Dassler, who paid them, perplexed. Five months later Vivaldo flew back home.

Although he did not have much of an inclination for brand management, Armin pondered about how he could win over not only wealthy but also poor people to Puma products. He was less of a rational thinker than his father, preferring to make decisions on the basis of gut instinct than to think in terms of contribution margins. For whatever reason, he felt he belonged to the working class rather than the jetset. For this reason alone, the position of sympathetic number two behind the arrogant global power Adidas gradually started to appeal to him. He decided that Puma's products had to move outside specialist sports stores. The price of remaindered stock was immediately slashed and the products sold off in major department stores and discount chains.

An important objective for Armin was to outperform Adidas when it came to innovation. He ploughed five to seven percent of sales into research and development. In 1982 he made an unexpected appearance at the conference of Puma's commercial representatives at the Novotel in Fürth. The assembled gentlemen gazed in astonishment at the head of the company, who stood before them in one of his many shepherd's check jackets. At that time, Dassler was having to treat himself to a new wardrobe fairly frequently, due to a gradually spreading waistline. He pulled a straw out of his case and began his speech: he said that he had first had to seek out an ice-cream parlour in Herzogenaurach in order to understand how the hinge on a bendy straw works. He then pointed at the grooves at the top end of the straw and reached into his case again. Out of it came a new football boot, the sole of which was able to bend using a similar principle to that of the drinking straw. This sole, known as the "Duoflex", is still used today in many football boots.

## Electronic trainers

In September 1985 Puma presented its latest invention: the RS computerized running shoe with integrated sensor and mini computer. Anyone who owned an Apple IIe or a Commodore 64 could connect up a cable, read out the running data and display it graphically on the monitor. This gadget, with its dubious benefits, came at a high cost: the price for a pair was 289 marks.

Puma continued to grow and sales soon exceeded a billion marks for the first time, a third of which originated from the licensing business. Armin had also managed to improve profitability, with 80 percent of shoes now being manufactured by licensed partners or by means of toll manufacturing in low-wage countries. A quarter of revenues were generated from the textile trade. At the beginning of 1983 the Franconian firm put a central warehouse costing 15 million marks into operation with the aim of improving logistics and deliverability. Employee numbers had declined to below 2,500, with half of staff employed in the three West German plants in Herzogenaurach, Reckendorf bei Bamberg and Bad Windsheim to the west of Herzogenaurach. "I still have a lot of catching up to do," Armin Dassler complained to *Spiegel* magazine, with one eye on Adidas.

His detested relatives now controlled around 60 percent of West German sports shoe retailers, with Puma managing just 30 percent. Armin Dassler believed there were hardly any opportunities for growth in Eastern Europe: his Uncle Adi had only just started up licensed production in the Soviet Union. Even in the USA, the new boom market, no real progress was being made. Nike had forced Adidas into second place and Puma remained in third position, together with Converse. Armin Dassler was furious when Norbert Blüm, West Germany's Federal Minister for Labour, had his photograph taken while playing sport in Nike trainers. He immediately drafted a letter in which he accused Blüm of putting West German jobs on the line. Commenting that even Pelé wore Puma, he offered the politician a pair of domestically produced sports shoes. Blüm responded that he would happily follow in Pelé's footsteps, on condition, however, that Puma forked out as much money as it did for the Brazilian. He proposed that the fee should go to a charitable association. Dassler preferred not to pursue the matter any further.

The cash battle between the Herzogenaurach-based sports equipment manufacturers continued to rage behind the scenes. It reached comical new heights in Cologne. There, one-time European champion decathlete and Adidas manager Werner von Moltke, a former Puma athlete and representative, had, by his own account, shaken hands on a deal to extend the sponsorship contract with 1. FC Köln. He claimed to have negotiated with the Board for five whole hours before reaching an agreement. Apparently, Dassler immediately offered five times the amount if the football club's representatives informed him that they were turning down the deal. Who can say no to that much money? The management justified the switch by saying that its decision was based on its "obligation to safeguard the future of the association". Only Harald "Toni" Schumacher, the goalkeeper, refused outright to wear boots bearing the Puma Formstrip. He had signed an exclusive contract with Adidas some time before.

*Advertisement for the RS Electronic computerized running shoe*

## 1.8 Club of the Vanities

*The best years: back yard kick-around, "Boom Boom" Boris, a visit to "You bet!" and a bit of leisure time*

Armin Dassler had barely moved into the boss's office following the death of his father when his peace was shattered by noise from the back yard. Lothar Matthäus, the 13-year-old son of the Puma caretaker and canteen manager, was using this area to improve his football skills. He lived in an unassuming brick house next door. Time after time Armin would fling open the window and bawl at him to go and find another place to kick around in. Lothar did just that and joined FC Herzogenaurach, Puma's own local team, as a centre-forward. The boy's exceptional talent soon became

*Puma hero Lothar Matthäus*

apparent. In 1979, when he was 18, Puma's PR manager Hans Nowak called his friend Jupp Heynckes, who had just taken over as trainer at Borussia Mönchengladbach. "Just take a look at him," said Nowak. Heynckes looked, and liked what he saw. He gave him a contract immediately. Lothar promptly terminated his apprenticeship as an interior decorator (monthly salary 450 marks) and just a few months later the back yard player was a firm fixture for the Mönchengladbach team. And there was more: in 1980, national coach Jupp Derwall called him into the national squad. His rapid rise reached its impressive peak when the team beat Belgium 2–1 in the final of the European Championships in Italy that same year.

From now on, Armin and Gerd Dassler treated "Loddar" as their own son – he became their trade mark. Their hearts filled with joy as, in his pronounced Franconian accent, he stammered such sentences into the microphone as "We mustn't bury our sands in the head." "Lothar Matthäus is virtually a global star, he can play on the left and the right, at the back or the front," is how Franz Beckenbauer is said to have praised him at the time. Two years later, though, the winner had dropped quite a bit down the rankings: he had lost his regular place at Borussia Mönchengladbach and in the national team and had parted ways with his girlfriend Sylvia (at least temporarily).

In 1984, Armin Dassler made a decision that was to have major consequences: Puma entered the tennis racket business. Although in Germany alone around 100 suppliers were wooing the players, the length-adjustable Puma "Mid-Size" was set to roll up the field. It was the era of tennis and the two German players of the century were growing up virtually unnoticed: Boris Becker and Steffi Graf.

Becker, from the town of Leimen near Heidelberg, was just 16 years old in 1984. Ion Tiriac, a former Rumanian ice hockey and tennis player, who had been managing players for some time, had already aired his enthusiasm about the sandy-haired young talent, then number 750 in the world rankings, to Armin Dassler a few months before Armin was able to meet the child prodigy in person. He explained how Guillermo Vilas, the tennis legend in Puma gear, had trained with Boris in Monte Carlo for five hours before finally throwing in the towel. Following the Puma Christmas party in 1984, the Puma boss asked Tiriac for a meeting with Becker, who until then had played with an Adidas racket. At this meeting – according to informed sources – the Rumanian demanded 400,000 marks from Puma – per season. Armin rejected this request. Tiriac took his charge and crossed the Aurach river to Horst Dassler, who was running the Adidas business following the death of his mother Käthe. He felt there was something afoot, grabbed the phone and called his cousin – a historic moment. They came to an agreement to prevent

*Boris Becker wins Wimbledon, 1985*

Tiriac from driving up the stakes and effectively taking them to the cleaner's. A short time later, Becker's protector contacted Puma from a telephone booth. Adidas, he claimed, were willing to pay the amount. Armin Dassler hit back and negotiated him down considerably. On 15 January 1985 the parties signed the contract. Just how much Puma paid in the end remains a secret to this day.

A year or so later, Armin Dassler outlined what happened in the *Bild* newspaper – a red-top, but famous for the excellence of its sporting news – as follows: "I called Tiriac: I said 'I have to have Boris.' He had just made it into the world's top hundred. I could sense it: he was destined to one of the all-time greats." Dassler could never have guessed or dreamt what would happen six months after the contract was signed. On 7 July 1985, a hot summer's day, Boris Becker played an ace against Kevin Curren with the score standing at 40–30. The spectators yelled and shouted, Becker fell to his knees. The 17-year-old had won Wimbledon and thus assured his place in the Olympus of the tennis world. In his hand was the tool of his trade, with the Puma logo emblazoned across the strings.

### The battle of the rackets

In the following week, customers stormed the sports stores. Within a few days, 10,000 examples of Boris' Puma racket flew off the shelves, selling at 199 marks each. No one was bothered that the racket featured the name "Guillermo Vilas" (the company had developed it originally for the Argentinian). Puma presented the rackets "B. Becker" and "Boris Becker Winner" before the summer was out. More than 300,000 of them sold, though they were much too cheap to yield decent margins.

"Boris is my baby, my youngest son," enthused Armin Dassler quite publicly. Meanwhile, the sons he had produced himself were already working in the business or were preparing to do so: Frank, the eldest, had studied law and subsequently went to the USA as Puma's President; Jörg enlisted pop stars as advertising icons for Puma clothing; and Michael was studying business management in Boston, USA. "My sons are to have an easier time of it," promised Armin, "I do not intend to stick around as long as my father."

Becker fever continued to spread. The Puma managers could scarcely believe it when they saw the pictures in the news reports as Pope John Paul II at an audience in the Vatican blessed not only the tennis ace, but also their silver Puma racket. At the start of April 1986 Ion Tiriac offered them an extension of the contract to five years. Becker would then collect the vast sum of 27 million dollars if he remained within the world's top ten. In return, he had to use rackets, shoes and outer clothing from the Puma collection. Half the board angrily rejected the dizzying demand. Brother Gerd presented Armin with a calculation showing that the firm would have to shift Becker products to the value of a billion marks just to recover the costs. Armin dug in his heels, he was banking on the boost to the company's image. On 18 April he signed the contract in Tiriac's apartment. Following the formal signing, the Rumanian took a diamond-studded Ebel watch from a white box – Ebel was one of Becker's sponsors – and presented it to the Puma boss. Two months later Boris won Wimbledon for a second time.

In 1986 the German TV station ZDF also had something to celebrate: the Saturday evening TV show *Wetten, dass ...?* (by 1989 there was an English version called *You Bet!*) was five years old. In the emerging era of private television, the show's creator and presenter Frank Elstner had hit upon a programme that kept the population glued to their TVs every week. On 27 September 1986 the popular game show was being held in Basel. Steffi Graf was a guest

*Dassler friend Frank Elstner, Boris Becker, trainer Günther Bosch (left to right)*

on the show. She was currently heading up to the top of the world tennis rankings. She placed a bet that in a penalty shoot-out two men with an excavator would be able to score more goals than Bundesliga players with their feet. Armin and Irene Dassler were in the audience, and they applauded enthusiastically. Elstner had invited them to the show to put Graf in contact with Puma. The next day, he arranged a meeting with Steffi's father Peter Graf in Armin's Basel apartment. Graf came alone and unemotionally recited his demands: over one million dollars each year for her to use a Puma racket, a further million for the shoes and another million for the clothing. Armin Dassler drank a glass of schnaps to curb his anger. Unlike Becker, Steffi Graf had not yet won Wimbledon. They went their separate ways empty-handed. Perhaps Graf would have been the better deal in the long run.

The white sport itself also became fashionable thanks to the popular appeal of the young tennis pop stars. Prophets foretold 30 percent growth rates on the sports fashion market. At the 1986 International Trade Fair for Sports Equipment and Fashion (ISPO), Puma launched its first sportswear collection – 600 textile items no longer suitable for stadia and sports halls, but exclusively designed for leisure. "The number of people buying casual sportswear for everyday fashion is increasing all the time," ascertained Helmut Fischer, the then advertising manager. Nevertheless, market observers did not believe the Herzogenaurach company could build up a permanent business "leg" in this segment: the power of the established brands such as Lacoste seemed too great. But Fischer stepped up the pressure. With support from the advertising agency Wündrich-Meissen, he backed a four-stage communication strategy: sponsoring associations, clubs and athletes; pushing PR work; placing classical print adverts, especially in the popular German magazines *kicker*, *stern* and *BRAVO*; and promoting sales in the stores. Ten million marks were available for advertising and marketing.

## 1.9 Out of Order

### *The fall of the Puma: slippery floors, a nasty surprise from the USA and the death of the arch-enemy*

Herzogenaurach was consumed by Boris fever – albeit only at Puma. There was a deep-seated anger on the other side of the Aurach at Adidas, which had failed to contract a shooting star thanks to the guile of its business adversary. Even Nike's managing director De Boer began to display the first signs of resignation: "I regard us as the third brand in Germany. A long way behind Adidas. And well behind Puma, too, thanks to Boris Becker, who has got our intended target group on side," he revealed to German advertising magazine *Werben und Verkaufen*.

Germany celebrated with Puma. There was a euphoria surrounding the charismatic "Boom-Boom Boris"; he made people feel they could achieve anything as long as they trained hard enough and really wanted it. The mood amongst the population seemed ideal for the flotation of Puma on the stock exchange – thereby resolving a huge financial problem. In November 1985, the Puma management decided to turn the limited partnership into a public limited company and to increase its capital in the IPO (initial public offering) by 14 million to 50 million marks, in order to underpin forthcoming investments. Armin and Gerd decided to retain 72 percent of the shares (of which Armin held 70 percent and Gerd 30 percent), with 28 percent earmarked as free float.

As the nation reeled in Boris frenzy, the Puma speculation bubble filled and the danger that it could soon burst went largely unrecognized. The rainmakers of the financial world were really pushing Puma, and painting a rosy picture for the future of the cat. Debt reduction? No problem. Only in passing did they mention that the "drop in orders from the USA indicates a clear downward trend". Investors thrilled to the great leaps of 20 to 30 percent in annual sales, and harboured no doubts that both the turnover and

Becker's string of victories would continue. Why Puma had not been able to build up much equity in the past was a question no one really dared to ask. Yet how could there have been anything left over in the past few years, when Armin Dassler was flooding the market with shoes for under 30 marks, and selling tracksuits whose entry-level prices were up to 30 marks below those of competitors, causing the gross yield to melt into nothing?

Before the cat stepped out onto the slippery trading room floors in Frankfurt and Munich on 16 June 1986, the shares were many times oversubscribed. The issue price of the non-voting stock was 310 marks, a week later the share was trading at almost 600 marks and on 14 August it reached a record high of 1,480 marks, apparently bolstered up by English fund managers. This was "the craziest share of all time," in the opinion of experts from the financial newsletter *Frankfurter Tagesdienst*.

*Puma star Maradona*

Everything went like clockwork. Even God was on the side of Puma. At least that's the way it seemed: it was 22 June 1986, the quarter final of the World Cup in the Aztec Stadium in Mexico City. Argentina was playing England. In the 51st minute, Argentinian and Puma star player Diego Maradona directed the ball into the goal with his hand. The referee failed to spot the error, leaving the score at 1–0. If there had been a hand in the game then it was "the hand of God," Maradona said later. A week later Argentina beat Germany in the final. Armin Dassler was wild with excitement: Puma had kitted out both the Wimbledon champion and the football World Cup winners. What could be better?

However, rational observers looked at the figures and started to express some first doubts at the sustainability of the new shares' price curve. Dark clouds were starting to gather on the horizon: the US business had collapsed by more than 50 percent in the first half. "Puma ohne Puste?" ("Has Puma run out of puff?") inquired *Stern* magazine, and described the share as overvalued even then. The Hamburg-based publication realized that the firm "urgently needed

*Clyde leisure shoe*

the capital injection in order to keep such a big wheel turning".

The Dassler brothers were clearly less concerned about their future. They withdrew from the top management slots and joined the Supervisory Board. On 2 October, Vinzenz Grothgar was elected CEO and Chairman of the Board of the new public limited company. The former director of the influential banking group WestLB and confidant of Deutsche Bank boss Alfred Herrhausen wasn't that interested in sport, preferring fine threads to tracksuits and feeling more at ease in the company jet than on the tartan track. When he took up office, all of a sudden the Puma headquarters was buzzing with auditors, controllers and analysts. The Board conducted operations as it saw fit and did not always regard it as a matter of course to keep the owners abreast of current events. Armin and Gerd Dassler found the omnipresence of capital increasingly unbearable.

### Trouble across the Atlantic

There was one main reason behind Grothgar's appointment: he was a US expert who was supposed to get the American operations back into shape – and quickly. The wholesalers had developed an autonomous existence that the Dassler brothers could not fathom, let alone direct. First of all, Grothgar set about regaining control: in November, he brought the West coast distributor, Pacific Sports Inc., into the Group. Then he decided to swallow up its East Coast counterpart Atlantic Sports Inc.

The crash on the other side of the Atlantic was the result of a flagrant error of judgment to which Armin Dassler and his cousin Horst at Adidas both succumbed: they underestimated the verve with which Nike and Reebok were starting to dominate the US market. Or rather they did not want to admit it, firmly believing that people would continue to appreciate German craftsmanship. "We just missed the boat," Armin Dassler later admitted in succinct fashion. "We were overrun by cheap products and we were stunned at their quality." Nevertheless, he still firmly believed in early 1987 that Puma would soon score points again over Nike and Reebok. At first glance, the situation did not appear so bad: the wholesalers' order books were fairly full. But there was one snag: shoes with the Puma logo were sticking to the retailers' shelves like lead. The Americans wanted to wear their own new hip brands, and not some run-of-the-mill pumps from Franconia. Retailers returned the Formstrip goods to the distributors en masse. Plagued by such setbacks, Puma barely managed to break even in 1986 and, in 1987, 75 million marks' worth of losses had to be written off.

The collapse hit Puma all the harder because it had not made a profit in Germany for years. The US business, on the other hand, had always yielded a good surplus. An accounting trick assured the rich harvest: the shoes manufactured in Taiwan were delivered direct to the USA. According to the books, however, they were first purchased by the headquarters in Herzogenaurach and then sold on to the USA. Puma Germany posted a commission of 22 percent for the transaction, and added a further nine percent in royalties to this already increased purchase price. Altogether, this method produced a hefty commission fee of 32.98 percent.

That was in the good old days, but then the well ran dry. In particular the up-and-coming Reebok posed knotty problems for Puma's decision-makers. Under its new owner Paul Fireman, who was 43 at the time, the American firm grew more and more dynamic by the day. Between 1984 and 1987, revenues of 66 million dollars shot up to 1.33 billion. The former Avon manager Fireman also knew what women (and men) wanted in terms of sports fashion: lightweight footwear for the booming aerobic and fitness sports markets. Actor Jane Fonda had triggered the wave when, five years earlier, she opened two studios in San Francisco, labelled her gymnastics "Aerobics" and then published her work-out book *I Feel Good*. From market research, Fireman knew that consumers only grew to love their sports shoes after a period of seven weeks. "Why?" he wondered, and discovered where – or more precisely, that – the shoe pinched. He experimented with softer leather and created the first sneakers that felt good on the initial outing. They were a huge hit, as 80 percent of all sports shoes sold were used purely as leisure footwear.

Nike, too, was making great strides. Its managers were concerned more with the better earners than the simple folk. Their strategy: to make Nike products so expensive that the craving for them would spread like wildfire. Anyone wanting to wear shoes like those of six-foot-six Nike basketball star Michael Jordan should be prepared to pay a tall price tag. Nike was already selling a cool lifestyle attitude five years before Puma caught on to the same thing. The question of whether the products' performance could justify their price was no longer the focus of sales pitches. The comparatively inexpensive "Borissimo" collection from Puma, on the other hand, had the coolness factor of grandma's feather bed. In addition to this blunder, there was another product group, the thought of which still makes Puma employees squirm to this day: the City Sport Shoe, a hasty decision by Armin Dassler, which was sold off cheaply, mainly in department stores. They had as much appeal as a line of clothing from a school uniform store.

### Bitter subsidies

The financial woes at Puma didn't only spark off a collapse in its share price. The Dassler family also ran into trouble for the very first time in the company's history. To compensate for the losses, Armin and Gerd pledged their shares in order to be able to raise a partner's loan of 62 million marks from Deutsche Bank. They passed this on to the public limited company as a subordinated loan, and it was converted into equity. At the same time, the brothers took the helm again on 9 January 1987: Armin, whose health had been hit hard by diabetes and constant alcohol consumption, assumed the post of CEO and Chairman of the Board. In February, Armin bought out his brother Gerd's shares. Grothgar departed for the Supervisory Board and attempted to end the crisis across the Atlantic as CEO of Puma USA. Confidence in the cat was gone. Analysts by the dozen immediately tipped the Puma share as a "sell": "The euphoria has died down," wrote the Frankfurt DG Bank, "regarding the stock price performance, buyers should wait until the price level has consolidated further."

As if that wasn't enough, cousin Horst of Adidas ended the truce with his relatives that had been in place since their days in France together: in March 1987, in the Budapest Hotel Forum, he spelt out to a small circle of selected journalists that the situation for Puma was worse than had been assumed to date, and there was little prospect of a turnaround. The fact that the banks had floated the company was "an absolute scandal" and placed the entire industry in a bad light. Deutsche Bank issued a prompt response. They said they had drawn attention "clearly" to the problems in the USA in the prospectus, and the introductory price of DM 310 was based on the substantiated proposal of an auditing firm. There had been no damage to initial subscribers since the current price was still above the issue price.

The old family warrior Horst Dassler was no longer just fighting for shoes and shirts, but for the survival of his company Adidas. Beneath his indignation was a deep fear that Puma might be swallowed up by a competitor, and a powerful rival might move in on the other side of the Aurach river. There were some firms, speculated Horst Dassler to representatives from the media, who needed a "major loss carry-forward".

The list of potential Puma hunters grew longer almost every day, thanks to new rumours. In fact, the Dassler brothers negotiated with Otto Beisheim, the billionaire founder of cash-and-carry chain Metro, and with the French conglomerate MTR plc. Beisheim wanted to pay 100 million marks for Puma. In the end both deals failed because Armin and Gerd could not agree on a price.

On 9 April 1987, the people of Herzogenaurach were dealt a blow which led to tears even on Puma's top management floor: Adidas boss Horst Dassler died aged just 51. His death came out of the blue. According to close friends, his body had been ravaged by several tumours. Five weeks previously, at the ISPO sports equipment trade fair, he had put in a surprise appearance at the Puma stand and had shaken hands with dealer friends of his. Unlike himself, the people thus honoured were unaware that it would be the last time. In Horst Dassler's case, too, it was only after his death that the importance of the power-mad networker for his company became apparent. Without him, the colossal tanker that was Adidas was left to flounder with no one at the helm. The company plunged deep into the red – just like Puma.

# 1.10 Chaos

### *The Deutsche Bank era holds sway: a costly financial boon, the brothers sidelined and constant shifts in ownership*

"If you would know the value of money, go and try to borrow some," advised US politician Benjamin Franklin back in the 18th century. The Dassler brothers paid a very high price for their 62-million mark loan: they had to hand over control of their business to the managers at Deutsche Bank. As a major creditor, the financial experts now ruled in autocratic style, but without any sustainable strategy. A lot of their time was spent putting in new levels of management and changing staff. Let's be clear right up front: they did not do their job a single jot better than the Dasslers. Quite the reverse, in fact. For Puma, it was the start of an unprecedented decline that lasted over six years. There was no longer any question of being in the black. The company lurched unchecked towards insolvency. Puma's decline is certainly one of the greatest instances of mismanagement by Deutsche Bank, which had dragged the already ailing sports goods manufacturers to the trading floor and equipped it with a constant flow of new managers. It was only when new CEO Jochen Zeitz managed to curb most of the bankers' power in 1992, thanks to a tough turnaround strategy, that Puma had some sort of future again.

On 19 October 1987, the first annual general meeting of Puma AG took place. The conference meeting room at the Munich Sheraton was decked out in fine style. However, the shareholders were certainly in no mood for celebration. Their mood fluctuated between disappointment and fury about the poor financial results and the lousy share price. For Armin Dassler, this day marked a personal low in his business life. He felt guilty because he had promised the shareholders a golden future at the time of the IPO. In order to eradicate this evil, he decided on a step that made stock exchange history: he paid 4.50 marks in dividends per share – from his personal assets.

It was the last major official act by a representative of Rudolf Dassler's family at Puma AG. With this day, the bank's representatives had sidelined the family for good. The Supervisory Board positions for Armin and Gerd Dassler were nothing more than a formality. Forced out of the company, they would never utter another word in public about their inheritance; instead, they appointed a Hamburg lawyer as spokesman.

Another man took over the chair of the AGM: Manfred Emcke, 54. Deutsche Bank had placed the management consultant with the mighty ego and the image of a turnaround specialist at Armin Dassler's side some time before – as an "adviser", according to the official line. Emcke was formerly boss at the Vorwerk conglomerate and the Reemtsma tobacco group, had turned around flagging family businesses and, like Grothgar, was a faithful vassal to the head of Deutsche Bank, Herrhausen. He was au fait with the rules of rhetoric for spreading confidence in hopeless situations, and made plenty of use of them at the General Meeting. His optimism was part of his new job: Emcke was to be the new Chairman of the

Supervisory Board. The hapless Vinzenz Grothgar cleared his desk the very same day and left the company.

Emcke had also brought a successor for Armin Dassler along with him: 47-year-old Hans Woitschätzke. "The right man at the right time," proclaimed Emcke about his choice. "With an orthodox man it just won't be possible," he said, in another dig at Dassler. Indeed, Woitschätzke, a trained printer who had really wanted to become a professional ice hockey player, did not appear to be the worst choice of CEO for the ailing company: at least he was able to demonstrate some experience in the sports sector. In 1972 he had founded the cross-country ski manufacturer Trak, and successfully produced skis with the "fish scale bottom". Nine years later he bought the insolvent Austrian ski factory Kneissl and revived its fortunes. He knew, he said, looking at Adidas, "how to fend off blows – even those below the belt." And Emcke proclaimed his optimism about the turnaround: "I believe I can do it faster than people think. Broadly speaking, the problem is resolved, we have a super concept." Just how wrong can a man be.

The idea of squeezing costs had already occurred to the Dassler brothers. The approximately 50 million marks they distributed each year to top athletes, sports associations and clubs had long been available. Apart from Boris Becker and Martina Navratilova, the superstars, every previously cosseted athlete there was ran the risk of losing his or her endorsement from Herzogenaurach with immediate effect. A bigger problem was that Puma still had no decent weapons to counter its assailants Nike and Reebok. The Germans only took a pointedly casual interest in the upturn in the two companies' fortunes. They continued to believe that the lightweight goods from abroad were nothing more than a passing fad. In 1985, Horst Dassler boasted: "1987 is set to be the big year when we intend to focus particularly on the USA and Japan." At that time, Adidas was still the number 2 in the USA – just one year later it was only number 4, with Puma in fifth place. Now the Franconians also feared for their supremacy on the domestic market, where they had a share of around 90 percent. "This monopoly must be broken," announced Anthony Churchill, Nike's viceroy for Germany. Reebok, too, sounded the attack. Reebok Germany's manager, Richard Litzel, had forecast sales worth ten million marks for 1987 – the target was achieved in just four months. Even up and down the country, at major retailers Sport-Scheck in Munich and Görtz in Hamburg, for example, the soft imports were ousting the sturdy products from Franconia.

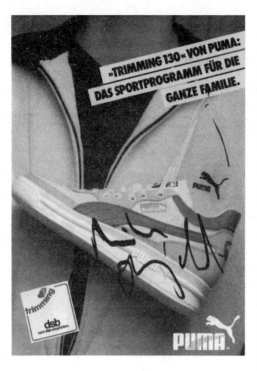

*Millions of sponsorship money down the drain with Trimm Trab*

Puma failed to make a recovery in the following year, 1988. Hasty experiments with fashionable collections consumed a lot of money and attracted no buyers. The products finally ended up on the bargain counters at Kaufhof, Karstadt and other low-cost department store outlets. In the USA, too, the picture was no better. Woitschätzke sent a friend to America, the lawyer Christopher "Toby" Smith, who was to conduct a management buy-out. The idea was that the bosses would buy the subsidiary, Puma would lend them the money to do so and the ailing branch would finally disappear from the books. A dubious business close to the edge of legality, particularly since Puma would have to continue to bear all the costs and losses – a fact managers kept from the shareholders. Nevertheless, in 1988 the team established the US company Sports Enterprises Inc. (SEI).

## Advent of the number crunchers

The Puma simply refused to make any great strides. All affirmations by Woitschätzke and Emcke that the situation was finally looking up proved to be unfounded. The CEO continued to put on a brave face in these difficult times. In the middle of the year he even offered prospects of a break-even result. But Woitschätzke had gone out on a limb and had to correct himself again just a few days later. Now he merely forecast being able to come "close to the break-even point" at best. More and more number crunchers from management consultancy firm Roland Berger wandered about the corridors, and trade journalists happily went on speculating as to when Puma would be bought up by an investor at a ridiculously low price. Of the loan granted by Dassler to the company, only 21.5 million marks remained. Woitschätzke announced that the collections would be drastically pruned, with about one third of the footwear and clothing to be cut without replacement. "They are firing small rounds and not bullets at the market," was Supervisory Board Chairman Emcke's scathing attack on his own team.

*"Dear" friends: Dassler (centre) with Jupp Heynckes, Udo Lattek, Otto Rehagel (left to right), shown here with US sprinter Evelyn Ashford*

Most of all, the Puma managers wanted to get rid of their most expensive contract: Boris Becker's. The ginger prince who had set the whole country alight just two years earlier had already passed the peak of his appeal, and made a name for himself as a tax evader and womanizer. At Wimbledon, Woitschätzke pressed Becker's manager Ion Tiriac to annul the 27-million mark contract concluded in 1984. The Rumanian suddenly seemed a whole lot less friendly and no longer issued invitations to his home in Monte Carlo. Following tough negotiations, however, he agreed to the separation. Boris Becker felt so at home with the Puma racket, though, that he used it again at the Davis Cup in Dortmund in the summer of 1988 – this time without the logo.

But there were other former big names that Armin Dassler had provided with hefty annuity agreements. For example, Udo Lattek, who had become the most successful club trainer in German football. Dassler had promised him an astronomically high minimum royalty for Puma articles: 180,000 marks per year right through to his 65th year. It was the later CEO Jochen Zeitz who overturned this agreement. Martina Navratilova and football legend Diego Maradona were also given their marching orders. Also well catered for were the former directors of the company, who enjoyed generous pension payments.

Woitschätzke attempted to alter the course somehow with a new, young team. The only problem was that he was unable to get rid of the old die-hards because the money was not there for severance payments. He appointed 44-year-old Bernd Szymanski, who came from Triumph-Adler, as central executor and assigned him responsibility for management control, finance, tax and personnel; soon, internally, they gave him the nickname of "Savings Commissar". Karl Taylor, 38, a PhD of South African descent and previously a manager at chocolate bar manufacturer Mars, now focused on the neglected corporate marketing division. Gerhard Scholz, 36, whom Woitschätzke had wooed away from skiing goggles manufacturer UVEX, took over exports. And for the German market he recruited Eberhard Körn, 37, who had worked for Procter & Gamble in distribution and who equipped his sales staff for the first time with a laptop by the name of "Pussi". Annual results remained pitiful: 800 million marks in turnover, 50 million down on the previous year, and once again way into the red: minus 12.4 million.

At the time, Armin Dassler still made the short journey from his home to the company headquarters in his Daimler each morning. He would sit down at his desk in his large office and his secretary would serve him a hot drink. He no longer had any say in what went on.

While the men in dark suits reduced operations in Herzogenaurach to a bare minimum and Deutsche Bank, which led the banking pool, looked desperately for an investor to buy the 72 percent stake of brothers Armin and Gerd Dassler, Nike really took off. Fans and employees of the company alike adored the new brand. They had the "Swoosh" emblem tattooed on their skin and went into a frenzy over their new basketball supergod Michael Jordan. Puma had finally dwindled to a loser brand. Anyone caught wearing the Formstrip on their shoes at school would be the butt of malicious remarks, or at best be regarded by others with sympathetic pity.

### A new owner

The firm Cosa Liebermann worked for Puma in Asia in the 1980s. The Swiss pairing of Johann Wälchli and Ernst Liebermann had established the company in 1912 in Japan as Liebermann-Wälchli & Co., a trading company mainly for clothing products. Since 1970, Cosa Liebermann had run a kind of Asian base store for the distribution of Herzogenaurach's stock. Managing director Guido Cherubini, who was born near St Gallen in Switzerland, produced good returns and had been a friend of the Puma family for many

*Puma "live" – weird fashion damaged the brand*

years. Yet he had nearly gone and spoiled it all with the Dasslers on the very first day. When he entered the Puma head office in Herzogenaurach in 1972, he stood chatting with a few staff members in reception. He let slip the name Adidas, enthused about their shoes and innocently asked: "Aren't they in this town too?" One of the employees replied: "If you want to be acquainted with Rudolf Dassler for longer than a couple of minutes, please never mention that word again. Just say NG." "NG?", asked Cherubini. "What does that mean?" " 'Nicht gennant' ('the unmentionable')," replied the Puma man. It was a good piece of advice: Rudolf Dassler and the man from Tokyo got along just fine. Cherubini was also a friend of Armin Dassler's. Dassler Junior suddenly became interested in Far Eastern prophecies and the wisdoms of Feng Shui. In order to improve procurement, which ranked as one of the biggest headaches in the company, they set up a company in Hong Kong called World Cat Limited.

In early April 1989, Cherubini flew to Franconia once more. A member of his Board of Directors, Claude Barbey, came up from Geneva. The two Swiss men had spent a long time beforehand discussing whether Cosa Liebermann should take over the 72 percent Dassler stake. They finally agreed on a definite yes. There was plenty of money around and both men felt the brand had high potential. The deal was completed on 13 April 1989. From that day forth, Armin and Gerd Dassler were no longer legally involved in Puma. According to the estimates, Cosa Liebermann paid around 85 million marks for its admission ticket. Measured by Puma's market value, they would have had to cough up over 300 million marks. However, that was pure theory, since the banks were owed 62 million marks. Armin waived the right to severance pay so as not to damage the company and wrote in a letter to the bank that he didn't want his money until Puma was bringing in profits again.

The Puma Board breathed a sigh of relief, but the relief over the new owners did not last for long. Three months later Cosa Liebermann was swallowed up by the large Swiss industrialist Stephan Schmidtheiny. He played with the big cat for just six months, then he too started looking for a new investor. Puma appeared to be jinxed. CEO Woitschätzke certainly lacked the rigour, ultimately, to turn around the company. The constant shifts in ownership also made it difficult for him to pursue one clear direction.

On 28 August 1989, Hamburg lawyer Werner Hofer was working his way through Puma AG's balance sheet. Hofer was a close business associate of Ingvar Wenehed, a top manager of the Swedish company Aritmos. The man from Helsingborg travelled around the world with one mission: to track down suitable candidates for the conglomerate's portfolio. Aritmos, which focused largely on the US market, owned brands that included Tretorn (tennis balls), Etonic (golf shoes) and Stiga (lawn mowers). The analysis of the figures brought Hofer to an amazing realization which he immediately passed on to Wenehed: Puma had a profit potential in excess of a million marks. All that was required was to take good care of the brand, then the company could soon be in the black again. Wenehed listened attentively and made a decision: he would buy.

On 27 November, Wenehed, Hofer and Puma's CEO Woitschätzke boarded a Lufthansa jet at Munich Airport and flew to Hong Kong to visit Cosa Liebermann boss Cherubini. The parties were in agreement in just a few hours: Aritmos was to take over 49.9 percent of Cosa Liebermann's shares on 30 January 1990, and acquire an option for the remaining 22.1 percent. With the split, the new majority shareholder was able to keep the heavily loss-making sports goods manufacturer off its books for the current financial year. In February 1991, the Swedes increased their stake to 72 percent.

On 30 November 1989, Wenehed and Hofer had arranged a meeting at Deutsche Bank at Stachus in the centre of Munich in order to ensure speedy completion of the Puma business. They were led into a conference room and waited for their discussion partners – in vain. After a small eternity, a spokesman for the bank entered the room and explained to them that the Chairman of the company, Alfred Herrhausen, had been assassinated and that therefore all meetings were cancelled. Alfred Herrhausen of all people, who had declared Puma a matter for top management attention. The deal could not be completed until several days later.

## Storm from the East

The year 1989 ended for Puma on the same miserable note as had the previous few years: sales shrank drastically again, to 520 million marks, and the company posted losses to the tune of 13.2 million. However, it proved to have been one of the most pivotal years in the company's history, and not just because of the constant change of owners and the death of the Deutsche Bank chairman. On 9 November, the first revolution on German soil led to the fall of the Berlin Wall. Millions of East Germans flowed into the west and visited the shrine of consumerism; many of them stayed. For Puma, an extended domestic market unexpectedly opened up which gave the managers new hope on the sales front.

The mood was positive in the country and everything was geared towards reunification. The Puma AG shareholders who had travelled to the AGM at the Munich Sheraton in July 1990 were unable, however, to celebrate unreservedly. "Puma has had an interest-free loan from me for years now," said one small shareholder, summing up his discontent. "This isn't my idea of being a shareholder – I would be as well to give to charity!" Hans Woitschätzke, the CEO, once more painted a rosy picture. "The point where the business will become profitable is within our reach," he resounded. With all kinds of rhetorical tricks, he tried to cover up the fact that Puma was already clinically dead.

The banks were no longer interested, Puma's debts were immense and there was no sign of light at the end of the tunnel. The bankers were pressing the company to increase its capital by a nominal 20 million marks and insisted that Aritmos had to guarantee to buy the shares should the placement fail. In the end, the Swedes bore the increase alone and held over 80 percent of Puma's capital.

*Armin Dassler – signs off*

Armin Dassler watched the decline from afar in his wood-panelled office. He gathered together a small circle of former colleagues. Together they discussed the situation and drank whisky in the adjoining bar room to wash away all the frustration. Late in the afternoon they switched venues, continuing their discussion 300 metres away at Dassler's own home, which was laid out like some vast valley station at the foot of an Alpine ski lift. The cavernous party room in the cellar was a memorial to better times for Dassler. Here, he had negotiated the contracts with Diego Maradona and Boris Becker. Football stars such as Lothar Matthäus and even Pelé, the football god, had dropped by. Udo Jürgens would bring along his latest records, they would sing and drink, and afterwards the hit singer would spend the night in Dassler's guestroom.

Dassler was like a wounded stag at bay. His nerves were shattered. The money worries, the threadbare US business and the exhausting talks with the financial institutions had all robbed him of his zest for life. Time and again he and his wife would go for a few weeks to Salzburg, where they had celebrated their marriage, to shake off the pressures that were weighing down on him. Soon his body capitulated as well. Cancer ravaged his liver and the doctors at the University Hospital in Erlangen transplanted the organ of a dead infant into him. They were unable to save him. On 14 October 1990, at 2.30 in the afternoon, Armin Dassler died in bed at home aged just 61. His wife and his sons Michael, Frank and Jörg were at his side in his final minutes. It was their decision only to allow immediate family at the funeral. Outside the family, only his driver, Manfred Langer, and Dassler's assistant, Elfriede Eck, knew of his death. On 17 October at 8am, four pall-bearers carried the mortal remains to the small chapel of rest at the cemetery in Herzogenaurach. One hundred dark red roses adorned the coffin. Two years later his last wish was fulfilled: the passionate fan of 1. FC Köln received a replica two-metre high tip of Cologne cathedral as a gravestone.

When the death of "Mr Puma" became public, a shockwave

surged through the corridors of the Puma headquarters. He had been admired by most of the employees. The fact that Armin Dassler had driven the company to the brink of ruin with his provincial style of management no longer mattered in their minds. This was the absolute end of the Puma and Dassler era. It would be years before a Dassler once again entered the company headquarters on Würzburger Strasse.

**2**

# The Return of the Cat

## 2.0 Leaping Back

Tuesday, 24 April 2007 – at the Maritim Hotel in Berlin's Stauffen-bergstrasse, the Puma logo is everywhere. The evening event of the "Go Live 2" international sales conference is in full swing in the large function room. On a shiny, polished black stage stands a blond man of 44. He beams across the expanse of the room, eyes sparkling. The light from the video screen, which displays a leaping big cat, bathes his body in the corporate shades of red. Jochen Zeitz, Chairman and CEO of Puma AG, has reached his goal – for the time being at least. "After 15 years, Puma has finally found its home," the 44-year-old announces to the auditorium. The guests – around 950 Puma employees from 72 nations – hang on his every word.

Zeitz then invites a man onto the stage who, with his company, has given Puma this new home. The man is François-Henri Pinault, also 44 and CEO of the French group Pinault-Printemps-Redoute (PPR). The two managers walk smiling towards one another and give each other a warm hug. They are old business acquaintances and new true friends, also kindred spirits in lifestyle. A few years earlier, Pinault had wanted to make the German CEO of his group subsidiary, Gucci. Zeitz considered the offer – and turned it down. Not that the high-end fashion house wouldn't have tempted him, but he was by no means finished with Puma.

Now Pinault is back. Two weeks earlier he had announced the intention of taking over the majority share of Puma, ideally even the entire company, through PPR. Zeitz had actively helped promote the deal in the background, and had welcomed it warmly in public. He really, really wanted PPR as the owner. The Gucci group. High society. Finally, the right investor had come along for his sportlifestyle and fashion company. Finally, a high-end fashion house rather than a stingy ex-coffee roaster like the last main shareholder, Tchibo owner Günter Herz.

On this mild April evening, Zeitz has been working for Puma for 17 years and 113 days, and has been CEO for almost 14 years. He has long been older than the target group for his products. Many of the employees attending the event were not even at nursery school when he became the youngest CEO of a German listed company. He built a team and moulded it. He made the products attractive and the employees themselves passionate about the shirts and shoes with the big cat logo, so that they would spread the Puma message far and wide. Tonight, he is once more doing everything he can to keep them on track and energize them. In doing so, he does not act as a team player – because that's not what he is. He is a self-reliant coach, always one step ahead of everyone else, determined, uncompromising and unyielding. A kind of Jürgen Klinsmann of the sports equipment industry. Like the former national football coach, who gave Germany the summer's fairytale of 2006, he has the ability to train young people into a world championship team. And, like Klinsmann, Zeitz remains unapproachable to the majority of them – however much respect and admiration they may have for him. Does anyone in the company really know Jochen Zeitz as a human being?

Day and night Zeitz toils for Puma. He constantly checks that everything is on track. After a radical restructuring programme, he has increased the market value of the company by more than 5,000 percent. He has filled the pockets of his employees and shareholders and earned a few million himself. He deserves to be celebrated for this success. No other manager of a DAX or MDAX concern has achieved such a performance curve.

In 1990, when Jochen Zeitz first joined Puma, nobody would have considered such a development possible. At that time, no analyst would have given as much as one cent for Puma. The shoes with the Formstrip were deemed totally uncool by youngsters and athletes; the products were piled high on discounters' bargain counters. The company with the long history was facing insolvency, worn down in the blind battle with its rival Adidas. Year after year sales were falling further and profitability had become a distant memory. The management team at the Franconian head office licked their wounds, washed down their frustration with copious amounts of alcohol or surrendered to their fate.

Zeitz achieved a minor economic miracle, as the following chapters show. They describe how he breathed life back into the fading big cat and helped it make a giant leap forwards. They also give an outlook on the Puma group's future prospects – on both the opportunities and the risks that may be lying in wait.

## 2.1 The Apt Pupil

*The rapid rise of Jochen Zeitz: a threefold shock, the Mannheim years, the first flop and CEO overnight*

It was a sunny autumn day in Munich, mid-September 1989. Many visitors to the International Trade Fair for Sports Equipment and Fashion (ISPO) were relaxing on the outdoor seating between the exhibition halls and turning their faces to the sun. The ISPO at this time was uncontestedly the largest and most important trade event for manufacturers of sports equipment. Anyone who wanted to be anyone on the scene had to show presence, and bring along a robust liver for stand parties and evening events running with booze. The visitors followed a daily ritual of establishing contacts, spotting trends and closing deals. The atmosphere in the industry this particular year was pretty subdued: yes, on the one hand, sales had rocketed – the German market alone had grown to 30 billion marks – but, on the other, nobody's products were really bringing in money any more. Cut-throat competition had driven margins down and down. Despite all their worries, the trade-fair participants had no desire to lose out on the fun of the ISPO: depression was concealed behind a false party spirit.

The blond six-footer in the dark suit striding purposefully down the aisles of the hall towards the Puma stand went practically unnoticed. No one recognized him, why would they? He was a nobody who had never previously had anything to do with the sports shoe or sportswear trade. The 26-year-old jumped onto the platform of the Puma area, adorned with its leaping big cat, and marched straight up to the reception desk. "Hello, my name is Jochen Zeitz. I'd like to meet Mr Karl Taylor," he said in English. The company's head of advertising, Helmut Fischer, who was behind the desk welcoming guests, surveyed the obviously German visitor. "Why is he speaking English?" he wondered. Then he realized whom he had in front of him. His colleague, Taylor, who until recently had been head of marketing at Puma, had raved to him about Zeitz. "I'm getting a new assistant from Hamburg," he had said, "he's coming from Colgate. A really fantastic guy." He brought the visitor up to date: "Sorry. You can't speak to Mr Taylor. He no longer works for Puma."

Taylor had been released out of the blue a few days previously. The Board harboured the suspicion that he had been involved in shady deals. Zeitz displayed virtually no emotion in response to the news. "Well, as far as I'm concerned that's it, then," he said with his cool Mannheim accent and turned on his heel. "Please wait a minute," Fischer called after him, "I'll introduce you to our board member in charge of sales and marketing, Manfred Häussler." Zeitz stayed and drank a cup of coffee with Häussler, who declared that Puma was well on the way to recovery and that there was already a new man in line to head up the marketing department. The restructuring was almost complete and it was now time to drive the brand forward so that it could go back into the lead. "I'd still like you to take up the position in January next year," offered the Puma director, and invited him to attend the next international sales conference in November as an observer. He was to see the spirit of optimism within the firm for himself. Zeitz agreed – he had no desire to throw in the towel right away.

Zeitz had no idea that he would soon be seized by grave doubts about the quality of his new employer. The sales event, held in a good, plain conference hotel in Biel in the Bernese Seeland of Switzerland, took his breath away. From the back row of the conference room he watched as uninspired sales people put up their slides and presented concepts that the Colgate man tagged as provincial. His future boss, Klaus Popp, head of marketing and a chain smoker, who had not crossed his path during his job interviews, stood before the auditorium and humourlessly rattled off a presentation on sales promotion. "I'm in the wrong film," Zeitz thought disconcertedly, and returned with all speed to Hamburg. Nevertheless, he was not ready to give up. The word "failure" does not feature in his vocabulary. "If you want to win, you shouldn't think about losing," is one of his sayings.

The winter air above Herzogenaurach was frosty and clear at around nine o'clock on the morning of 2 January 1990 when, a good month later, Zeitz strode into the foyer of the Puma headquarters in Würzburger Strasse. Once again, he wore a dark suit and, once again, he marched straight up to the reception desk. "My name is Jochen Zeitz," he said, "I start work in the marketing department today." "Zeitz, Zeitz...," the receptionist muttered as she leafed through her documents. "I'm sorry, there's no mention of you here." "You are joking, aren't you?" said the young manager. At that moment he would dearly have loved to grab his briefcase and left the claustrophobic little town behind him as fast as he could. But even at this point, his ambition was stronger than his frustration.

"Shocking," he thought. This was already the third time he'd been disappointed by his new company, before he'd even done a single day's work. First, the incident at the ISPO. Then, the conference from hell. And now this: his first day – and nobody had any idea who he was. He had imagined the start of his new career would be rather different.

### Son of Mannheim

Jochen Zeitz had never actually had the ambition to work in a business, let alone become a manager. He wanted to be a surgeon. He was born on 6 April 1963 in Mannheim, Germany. His father was a gynaecologist and his mother a dentist. His parents lived lives befitting two members of the educated classes with Protestant discipline, and brought up their daughter and two sons accordingly. Although they had not seen much of the world, they were thoroughly cosmopolitan. Fashion was unimportant to them. In his own practice and as the senior consultant in the Diakonissen hospital, his father worked hard, delivering more than 1,300 babies each year – it didn't leave much time for the family. Jochen went to the Karl-Friedrich-Gymnasium grammar school on Roonstrasse, the oldest school in the town and with a traditional leaning towards the classics. He learned Greek, Latin and Hebrew and opted for History and Biology as his main subjects, with Protestant Religion and German as subsidiaries. Even today, he sometimes wakes up in the night from a dream that he has got to take another Latin exam. It is the only nightmare that haunts him.

At the age of 16 he acquired his hunting licence – hunting is part of the family tradition. And, whenever he had the time, he would grab his guitar and play rock 'n' roll with his band for 300 marks a night. He had an athletic figure and broad shoulders from an early age, not least because he played American football in the rough first league team of the Mannheim Redskins. It was a tough sport, but nevertheless, he did not exactly belong to the tough guys of the 1980s. He felt most comfortable in a pair of nice Levi 501s and a Lacoste or Ralph Lauren polo shirt, more the uniform

*Zeitz playing American football, aged 17*

of a preppy. He had covered the seat of his Vespa with a pair of old jeans. But he also already wore Puma shoes – the "King" and "Maradona". In his view of the world, the brand stood for individuality.

Zeitz passed his school-leaving exam with a grade of 1.7 (on a scale of 1 to 6, with 1 being the best). He graduated as one of the best of his class, but it was not enough to allow him to study medicine, for which he would have needed a score of 1.4. Later, in an interview, Zeitz mentioned that his greatest disappointment in life was not to have been able to study medicine in Germany. On no account, however, did he want to lose sight of his ambition to become a surgeon. He was spared military service because of a back problem, and moved to Florence, Tuscany, to have a go at an Italian university. At that time, his foreign language skills were not particularly well developed. He had learned Italian in the summer holidays when he was 17, and when he left school he was just about able to speak broken English. It was in Italy, however, that he discovered his talent for languages as he swotted up on his vocabulary for the entrance examination. Today, he can converse more or less fluently in English, French, Italian, Portuguese, Spanish and Swahili, which gives him the inestimable advantage of virtually always being able to conduct negotiations with top-level personnel in the sports business in their native tongues.

After two semesters of hanging around he felt the urge to try something different. On the advice of a friend, he enrolled to study at the European Business School, specializing in marketing and finance. The EBS at Schloss Reichartshausen in the Rheingau ranks among one of the few elite private universities in Germany. It was the right place for him. "Jochen is very intelligent, he has a very high intellect and his mastery of management through communication is virtually unrivalled," was the assessment of his tutor there, Manfred Bruhn, who went on to become professor of Marketing at the University of Basel. During his studies, Zeitz completed internships at Deutsche Bank and BASF in Germany, at

Dresdner Bank and Rothschild in Paris, at Mercedes in California (where he even sold a car to Madonna) and at Schott-Glas in Brazil. He took holiday jobs preparing profitability analyses, developing strategies for the expansion of factory capacity and drawing up finance and marketing plans. At the end of his course he was awarded the top grade for his dissertation and left the EBS as one of its best graduates.

Today he is still constantly full of energy, always trying to progress something or other. Should he find himself at a loose end, through no fault of his own, he begins to jig his legs vigorously. His mother then still says to him: "Jochen, calm down!" He is in his element when multitasking. Laptop on his knee and telephone to his ear: dealing with e-mails and telephone calls simultaneously is one of his most highly developed skills. He cannot bear to waste time. He very rarely sits down to watch television – he soon gets bored with series and shows – and much prefers to watch his own choice of films on DVD, but even then his laptop is normally running in parallel. And he only ever switches on Günter Jauch's German version of *Who wants to be a Millionaire?*, which he likes to watch every now and then, if he can eat dinner at the same time.

Before even graduating, Zeitz received a job offer from the American group Colgate-Palmolive. The German head of personnel at the time, Elk von Reisswitz, had given the EBS students some training in how to behave at job interviews. Zeitz made a positive impression on him and von Reisswitz offered him a place on a trainee programme with Colgate in Hamburg. The apt pupil thanked him, but declined because he wanted to work abroad. He promptly received a better offer: a job in new product development on Park Avenue, New York, reporting directly to the head of the company. Zeitz did not hesitate: America, the land of great, untamed liberty – that was precisely what he wanted.

The move to the Big Apple proved to be a double stroke of luck for him. He not only became acquainted with the fundamentals of modern marketing and new product launches in practice, but also with Birgit, who would later become his wife. She was the sister of a university classmate, four years older than him and visiting New York at that time. She came from a fashion house in Jülich, had studied Communication Design and managed purchasing and marketing for the family business. The couple married in 1992 in the church of Nideggen in the Eifel hills, close to where his father-in-law goes hunting. Zeitz's boss at Colgate invited him to stay in the USA for another two years. However, not wanting to tie himself down to America too young, Zeitz was ready to return to Germany and transferred to the Hamburg office. There, as product manager, he took care of the products with the Colgate label: toothpaste and all that goes with it.

He was not unhappy in his work, but neither was he exactly enthusiastic about it. Somehow, the fear was creeping over him that he was not making quick-enough progress with his career. So when a head-hunter phoned him in the late summer of 1989 and offered him a job at Puma as the Business Manager for Footwear, he listened attentively. In future he would be responsible for the kind of shoes he himself wore out of conviction. It was a challenging task, on which the future of the whole company depended. Footwear still counted for two-thirds of the group's sales, while textiles played merely a subordinate role. All the same, though: New York, Hamburg, Herzogenaurach – it did not sound exactly like a dream career. However, he encouraged himself with the thought: "You're young, if it doesn't work out, at least you'll have tried." He had absolutely no intention of living in the Franconian backwoods, so he looked for a place to live in Nuremberg.

### Arrival in the backwoods

The first few days at his new company again plunged Zeitz into serious doubt as to whether he had been right to give up Colgate. He soon realized that the optimistic business forecasts that CEO Woitschätzke and marketing manager Taylor had presented at his job interviews were nothing more than waste paper. The company bore no traces of the innovativeness they had raved about. The board member in charge of sales and marketing, Manfred Häussler, who had come to Puma on the recommendation of Deutsche Bank, was at loggerheads with the CEO, which made it doubly difficult to implement fresh marketing ideas in the company. In frustration, Zeitz called his former head of personnel at Colgate in Hamburg and asked him what he made of the tricky situation. "Come back, you're not going to get anywhere there," advised von Reisswitz. Nevertheless, Zeitz stayed, going back would have meant having to concede a bitter defeat. He wanted to win through.

Zeitz tried to work in the way he had learned to do things at Colgate. In the neighbouring office sat dyed-in-the-wool Herzogenauracher Erwin Hildel, who was responsible, amongst other things, for market research. The task did not challenge him a great deal, as a systematic approach was not traditionally called for in this area at Puma. On the contrary, Armin Dassler had once written on a market research book: "What's the point of this rubbish? I am the market." One day, Zeitz went into Hildel's office and asked him: "Can you please let me have the market research reports for the last three months?" Hildel replied: "Three months? Dream on!" Despite the fast-moving trends in the market, they had half-yearly figures at best – if any.

This was a strange situation for a young manager who considered American-style market reports to be the measure of all things. Puma's employees, however, still preferred to peek surreptitiously at what was happening on the other side of the Aurach, or sound out acquaintances on what was new at Adidas. Although the Dassler family had long since left the company, the brothers' feud lived on in the minds of the staff. According to established tradition, the letters "NG" were still written below the blue Adidas line on the sales charts that Hildel received from the German market research organisation Gesellschaft für Konsumforschung (GfK). "What does that stand for?" Zeitz wondered. "It means 'nicht genannt', the 'unmentionable', and is another way of saying 'Adidas'," an embarrassed Hildel replied. "What a load of nonsense," Zeitz grumbled, "as from now the competition will be referred to as Adidas."

While the business had ground to a halt, the staff carousel continued to turn merrily. People came and went without there being any fundamental changes to the company's hopeless situation. Häussler moved to Hamburg to the cigarette manufacturer Reemtsma and Zeitz's boss Klaus Popp, who had previously worked for Herta sausages and who had made a bad impression on Zeitz at the Swiss conference, continued his attempts at managing the marketing department. Zeitz considered him to be unqualified and ignored him whenever he could. He seized the helm himself and acted, de facto, as the department head. Popp did not stop him and puffed away on his cigarettes in peace. Soon Popp too was out of the way – Zeitz, observers claim, had put pressure on the top management to remove him. And, suddenly, the now 28-year-old was quite officially the sports equipment manufacturer's top marketing man, despite the CEO's fairly sceptical attitude towards him: Zeitz was regarded as a Häussler man.

The months passed by without anything decisive happening in the troubled company. The team was primarily concerned with itself, and anyone who had not already resigned in spirit took an active part in the favourite preoccupation of the day: blaming

*One of many variations of the logo*

each other. Zeitz had not known anyone when he took up his position at Puma and, therefore, did not have to show consideration for anyone. One day, employees watched through their office windows as the go-getting blond strode across the grounds with a camera and took photographs of cars. They couldn't work out what he was up to. A few days later they discovered the purpose behind the photo shoot: using the photographs, Zeitz showed how different the Puma logos were. Whether on vehicles, packaging or in brochures – all the departments had changed the shape and colour of the logo as they saw fit, whenever the fancy took them. There was no trace at all of a uniform corporate identity (CI). The marketing boss laid down rules: from then on, the puma was only to leap in the way it still does today, and only the dark Puma green was permitted as a colour. "Nobody is to mess around with the logo any more," were his instructions. He later replaced the green with the red that is the corporate colour today, which seemed more modern to him.

Zeitz also taught the Franconians how to build up sales pressure in the shops. Until then, nobody had given any thought to a clear message at the point of sale. From that time, however, all promotional materials had to be "Puma-like" – from the sales stands through to poster frames. Zeitz also drew up marketing plans. His employees had to change their way of thinking: although they had given consideration to promotional measures in the past, they had never learned how to approach the market in a tactically skilful manner.

Zeitz stepped on the gas – but was nevertheless unable to pick up speed properly. The banks showed little understanding of emotional marketing, which had a cost attached. They preferred to see their money back. Certainly the share price had increased since the Holland-based Swedish group Aritmos had taken on the role of majority shareholder – but the figures behind the share remained lamentable. Chairman Hans Woitschätzke had not managed to turn things round and would defend himself with regard to the press before he was even attacked. It was incomprehensible, he said, how a company which at that time had "such a plain, small company infrastructure" could have become so large and well known. Once again, he took pains to declare that Puma was on the road to recovery and would even post profits in 1991. In reality, however, the situation was more serious than even the pessimists feared. The majority shareholder Aritmos was particularly displeased about the American front name Sport Enterprises. Overall, the bottom line for the years under Woitschätzke was sobering. Since he had taken office, the specialist retailers' confidence in the brand had dropped like a stone. The situation would probably have been even more dramatic if the dealers had not treated the Franconians to some goodwill for old times' sake. The boring products with the big cat logo no longer suited the times. In addition, the attempt to increase profitability quickly by switching to cheap production in Asia had exacerbated the situation: quality declined rapidly. Customers stormed into the shops and angrily returned shoes with the soles coming off.

Puma's whole business was standing on extremely thin ice. Since 1990, the equity capital had dropped to 42.1 million marks, below the subscribed capital of 50 million marks. Aritmos was becoming very, very scared. Within a matter of weeks, the principal shareholder lost confidence in the CEO, and by the end of April 1991 Woitschätzke had to go – officially, he stepped down for personal reasons. His successor was a Swede by the name of Stefan Jacobsson, who had previously managed the business activities of Aritmos' US subsidiary Tretorn.

## The end of the tracksuit

In the early 1990s, an article appeared in the American magazine *Sports Illustrated* about a horrifying incident. It told the story of 15-year-old Michael Eugene Thomas from Maryland who, with 100 determinedly saved dollars, had fulfilled a dream: to buy a pair of Nike "Air Jordan" basketball shoes. The model came from the product line of black basketball star Michael Jordan, who was hero-worshipped in the black neighbourhoods of America. Every evening, the high-school student cleaned his new sneakers lovingly, polishing away the tiniest scratches and pulling the thick laces flat.

"Before I let anyone take those shoes, they'll have to kill me," he had said. Scarcely two weeks after he bought the shoes, the police found his body in a wood near his school. The shoes were missing from his feet. The murderer was quickly found – his name was David Martin, a fellow student two years older than the boy, who did not have 100 dollars for basketball shoes and had therefore strangled Michael with his bare hands in order to rob him. The magazine reported nine additional "sneaker murders". The whole of America was shaken.

The story from Maryland made it shatteringly clear that sports shoes and sportswear had long since left behind their status as articles of purely practical value worn for physical training. They had become desirable cult objects with an emotional potential that could hardly be overestimated. Zeitz had already had the opportunity to observe this phenomenon during his time in New York. An increasing number of young people strolled through the streets of the city with heavy sneakers and hooded jackets. They wore clothes with names like "Torsion", "Hydrolite", "Gel Stroke" and "The Pump", which they bought not only in sports shops but also in the "young fashion" sections of department stores, where aggressive heavy-metal music pumped out of the loudspeakers. The most important aspect of the clothing was no longer the athletic touch, but the brand logo which the youngsters showed off as a status symbol. They no longer wore them to sports halls or stadia, but to school, the disco or hip meeting places. Even in Germany, more and more people were prepared to reach deep into their pockets for the right image. In the fashionable shops of Berlin, Hamburg and Munich a pair of shoes with air cushioning would cost up to 400 marks. Sport had become fashionable and American companies such as Converse, British Knights, L.A. Gear, as well as Reebok and Nike, which had knocked Adidas off the top spot in the world rankings in 1989, were profiting handsomely as a result. Increasingly, even leading fashion designers were using the cut of sportswear and sending their models down the catwalk in sneakers: Jean-Paul Gaultier, Karl Lagerfeld and Katharine Hamnett, to name but a few.

Only in Herzogenaurach, at the headquarters of the two giants of the market, Adidas and Puma, was there little indication of this change in the times. As in the 1980s, the Franconians threatened once again to let an opportunity pass by. And yet, the market researchers had presented clear figures: only 20 percent of all sports items sold were actually still used only for sporting purposes. For a long time, however, the product developers of both companies resolutely ignored the new consumer behaviour. They continued to focus on quality and functionality in the dusty old tradition of the Dassler-Sportschuhfabrik, and preferred to develop expensive products for specialized sports rather than hip sportswear for rap and techno fans. And, if a designer ever did feel the urge to slavishly follow the American trend, the results were usually weird leisure products in pink or racing green which pitiable athletes had to wear in front of the television cameras.

The Adidas managers had been putting up a particularly strong resistance to any closer encounter with the spirit of the times ever since French entrepreneur Bernard Tapie had purchased the ailing family firm for 440 million marks in 1990. The man from Marseilles wanted to transform Adidas into a fashion company and bring in famous designers such as Kenzo to achieve this end. The management, however, attempted to respond to the prophesied trend of 1990s society with a new line by the name of Adidas Equipment: a return to functional sports clothing without any of that fashion nonsense. "It's time to get back to what is essential," read one pithy advertising slogan.

Puma had more important things to worry about. The vulture of bankruptcy was circling ever lower over the company. At the height of the troubles, its accumulated losses carried forward amounted to 210 million marks. In the finance department, accounting chief Dieter Bock, later the finance director, had all profit contributions calculated at the customer and item levels and drew up reports listing the products and dealers on which the company was losing money. He sounded the alarm forcibly, yet the Board's response was casual. Bock gradually lost all interest in Puma. Nobody at management level seemed to want to know the answers to the questions: "where is our goal?" or "which direction should we head in?" any more.

And then there was that young Vice President of Marketing Jochen Zeitz, who was constantly demanding money for new campaigns to catapult the brand into modernity. The worldwide marketing budget was only 14 million marks. Competitors from America would probably blow this sum in just two weeks. Zeitz had to spend most of his meagre funds paying for inherited burdens from the Dassler era. The national sports initiative "Trimm-Trab" ate up 500,000 marks per year, and football clubs like Werder Bremen and Mönchengladbach were entitled to approximately the same amount. Personally contracted football stars such as Rudi Völler, Udo Lattek and Lothar Matthäus received between 80,000 and 150,000 marks in consultancy fees. It was virtually impossible to think about forward-looking global marketing strategies, though it would have been a matter of urgency to bring the brand into line worldwide. The heads of the different countries and licence holders did as they pleased, creating collections according to their own ideas. The subsidiaries in Austria, Switzerland, France, Australia,

Linford Christie - Heike Drechsler - Merlene Ottey - Colin Jackson

*"Turn it on" campaign*

Spain, the Far East and the Benelux countries no longer yielded any profits. Only the licences in Japan and England still contributed 20 million marks a year to the kitty.

From the day he presented his ideas for the future of Puma to the international team in a small hotel near London, however, Zeitz also found his first admirers and supporters in the company. His words about a single corporate identity and a desirable European brand continued to ring in the ears of many of those present. When he had finished his presentation, he received a standing ovation. Many frustrated colleagues came up to him and hugged him with tears in their eyes. Sentimentality would normally make him nervous. He felt anything but comfortable in the role of saviour. Emotions were running so high, however, that even he had to suppress a few tears on this occasion.

To prevent the lights from going out for the last time on Würzburger Strasse, Aritmos threw another 80 million marks in total at the firm. The new CEO, Stefan Jacobsson, continued to woo the confidence of the AGM in the style of his predecessor: he proclaimed a change for the better and promised shareholders soaring sales and black figures. Once again, the opposite happened. In the second half of the year, business collapsed like a soufflé. "We have never experienced such an extreme slide before," conceded head of finance Szymanski despondently to the press. Even in its native country of Germany, the merchandise with the big cat logo no longer stood a chance against the way-out competition from overseas.

## The episode with the disc

There are days when even those who have really been through the wringer have the feeling that they can conquer the world. Such a day came in spring 1992. Early in the morning, marketing boss Zeitz and head of advertising Fischer entered the Starlight Express theatre in Bochum, where normally actors on roller skates

*The Puma "Disc" – the big hope*

staged Andrew Lloyd Webber's musical about the battle fought by Rusty, the loveable little steam engine, against his powerful opponents, Electra, the electric engine and Greaseball, the diesel engine. However, the Puma managers had not hired the theatre because it was symbolic of their own position, but in order to present their number one hope to the dealers: the Puma "Disc", a new sports shoe which had no shoelaces, but was done up by a turning mechanism. This was a high-tech product, something that would finally be competitive again on the world market. Puma had bought the disc fastening exclusively from Swiss patent holder PDS Verschlusstechnik AG. The preparations for the market launch had been running full steam ahead for weeks, Zeitz and Fischer had even had expensive TV advertising produced. A budget of three million marks had been estimated for the launch – a dizzying amount of money in view of the company's drooping performance. To ensure that no money was wasted on trivialities, Zeitz and Fischer shared a hotel room with the consultant from Godenrath Preiswerk, the advertising agency. Zeitz was convinced that the "Disc" would have the power to wake the big cat from its deep slumber.

The event had all the quality of a Hollywood party. "Turn it on", ran the advertising slogan which Zeitz himself had developed. The message to be put across to the audience was that "by turning the disc, you and the shoe become one". With interruptions from product presentations, roller skaters raced across the big stage, powerful music pounded from the speakers and lasers projected the new shoe into the dry-ice shrouded hall. A dream team of top athletes vouched for the quality of the running shoe: German Heike Drechsler, who in the same year had won Olympic gold in

Barcelona in the long jump: British hurdler Colin Jackson, who won the World Cup in the 110 metre hurdles wearing the "Disc"; British sprinter Linford Christie, who later even wore contact lenses emblazoned with the Puma logo; and the Jamaican athlete Merlene Ottey. Even the most sceptical dealers among the guests clapped enthusiastically and the Board also applauded the pantomime. "Bingo," thought Zeitz on the evening of that exhausting day.

He had wanted to show that Puma was back. And the message seemed to have been received and understood. People who had seen the advertisement on TV rushed to the shops in droves demanding the new Puma shoe, at a price of 120 marks and more. Such a thing had not happened since Boris Becker's departure in 1987. However, what had initially appeared to be a huge success ended as a flop. The "Disc" did not work properly. Marketing boss Zeitz had put pressure on to have the shoe released for the launch – the experts had assured him that it worked perfectly. Unlike in the special productions for the professional athletes, however, the mechanism kept jamming in the mass-market version. Customers and dealers were disappointed and angered in equal measure. Zeitz raised Cain with those responsible. The best comfort he was able to offer himself, however, was that it was not marketing but production that was responsible for the failure.

The unsuccessful episode with the "Disc" was not the final failure in the history of the company – in this respect the company was no different from any car manufacturer, however prestigious, that has to start product recall campaigns. From time to time, Puma products failed to function properly despite extensive laboratory tests – no wonder, given the high number of new launches. In 2002, for example, at the football World Cup in Japan and South Korea, there was a mishap with the high-tech football boot "Cellerator Shudoh". Only after the first boots were dispatched did problems emerge with the upper, meaning that parts of the delivery had to be exchanged.

### Hostile takeover

The tunnel in which Puma found itself after the Bochum presentation was long and dark. There was not the slightest chink of daylight visible in the distance. The team's hope of survival was fading day by day. To crown it all, principal shareholder Aritmos got into financial difficulties as well. The shareholdings in Tretorn, Etonic, Abu Garcia and the other small firms turned out unproductive. But it was the Franconian company's red figures that delivered the really nasty shock. Aritmos boss Ingvar Wenehed tried another change of team. On 31 January 1993, he fielded a man by the name of Niels Stenhoj in the place of the popular, but way too uninspired, Stefan Jacobsson after only 21 months. Jacobsson, who had signed a five-year contract, collected a high severance payment which inflicted further pain on the company and the banks. Zeitz had got along well with the pleasant-natured manager. "If I had stayed around longer, you would have been my natural successor," the Swede later revealed to him.

*Zeitz's trademark: athlete Linford Christie wearing Puma contact lenses*

Originally from Denmark, Stenhoj had been in charge of operations for Aritmos at US subsidiary Abu Garcia, a sports fishing tackle specialist. Just why he of all people was thought to be the right man for Herzogenaurach remains a mystery to Puma's elder statesmen to this day. Perhaps because of his favoured Rambo act. The 86 days he was to remain in office were one long nightmare for many. The new CEO displayed neither competence in the business nor a feel for the market.

Meanwhile, dark clouds were gathering above Aritmos. In financial circles, the Group was regarded as seriously ailing and was consequently being hailed by investment bankers as a takeover target. Located 560 kilometres to the north of Aritmos' head office, in Stockholm, was the headquarters of Proventus AB, whose business, like that of Aritmos, consisted of equity holdings and investments. The Group had grown into a heavyweight with a stock market value of half a billion euros. Manager Robert Weil had founded Proventus in 1980 on the principle: "Change is the only constant in our world". Weil's parents originally came from Germany, but had been forced to emigrate to Sweden at the end of the 1930s because his father was of Jewish descent. Now the son ruled the empire with the severity of a Godfather and the curiosity of an entrepreneur. He saw himself as a businessman, wanted success, nothing else, and was not averse to staging the occasional ambush to achieve it. But he also liked to show his relaxed side: even in important meetings it was not unheard of for him to fall asleep. On such occasions, his manager Mikael Kamras would listen to the presentations for him.

Kamras took care of foreign affairs for Proventus. The charming man with the winning appearance came across as a level-headed business partner whom people could trust. At the end of 1992, he arranged for an analysis of the Aritmos portfolio to be drawn up for his boss. The decision was made after Christmas to enter the flagging holding company by the back door and to transform the company's less risky interests into profitable subsidiaries. In the Swedes' eyes, Puma, of which Aritmos now held over 80 percent, was extremely interesting and at the same time highly dangerous. The immense losses run up by the Franconians over the years in an expanding market were a source of headaches for the Scandinavians. Weil instructed Kamras to take care of the acquisition – and at the same time to dispose of Aritmos' boss, Ingvar Wenehed.

On 26 January 1993, thousands of kilometres away in the Marriott Hotel in Orlando, another Swede was thinking about Aritmos: Thore Ohlsson, 50, a former manager of the group. Twelve years earlier he had sold his own sports goods distribution company to Aritmos, signed up with the purchaser, and then managed the new Tretorn subsidiary in the USA. He and Wenehed had grown into a powerful partnership and were good friends. Nevertheless, when the CEO was looking for a deputy, he passed over his trusty colleague. Disappointed, Ohlsson resigned in 1990 and went on to work in a variety of posts, most recently for a provider of golf equipment. A trade fair was taking place in Florida at the time. In the evening, when he went to pick up his key at reception, he was given a message: "Mr Ohlsson, please call Mikael Kamras, CEO of Proventus, Stockholm, tomorrow afternoon on the following number. Thank you and regards." Ohlsson was surprised. "Kamras?" He had no idea what Proventus wanted from him. The following afternoon he picked up the phone. Kamras revealed their interest in Aritmos to him, and made approaches to him. They agreed on an interview in early February in snowy Stockholm.

A week or so later Ohlsson once more packed his suitcase at his home in Falsterbo, a village in southern Sweden. As he headed for the front door, he came across a note his wife had left him: "If they ask you if you want to go and work for Aritmos, say No! Promise me!" read the message in block capitals. Ohlsson smiled reflectively. He later framed the letter. At the meeting, Weil and Kamras came straight to the point: Ohlsson was to replace Wenehed and become the new boss in his old company Aritmos. Ohlsson felt flattered – and immediately declined the offer. He thought of his wife's note. Weil and Kamras gulped. They had not expected a refusal. When they shook Ohlsson's hand at the close of the meeting, Weil whispered in his face: "We'll get you yet, Thore."

At Puma in Herzogenaurach, heads were now definitively under water. Despite all efforts, the brand had fallen into total insignificance. The disposition of the new CEO and Board Chairman Stenhoj prompted even the most willing and optimistic members of staff thus far to look around for new jobs immediately. Completely clueless and helpless, the CEO took refuge in his Rambo tough guy role. In board meetings he would bang his fist on the table like a Stalinist to seal his decisions. Zeitz, who really hates throwing in the towel and was sticking it out at Puma for that reason, got together with his colleagues Martin Gänsler and Ulrich Heyd in a Tex-Mex bar and washed away his disappointment with so much tequila that he still had a fierce headache the next day.

At the next ISPO, Zeitz received an invitation to attend a dinner with Aritmos boss Wenehed and other company royalty in the elegant surrounds of Boettner's restaurant in Munich. He witnessed how the big guys liked to party, but also found out that the Swedes were evidently only now realizing just how much trouble Puma was in. When the gentlemen left the bar, Wenehed turned to the marketing man: "So, how was it with the big guys?" Zeitz smiled politely and kept his thoughts to himself. What he did not know was that on that same evening, the negotiators of Proventus in Stockholm had agreed with one of the Aritmos shareholders on the purchase of a 25 percent share. The option to buy was valid for a week. Proventus boss Kamras had to move fast. He was determined to see Thore Ohlsson at the top and called him the following afternoon at the ISPO on the stand of sports equipment producer Spalding. The discussion about their future working relationship lasted ten minutes – then Ohlsson accepted. His wife had been trying to convince him for two weeks – with no particular success. In the end, it was clear to her that he really wanted to do it. From that moment onwards, she wholeheartedly supported her husband in his new job.

The personnel issues were settled, Proventus closed the deal and bought a further 19 percent of Aritmos from smaller investors. A week later, the new principal shareholders informed Ingvar Wenehed that his work at Aritmos was done. He had been totally unaware of the jostling for power and the hostile takeover, and displayed surprise at his own downfall. Then he made demands:

firstly, he demanded a place on the Proventus supervisory board and secondly, under no circumstances was his successor to be called Thore Ohlsson. Kamras agreed on the first point and categorically rejected the second condition. It signalled the start of a battle: since the personnel decision still had to be approved at the AGM on 27 April, Wenehed refused to clear his desk. Ohlsson had to move into an adjoining room and share a secretary with his former partner, now his enemy.

### A surprising offer

This did nothing to sap Ohlsson's energy. Without formal authorization, he travelled to Franconia in early March to seek a meeting with Puma executives. He spoke with CEO Stenhoj, who was currently greatly occupied with his relocation from New York to a Nuremberg apartment rented by Puma. He even arranged for his white Saab 900 to be shipped over, costing the firm 27,000 marks. He had not yet signed his contract – not a wise move, as it turned out.

Stenhoj convened a meeting at short notice for the Swedes' visit. The divisional managers were to present their goals for the coming year to him and the guests. On the instructions of the CEO, only the person presenting was allowed in the room. However, when development manager Martin Gänsler outlined the situation with great frankness and showed himself far more competent than the CEO, he aroused the interest of Kamras and Ohlsson. To Stenhoj's annoyance, they asked him to remain in the room. They wanted him to come along the next day, too. Gänsler was actually on holiday, had the decorators round and could not cancel them for a second time. He was in an embarrassing situation. "If we can start tomorrow at 7 am, I can make it," he said cheekily. The Swedes gave the nod.

The following day the marketing presentation was on the agenda. A few days earlier, Zeitz had gone with his wife to visit his parents-in-law. He felt extremely ill and was suffering from bouts of flu-like fever. Gänsler called him: "You have to come – without you we can't do anything here." Zeitz came. As his pal waited with a red nose and swollen throat outside the door to the conference room, Gänsler feared that he would not make it through the event. Yet, despite his fever, Zeitz put in a stellar performance. The Swedes' eyes lit up. Gänsler could sense it: Stenhoj's time had passed – and Zeitz's time had arrived. Intuition told him that a major career advancement was in store for his young blond colleague – and perhaps for him too.

After the presentation, Ohlsson called on Gänsler again in person as well as on product manager Hubertus Hoyt and Karl-Heinz Driediger, who had been appointed finance director following the departure of Bernd Szymanski for Escada in February. And he knocked on Jochen Zeitz's office door. "I find that you are doing a good job," said the Swede. Then they held a lengthy discussion about the mistakes and opportunities in the company. Zeitz hinted at his thoughts of leaving the company. "Stay!" Ohlsson urged him as he walked out the door, "wait a little longer."

At the end of that day the Aritmos boss designate left the company with mixed feelings. He had been introduced to dynamic men with the will to change, and in particular one young marketing and sales manager who was a strictly analytical

*Resurrection: Puma poster from 1992 showing Maradona*

thinker and, in his opinion, was destined for greater things. However, he had also made the unpleasant discovery that Puma was in disastrous straits and the employees were sending job applications to the competition by the dozen. He filed the CEO in the drawer labelled "Dead wood".

A few days later, on 13 March 1993, Zeitz and his wife Birgit were sitting at the breakfast table in their Nuremberg flat when the phone rang. Ohlsson was on the other end of the line. "Think about what needs to happen for Puma to turn the corner," he asked him. "In my area?" Zeitz inquired. "In all areas," replied the Aritmos boss. "And don't mention a word of this to colleagues, even Stenhoj." Zeitz was asked to go to Malmö for an informal meeting the following week. The strange constellation bewildered him: he was being asked to supply a shareholder, who was not yet legally in that position, with internal information over the heads of his own bosses. The first thing he did was book a day's holiday. Then he said to himself: "What the heck, it's worth one final attempt."

In the days that followed Zeitz barely saw the light of day.

Working almost round the clock in his office, he prepared his slide presentation for the forthcoming meeting. As an icebreaker joke, he had sketched the picture of an emaciated cow and written below it: "We no longer have a cash cow, just a very thin one." On its udder hung bankers, consultants and everyone else who bled Puma dry. Because drawing is not exactly one of his strengths, he asked his colleague next door, Erwin Hildel, to create the metaphor on his Macintosh using a drawing software program.

On Thursday, 18 March, Zeitz flew with Lufthansa from Nuremberg to the Danish capital Copenhagen. There he got into a helicopter that carried him to the Swedish city of Malmö, 40 kilometres away. He took a taxi from the airport to the four-star hotel Master Johan in the city centre, where the meeting had been arranged. Three senior managers were already waiting for him in the lobby of the friendly, bright hostelry: Proventus Managing Director Mikael Kamras, the future Aritmos boss Thore Ohlsson and his trusted man Staffan Svenby, who was to occupy a position on the Supervisory Board in the new Aritmos team. The three managers stood up, shook his hand and asked the usual small-talk questions about his journey and how he was feeling. Then the group moved on to the reserved meeting room. Zeitz felt pretty uncomfortable. "What have I let myself in for?" he wondered. "Well, maybe in the end you can still do the company some good."

The foursome in the dark suits discussed Puma's future for an hour, very seriously and intensely. Zeitz was utterly direct and criticized his employer so vehemently that his audience's eyes popped. Presenting is one of his great strengths to this day; he does not convey his emotions by facial expressions or gestures, but by the keen-edged clarity of the spoken word. At the end of his speech, a short silence prevailed. Then Kamras asked him: "In a word: what do you think could save the brand?" Zeitz thought for a moment. His sharp brain had immediately realized that the Swede had asked him the key question, and that the answer would decide his own future as well. However, he had faith in himself and his analysis, and did not draw back. "At the end of the day, Puma has only one chance: first of all, radical cuts have to be made to drive costs right down, and then there has to be a clear business plan to make the brand step by step into what it needs to be: desirable." The managers' faces relaxed. Zeitz had entirely convinced them. Relief spread through the room, a sense of optimism. "Could you imagine taking on the job yourself?" asked Kamras. Zeitz looked up, surprised. Were his ears deceiving him? Before he could answer, Ohlsson spoke. "We don't have to discuss it in detail right now. Let's take a break first."

During the break, the 29-year-old's brain was in whirl. He thought of the depressed atmosphere in Herzogenaurach, of the many failed managers, of the highly paid management consultants roaming the corridors, of the seriously dismal figures. But he also thought of the clever colleagues he trusted, Martin Gänsler, Hubertus Hoyt, with whose support he could envisage a regeneration. Back in the meeting room, Ohlsson pressed for an end to the meeting, he had a flight to catch. "I think I could help," were Zeitz's rather abashed parting words. The Swedes assured him of support and swore him to absolute secrecy, in view of the fact that Aritmos' AGM was still to come. Not a single word about the meeting was to be spoken outside that room.

As he got into Ohlsson's silver Audi A6 Quattro, which was to take him to the heliport, he played the events over again in his mind: Is it true, did they say they wanted me to be CEO of Puma? Meanwhile, Ohlsson conducted a long conversation on his car phone. Zeitz understood not a word, Swedish is not one of his languages. Then the man at the wheel hung up and turned to his passenger: "Jochen, I would like you to implement the changes we have discussed. We want you to take over Puma, if you know what I mean." Zeitz felt a fresh surge of adrenaline. He was going to be the CEO of a public limited company? Head of a company with a tradition going back 55 years? Ohlsson also immediately offered him a decent salary. "Okay," said Zeitz blankly, "that's fair."

"I'll believe it when I see it," the rationalist decided to himself. He didn't even call his wife Birgit to tell her about what had passed in Malmö. Not until shortly before midnight, when he entered their flat in Nuremberg, did he tell her about the nerve-shattering offer. She burst into tears. Zeitz couldn't quite work out whether they were tears of joy or of sorrow. She knew they would be facing a very tough time, with far-reaching consequences for their life together.

The days of high emotion were followed by weeks of silence. Even on his 30th birthday, on 6 April, thoughts of the secret deal were clamouring in his head. It wasn't easy for the busy marketing boss with so many demands on his time to act at the workplace as if nothing had happened. The day of Aritmos' AGM, 27 April, dragged nearer at a relentlessly slow pace, like Christmas Eve and Santa Claus had done in his childhood. When the almost 300-strong group of shareholders convened in the conference room in

Helsingborg and the Supervisory Board chairman opened the meeting, Proventus with an official stake of 44 percent was Aritmos' biggest shareholder and Thore Ohlsson, as expected, was appointed Managing Director of the new subsidiary. Ingvar Wenehed was thanked for 13 successful years and the Board was discharged of accountability for its activities in the previous year. Kamras and Ohlsson, who were mixing with the public, breathed sighs of relief and drove immediately to the airport, where they just managed to catch the flight to Nuremberg. They did not want to lose one more day before initiating the turnaround at Puma with their new hope, Jochen Zeitz.

The next morning, Ohlsson entered the office of the CEO designate and informed him of an unexpected problem: Aritmos' Supervisory Board had voted unanimously against the dismissal of Stenhoj, who had only been in office for a few weeks, and against Zeitz's appointment. The creditor banks did not consider the switch a good idea either. The gist was: "We are not going to make ourselves ridiculous in front of our shareholders with a 30-year-old who has never managed a public limited company before." Nevertheless, Ohlsson assured him, a decision had been taken and he would execute it. The Swedes then spent hours on the phone to the Board at home from their candidate's office and from the conference room. They piled on the pressure: "We're going to do this whether you like it or not." After two hours, the first Supervisory Board member caved in. This was Lennart Nilsson, head of the Cardo industrial group. The next to weaken was Saab CEO Lars Kyhlberg. Finally, Per Sorte, Financial Director of the Cerealia food group, also agreed. The secretaries in the board members' offices, who kept having to dial new numbers, hadn't a clue about the personnel battle that was being fought during these hours.

Kamras left that evening, and Ohlsson invited Puma boss Niels Stenhoj to dinner in Nuremberg's Maritim Hotel. The two knew each other from the old days at Aritmos, but had never been friends. He dispassionately informed Stenhoj of the situation. Stenhoj appeared calm. He had been dealt a poor hand, and there was no point in bluffing. Because he hadn't yet signed his contract, he had to agree to an unusually low severance deal.

One of the first to hear about the change of management was Dieter Bock, head controller and subsequently finance director. Deutsche Bank had arranged an extraordinary meeting of the bank pool in Nuremberg on 29 April. Bock had spent days preparing a presentation for Stenhoj. The day before the meeting, at twelve noon, he was to meet with the CEO one more time to go through the details with him. Shortly before twelve, the secretary called and said the meeting might be running a little late. Time passed. At 4 pm, she rang again and asked Bock to come up to the boardroom. Bock peered cautiously through the door. IT expert Klaus Bauer was already there, sitting before the mahogany-panelled wall with big question marks in his eyes. All at once, the door opened and board member Ulrich Heyd came in with Jochen Zeitz. Bock and Bauer looked at each other incredulously. Heyd cleared his throat and announced that Stenhoj had just resigned and that Jochen Zeitz was the new CEO. "Our jaws dropped," Bock recalls. He registered the information, but was emotionally unable to process it.

Shortly afterwards, Ohlsson called in the rest of the Puma management team. He delivered a short report on the position of the company, looked into what had until then been the uncertain future, and presented Jochen Zeitz as the new company boss. When his last words had died away, those present froze in icy silence. You could have heard a pin drop. Zeitz stood among the group and felt lonelier than he had ever been in his life. The meeting broke up as though nothing untoward had happened.

Once more, Puma experienced a sharp break with the status quo. For the first time in history, the shareholders were entrusting a greenhorn rather than an experienced corporate captain to restructure the group, albeit a greenhorn who was seen by many observers as an up-and-coming talent. He had not much more to show for himself than his intellect, his uncompromising determination and a few years of experience in marketing and sales. His starting position was as bad as it could possibly be: the 1992 fiscal year had closed with sales of 512 million marks – more than ten percent down on the previous year. Licence revenues had also seen a dramatic slump. The consolidated loss came to a total of 12.6 million marks. The company was almost constantly operating over its overdraft limit in order to cover wages and materials. Zeitz knew he had only one chance: he had to throw every scrap of ballast overboard to save the tanker from going down.

It was 1 May 1993, Labour Day in Germany. Puma's employees were enjoying their day off and cycling through the meadows around Herzogenaurach, where the first lilies of the valley were in bloom. For Jochen Zeitz it was his first day as Chief Executive Officer and Chairman of the Board of Puma AG. He had a lot of work to do. The next day, a meeting of the bank pool had been set up at the Deutsche Bank office in Nuremberg. In actual fact, the new CEO Niels Stenhoj was supposed to be introducing himself to the financiers, but he was already history. Zeitz had decided to keep the appointment, present a brief business plan and ask the gentlemen in the pinstripe suits to have patience. It was clear to him that he had to win time, scrutinize the position of the company in every detail, before he could answer the bankers' inquisitorial questions to their satisfaction and present them with a restructuring plan.

The bank's conference room was furnished with a heavy wooden table and big leather armchairs. Wherever Zeitz turned, he was looking into faces of grave maturity. The dark-suited representatives of the 13 creditor banks created the atmosphere of a funeral service. The ladies and gentlemen had been warned in advance, but still looked aghast at the youthful appearance of the new leader of Puma Rudolf Dassler Sport AG, and concerned about the high debt levels he was tasked with reducing. "How old are you?" asked one of the men over again. The question was rhetorical. Zeitz came to the point straight away. He introduced himself: he had been with the firm for two and a half years, was currently vice-president in charge of marketing and sales and had got to know the company very well indeed. Then he presented the unvarnished facts about it. "Aren't the new shoes selling as well as your predecessor told us?" the WestLB representative wanted to know. "No," said Zeitz. "But the subsidiaries are pulling out of the slump?" asked the man from BNP Paribas. The CEO shook his head. He also rejected all his predecessors' other window-dressed representations as unrealistic.

The banks' envoys sat up and listened in horror. The Puma boss's presentation triggered a heated debate: should they give the new CEO a chance, or drop Puma financially once and for all? The spectrum of opinions ranged from emphatic consent to utter rejection. In the end, they agreed to continue – with a heavy heart. They had really wanted an experienced turnaround manager.

Finally, Zeitz asked the bankers to adjourn the meeting until 26 July. He would present a full restructuring programme to them then. The new Puma chief drew a deep breath and left the Deutsche Bank office with all speed. He had a mountain of work in front of him and no more time to lose. At the second meeting, he then put the company's hair-raising position on the table. The losses, he said, could only be stopped by laying off 40 percent of the workforce. A bigger credit facility would be needed for the restructuring, as it would eat up another 69 million marks.

## 2.2 The Lives of Others

*Zeitz's dream team: the purchasing biker, unrelenting number-crunchers, two globetrotters, and a gentle adversary*

Though Zeitz still didn't know exactly how he would turn the corner at Puma, he did know who he would be working with. In times of crisis you realize who you can count on, and there had been plenty of opportunity to do that in the past three years. Amongst the men who had been behind the effort from the start were Dieter Bock, general manager of financial accounting, Klaus Bauer, head controller and IT expert, Ulrich Heyd, board member and company lawyer, and advertising chief Helmut Fischer. They were joined shortly afterwards by the dashing, multi-talented Horst Widmann, previously Adidas founder Adolf Dassler's right-hand man and now on Puma's payroll. But the number one spot on his list of confidants went to another individual who still holds that place to this day: Martin Gänsler, dyed-in-the-wool salesman, whom he subsequently appointed his deputy.

As already mentioned, Jochen Zeitz has an astonishingly keen nose for hiring the right people. Along with his rigorous approach, this characteristic ranks amongst his greatest qualities as a manager. Even to this day, he insists on looking through all applications for key positions in person. He has never made a real mistake yet. As a new CEO, he needed no consultants at his side – he had long since mapped out the way forward – instead, he needed employees who were willing to go his way. Once more he demonstrated his people knack, and assembled a team that by 2007, had increased the value of the company by over 5,000 percent.

The spirit that welded the team together in the difficult years and held it together afterwards is undoubtedly one of Puma's most important success factors. A team was forged behind guiding spirit Zeitz which believed in the brand, in the CEO and in itself and which was ready to push itself to the very limits of its strength. In the years of restructuring especially, the lights were on in the offices virtually round the clock as employees figured out the details of cost-cutting plans or strategies. Even in the late 1990s, the personnel director would pass through the corridors late at night reminding the Puma staff that there were such things as core working hours.

It seems, then, that the Puma workforce has earned a place in the annals of German stock exchange history as a dream team. Strikingly, it was not elite university graduates who clicked into key positions but the locals, the pragmatists, some of them off-the-wall characters with crazy career backgrounds. Some of them, still movers and shakers of the Group today, will be introduced in more detail below. These include the head of the Works Council, a woman who by and large steered clear of ideological thinking, and spent almost 14 years as the counterbalance to the CEO's shareholder value-driven entrepreneurship, yet backed him up at the same time.

### Martin Gänsler, the indefatigable sourcing manager

Martin Gänsler bears a close resemblance to one of German TV's most famous detectives and has a penchant for dark clothing. He had already been in charge of products at Puma for quite some time when Zeitz got the top job. Zeitz appreciated his terrier-like quality of being able to sink his teeth into anything, no matter how small, in order to move mountains. He knew the production technology and sourcing channels in the sector like the back of his hand. Over the course of the years, Gänsler, a pragmatist without a big ego, was to develop from sparring partner to check and balance for the intellectually heavyweight company chief. He jetted tirelessly around the world to get the best deals for the firm. Status symbols do not mean much to him, and to this day he lives in a simple studio flat in Herzogenaurach. Many Puma employees maintain that it is a blessing to have him, and they were shocked when Gänsler announced his retirement from the company as per the end of 2007. He would now much rather spend time at his hunting lodge and farm at Gersthofen near Augsburg, looking after his dogs, horses and rabbits. Or cruise around all over the place on his Harley-Davidson. Or grow grapes on his small farm in Tuscany.

Gänsler was born in Augsburg on 1 December 1953, an illegitimate child. A few years later his mother married a prominent sports equipment retailer of the town, who owned a long-established business in the centre of Augsburg. Gänsler, who had always been keen on sports, thought his mother had made a cool choice. He left school and started a retailing apprenticeship with his stepfather. It was at this time that he discovered his love of selling. At the same time, he also completed courses as a state-certified skiing instructor and a diving instructor. But his idyll did not last for long. There was a dispute with the owner's daughter from a previous marriage, who treated Gänsler as an interloper. In the end, the owner had to pay out on a shareholder agreement. The sports store could not sustain the loss, and ended up in financial difficulties. A new business partner arrived on the scene, and Gänsler could not bear him. He took a time-out and decided to go on alone, combining hobby and career. In summer he wanted to work as a diving instructor and in winter he wanted to be out on the ski slopes. However, he quickly came to the realization that this life was not for him. "I am far too much the settled type for that," he says.

In 1977 he moved to Sport-Ecke, a sports retailer in Augsburg, and saw an opportunity there. The owner's wife had built up a ski school belonging to the firm.

*Martin Gänsler, deputy CEO, with Michael Schumacher (at left), 2004*

As she wanted more time to look after her children, Gänsler was to take it over. He gradually worked his way up to deputy manager. Sport-Ecke was the premier sports business of the town, but really too small and claustrophobic for him in the long term. He wanted to be out on the other side of the counter and get into field sales. In 1980, when Puma advertised for sales staff in the *Augsburger Zeitung* newspaper, he applied straight away. He knew the company's strengths and weaknesses. Until then, Puma had worked mainly with commercial agents, but now it wanted to have its own field sales force. Gänsler was invited for interview, hired, and from then on was responsible for field sales in the Swabia area of Bavaria. There was a fixed salary of around 3,500 marks – less than he had been earning – and a reasonable sales commission of 0.25 percent. But Gänsler was a good salesman, and after a few years was able to double his earnings through the commission because his sales area territory was extended to include Baden-Württemberg. He drove around the country in his company car – a Peugeot Break – with the boot crammed full of shin-pads, shirts and shoes. He would stay overnight in musty guesthouses for 18.50 marks. He would clatter over town centre cobblestones with his portable clothes stands hung with bags of clothes, and climb spiral staircases to the retailers. Wherever he went, he had to create opportunities for the widest possible spread of Puma products. "We don't need your stuff, we have Adidas," was the constant response from the dealers. "That was a battle of companies," says Gänsler.

In 1987 he came off the street and went in-house. In his last two years in the field – the time when Boris Becker became a Puma star – he had secured rich spoils. Very early on Gänsler noticed that things were going downhill rapidly at the parent company in Herzogenaurach. With his ability to build effective networks he had quickly established relations right up to top management level. He continued to believe in Puma's core element: the ability to design good footwear. However, it did bother him that the firm was being run like a German provincial company. In the eyes of most employees, there was Germany and nothing else. "We must seize trends, bring our products up to date and launch them with modern marketing," was his call to the managers in charge. The managers of the new principal shareholder from Sweden listened attentively to the street fighter – and promptly went their own conventional ways.

Gänsler was promoted to Product Manager Footwear, with overall responsibility for the entire range of boots and shoes – yet lost all motivation in this position, too, a few years down the line. The never-ending in-house intrigues wore him down. Moreover, the constant staff changes and lack of a clear line had led to chaos. Nobody really had any grasp of how the different departments were muddling along, each in its own little corner. The "sourcing" network plan hanging in one of the offices extended over three and a half walls. Management consultants were ubiquitous, tossing buzzwords like "extended workbench" into the offices, changing or cutting something here, adding something there – before going on their way again. In 1988, Gänsler submitted his first travel request for Asia in order to optimize sourcing. If we want to change things – he argued the case with his boss – then the key lies in Asia. The manager rejected the application, saying Gänsler was too inexperienced for the task. Asia seemed a world away to the men of Herzogenaurach in those days, and they would not be able to buy German bread there either. They preferred to keep a distance.

It was months before Gänsler was able to get his idea accepted, and fly to Taiwan and Korea for the very first time. He paid spontaneous visits to factories that were strange to him, and negotiated with producers he had never met before. While these days new Puma employees are accompanied on their first big trip by an experienced colleague, he received no support whatsoever from the management in Herzogenaurach. It was a frustrating and instructive experience for him, but he returned to Germany strengthened by his trip. He had learned to negotiate purchase prices. And he had found out how quickly an idea can be converted into a product in Asia. Puma's then design manager on the ground was a Japanese man who was on the payroll of Puma partner Cosa Liebermann. He was based in Thaichung, the footwear stronghold of Taiwan. Gänsler explained his design ideas to him, and went on to Korea. When he returned to Thaichung a week later, the prototypes of the shoes were waiting for him. Nevertheless, the sourcing strategy at Puma did not change – for the moment at least.

Gänsler became aware of the young Jochen Zeitz for the first time in 1989 at the company's International Meeting in Biel. "The big blond", as Gänsler called him, who had been invited for a taster weeks before he started his job, looked pretty lonely to him. Gänsler realized that he was about to become a new colleague of his – product management reported to marketing. When Zeitz moved into an office on the same floor as Gänsler's weeks later, he got to know him better. "A really great guy," thought Gänsler. Soon they were linked by a common faith: they – unlike many others – were convinced that something could be made of the fallen Puma brand. And they worked flat out to achieve this. Gänsler observed how Zeitz conquered his division uncompromisingly, but with sound arguments. How he revamped and revived the old-fashioned green shoe packaging. It was professional marketing – and Gänsler liked that. He is just the right man for Puma, he reported up the grapevine to the top. As Zeitz was getting hotter and hotter, however, Gänsler was preparing to leave. He could no longer stand the Franconians who, to him, appeared so noisy and bad-tempered and wasted their energy building networks with people who believed only in the good old days. And he could no longer stand dealing with the board member responsible for his area, Manfred Häussler. He did not credit the man, who later became head of Reemtsma and was implicated in a money-laundering scandal there, with any competence and he did not like him enough to go and have a beer with him. One of the two had to apply for Gänsler to take to someone.

Gänsler's head was full of grand plans: he wanted to launch his own footwear collection. It would consist of leisure footwear for children and adults, based on professional tennis shoes. He had built up plenty of contacts with manufacturers and dealers in the course of his career in the sports equipment sector. Designers put his ideas down on paper and the goods were produced in Italy. He chose footwear chains as the distribution channel. He sold 160,000 pairs in one year alone. He could have sold a lot more – if the

Italian manufacturer had delivered. Gänsler found out for the first time how hard times can be if you have orders, but no merchandise. He had to dig into his savings to pay debts. Alone in his quiet little room in Augsburg, he began to think the move to self-employment might have been the wrong decision.

Just four weeks after his departure from Puma the phone rang. Zeitz was on the other end. The big blond wanted to know whether he would be willing to come back – at least as a freelance consultant. Gänsler agreed and immediately fell into the time trap: the two jobs put far too much of a strain on him. Things were happening at Puma. The Swedish owners appointed a new CEO called Stefan Jacobsson. The organization was now no longer known even to the Germans as the "Firma", but as the "Company". English became the company language and Zeitz's job title suddenly became Vice President Marketing and Sales. Gänsler had hopes that Franconian narrowness might finally crack wide open. After eleven months, he decided to return to Herzogenaurach and became Vice President Footwear. He had no idea at this stage that Zeitz might one day become CEO and he would be his deputy.

### Dieter Bock, the home-rooted financial juggler

When Dieter Bock was born on 2 July 1958 in Herzogenaurach, Puma did not figure in the parental home. His family lived modestly in the small Franconian town, and believed it was more important to get a decent apprenticeship than a hefty salary. The family had nothing to do with the two local sports equipment manufacturers. Dieter grew into an ambitious lad, who could release quite a charge of energy in achieving his goals. After leaving school he completed an apprenticeship as a wholesaler in a local electrical business. He enjoyed his work, but at the end of his training in 1976 the company went into insolvency. Bock had no problem finding another job. He applied for a position at Puma as an accounts clerk and was taken on after his military service.

It was an exciting time for the young financier. For the first time under the Dassler regime, the company was really selling products with its low-price strategy. But even Bock, the mere accounts clerk, realized that it was hardly possible to make a profit that way. The gross margin, in other words the percentage share of sales left after deduction of the cost of goods sold, was less than 30 percent – far too low for the industry. But no one in the company was really interested in financial theory. There was no long-term strategy – apart from catching up as far as possible with big brother Adidas.

At first, Bock was made controller of the licence business that his colleague Heyd had built up and organized in the 1970s. Healthy profits flowed into Herzogenaurach in the early 1980s, particularly from Japan and the USA. In 1983, Bock was appointed group manager of balance sheet accounting. In this stage of his career he became aware for the first time of the astronomical contracts that had been concluded with Boris Becker and the other sports stars. Four years later, he rose to the position of deputy accounts manager. From his office, he could follow the dramatic scenes that were played out around the members of the Dassler family. The new company headquarters, Armin Dassler's dream, had just been completed when the banks decided to drive the family out of doors and sell their share package. Anyone who had been associated with the Dassler family in any form had

*Dieter Bock, finance director*

been dealt a poor hand. Bock felt compassion for the family. The Dassler sons had to leave the firm and Armin Dassler cowered, a broken man, in his wood-panelled office, where the smell of paint still lingered.

From that time on, the young Bock no longer felt at ease at Puma. None of the new managers identified with the brand – how was he supposed to? No one seemed to have any motivation to think beyond the day – how was he meant to develop commitment? The board members who came and went seemed to him to be only interested in making a fast buck, which is not exactly one of the Franconian virtues. New managers appeared, bringing a throng of dependants in their train. A plethora of managerial levels with highly paid positions was created; the consequences were most evident in the finance department: they were living way beyond their means. In today's era of shareholder value, the finance departments hold the reins on spending in the public limited companies, but warnings from number-crunchers like Bock counted for little at that time.

Miserable though he was, Bock stayed put. After all, he had a family to feed and had built a house in Herzogenaurach that had to be paid for. Yet the man who had come to Puma young and hungry, who wanted to work round the clock and make a career for himself, had already left his employer in his own mind at least. He harboured no thoughts of going to Adidas. It was not until 1992, when the last chink of hope at Puma was threatened with extinction, that he sent out his first job applications. Success soon followed. In early 1993 he received a top offer from a company in the same region. He went to the office of Martin Gänsler, whom he trusted, closed the door behind him and spilled his thoughts about moving on. Gänsler looked him straight in the eye: "Please don't do anything rash. Give us a bit more time." His bearded colleague had contacts even with the Supervisory Board. His gut feeling had clearly alerted him to the fact that change was once more imminent at the top.

Three months later, Zeitz was presented to management as the new chairman. Within 30 minutes of his first appearance in the role, he called Bock and asked him for a personal meeting in his office. "I trust you," he said, "and would like us to tackle the turnaround together." He wanted to keep the last word on marketing and controlling so as to be able to spur on or rein in business developments if required. Zeitz had previously asked around within the company and obtained a thorough picture of Bock's skills and loyalty. Since that day, the two have worked very closely together. Bock became manager of the entire financial accounting department and, in 2001, received the high honour of appointment to the Group Executive Committee, with responsibility for finance. In August 2005, the CEO awarded him the highest office of all: the Franconian number-cruncher advanced to become the Vice President Finance of Puma AG.

### Horst Widmann, the networking foreign minister

If you go looking for Horst Widmann, you are most likely to track him down in some airport lounge between Frankfurt, Ghana and Bahrain. He is constantly on the move. He is one of the members of Lufthansa's HON Circle, a select few who are picked up from the aircraft in an S-Class Mercedes or Porsche Cayenne and who can while away their waiting time in relaxation rooms over lobster and champagne. You can only become a member of this pampered circle if you amass 600,000 miles in two consecutive calendar years.

Seat 1A is his regular place on the plane. He started his career in the sports equipment sector at the side of Puma's biggest rival: Adidas founder Adolf Dassler.

Widmann, a small man with a stoop, born in 1941, originally completed a traditional German apprenticeship in business. At Nuremberg toy factory Schuco, he worked his way up to development manager. He was contented with his life. At the weekend, he reported on the regional football matches for German football magazine *kicker* or played football himself. He progressed as far as the southern German representative team. During a reporting assignment at the training camp for the German national football team, he got to know Adi Dassler, who was discussing a broken stud at the edge of the pitch with Wolfgang Overath. At lunch, Dassler happened to sit next to the entrepreneur. Widmann, a plastics expert, plucked up the courage to speak to the famous man, and tried to explain to him how the union between studs and sole could be improved. Dassler looked up, mumbled a few words to himself and turned away. The first contact was not very promising.

*Horst Widmann, foreign minister*

Six weeks later, Widmann took a telephone call. The Adidas boss in person was on the other end of the line. "Get over here right away!" he said. At six o'clock in the evening, Widmann was standing outside the patriarch's villa in Herzogenaurach.

"Can you implement the new stud system for us?" Dassler asked him. Widmann said yes: Schuco went on to supply four million studs to Adidas.

Dassler began to appreciate Widmann's skills and it wasn't long before he called on his creative powers for a second time. At the Olympic Games in Mexico in 1968, the running competitions took place on a tartan track for the first time. It became apparent that the stadium designers' innovation was taking a heavy toll on the Adidas athletes' joints. The sharp spikes dug deep into the plastic and put a strain on the anatomy. A new technical solution was needed. "Come to Adidas," said Dassler. "It doesn't matter what you are earning – I will give you three times that." Widmann duly came, remedied the problem and was very happy with his monthly salary of 10,000 marks plus a company car – an absolute fortune at that time.

He worked for Adidas for 22 years and spent the first ten as Adi Dassler's personal assistant. In the 1970s and 1980s, business was humming along – until Adidas, too, underestimated the new contender Nike. Although the Germans were already represented in the leisure sports segment with their jogging shoe "Achill", and sold around 30,000 pairs in 1975, even Widmann got the vast new market wrong. When the US dealers ordered 1.2 million of them, Dassler rejected the contract. He would have had to build new factories and this investment seemed to him too risky. As a result, no one stood in Nike's way. Despite such fatal errors in his thinking – Puma suffered from the same thing – Widmann does not have a bad word to say about his former boss to this day. He found him friendly and fair, and Adi treated him like his own son. After his death, Widmann became head of development and automatically a PR protagonist. Until the end of the 1970s there was still no staff department at Adidas for marketing or promotions. Footwear designers travelled around the world, arranged for the products to be tested and pressed them on athletes at the side of the track. Widmann was entrusted with this form of PR work.

Puma was not Widmann's focus at this time. The two companies played dirty tricks on each other whenever the opportunity arose, but from Adidas' perspective the small unloved brother was miles behind, and therefore unworthy of further consideration. In the football sector, however, Puma was a serious thorn in Widmann's side: the company had contracted Borussia Mönchengladbach, the star team of the decade. And it gave individual sponsorship to attractive players such as Pelé, Eusébio, Johan Cruyff and Günter Netzer.

When the French financial investor Bernard Tapie bought Adidas in 1990, and Swiss René C. Jäggi, a reinforced concrete draftsman who then went on to take a degree in sports, was at the helm and steering to order, Widmann left. He couldn't be bothered anymore. The Frenchman wanted to put less money into design and more into marketing. Widmann asked for his contract to be dissolved early. On the other side of the Aurach at Puma, this was the era of Hans Woitschätzke. Widmann knew him from old times at the ski company Kneissl, and had done a lot of business with him as an Adidas representative. "You can start here tomorrow," said Woitschätzke. At dinner, the Puma boss made him an offer he could not refuse. At lunchtime on the Friday he received the OK for his move from Adidas boss Jäggi, and on the Monday morning, Widmann moved into his new office at Puma, working as Vice President and right-hand man to Woitschätzke. Sacrilege. For the first time, a prominent manager had changed sides. Within a year around 20 Adidas employees followed him.

The gruff-seeming man, who appeared to come from another era, proved to be a talented communicator from the outset. His network of acquaintances extends deep into Eastern Europe, Asia and Africa. In the preparations for the 2010 football World Cup in South Africa, which Puma boss Zeitz is treating as a domestic event on account of Puma's many deals with African teams, Widmann is looking after nearly all contacts and contracts.

### Helmut Fischer, the advertising man who links past and present

Some people are handy to have in any company, because they are capable of holding everything together. Such employees are able to forge links between the past and future. They take care of the history of the company with the same zeal as they do its continued development. They are usually easy-going, committed, ready to help and always open to their colleagues' troubles. They provide warmth in a world dominated by cold numbers. They are people like Helmut Fischer.

He was born on 21 December 1949 in Herzogenaurach, the eldest son of Adidas shoe-factory worker Josef Fischer and his wife Margarete, and started work at Puma on 1 February 1978. Connections helped him with his entry to the profession. His father-in-law was a school friend of Rudolf Dassler's son Armin, who had been running the company since his father died in 1974. Fischer's father-in-law was already working for the Dassler brothers before the war, and opted to go with Rudolf Dassler when the two went their separate ways in 1948. The loyalty paid off for his son-in-law: Fischer was allowed to attend the Nuremberg advertising college Bayrische Werbeakademie between 1978 and 1980, and simultaneously build up Puma's first advertising department. He was officially appointed advertising manager in 1980 and remained in this position for over 25 years, albeit with responsibility only for Puma Germany under Jochen Zeitz.

Marathon runner Fischer counts as one of the last traditionalists at Puma. In addition to his duties as advertising manager for

*Helmut Fischer running a marathon*

Germany he is responsible for maintaining the archives and organizing old photos and brochures – he has spent decades collecting footwear and autograph cards of Puma's most successful contracted athletes, and he makes sure that the founder of the company is remembered with respect. As a young lad, he met Rudolf Dassler in person. He was impressed by his imposing appearance, his *bon viveur* manner, his entrepreneurial achievements. As a child he would look on in amazement whenever Rudolf drove through the small town in his big Mercedes saloon, always impeccably dressed. He regrets that the top management in many cases couldn't be bothered with the history of the company – it was Zeitz who, after many years, allowed a Puma museum to be opened in the planned new German headquarters. Fischer had pulled every string available to him with the town administration to have the street where the new company offices are located named Rudolf-Dassler-Strasse. Zeitz stubbornly ignores the street name and, instead, always uses his own coinage: "Puma Way".

If you want to understand how life worked in a divided city, you should take a tour of Herzogenaurach with Fischer. It soon becomes clear that the "Herzogenaurach Wall" between the Puma and Adidas zones is still very much there in the minds of the population. From the glass entry gate, it follows a line along Würzburger Strasse down past number eleven, the birthplace of Lothar Matthäus. Then across the street up the hill to Hirtengraben, the location of the house where the Dassler brothers were born. Here, in their mother's laundry, they worked on their first pairs of shoes. The words "Fritz Dassler Lederhosen" are written on the outer wall – the impoverished "other" brother had tried to build up his own business. Today the house is privately owned – for Fischer, another indication of how little regard the Dassler clan had for its heritage. The border between the two faiths ran a few hundred metres away on the Postplatz, where there is now a roundabout and the Aurach river flows by. From this point you can view the mighty Adidas building, compared with which the Puma headquarters seems a bit pathetic. In the local heritage society hangs a portrait of Christoph Dassler, the father of the estranged brothers. And in the local museum immediately adjacent to the church, devotional objects from years gone by are on display. They are contained in two glass display cabinets, which of course are set at a safe distance apart – one for Adidas and one for Puma.

### Klaus Bauer, the virtual HR manager

"Puma? Never!" Klaus Bauer summarily dispatched his boss Bernd Szymanski. Szymanski had just resigned from the Nuremberg type-writer and computer firm Triumph-Adler after it had been sold to Olivetti, and signed for the sports equipment company in neigh-bouring Herzogenaurach as the new financial director. He wanted to take his trusted IT chief with him. "If it had been Adidas, gladly," said Bauer, "but I have never worn Puma in my life." Besides, he had other plans – he wanted to go abroad and see the world. Szy-manski proffered an inducement: "At Puma, as well as being in charge of cost accounting, you can build up a sourcing organiza-tion in Hong Kong." Hong Kong? That proved irresistible. On 2 January 1989, Bauer started at Puma. But he only signed a two-year contract. If someone had told him then that he would stay on for over 15 years and play a key role in the Puma story, he would have laughed very loudly.

Bauer, born in 1955, completed an apprenticeship in indus-trial business after leaving school, and subsequently went on to study business. Over the years he developed a keen eye for situa-tions in which money was being thrown down the drain. At Tri-umph-Adler, avoiding extravagance was part of the company philosophy and even the tiniest screw had an article number to enable it to be recorded properly. He also knew how to create lean operating processes with modern information technology. His first impression of Puma was disastrous: ancient computer systems stut-tering away to themselves. And when he attended the ISPO for the first time in February 1989 he was flabbergasted. The moribund company was taking up an entire hall to itself. "How ostentatious," he said, shaking his head in disbelief. "I felt like I was in Holly-wood: it was all just show."

For months, Bauer toiled hard in Asia to get an efficient sourc-ing organization up and running. An exciting job – nevertheless, he did not want to extend his contract in 1991. Puma was almost

*Klaus Bauer, head of personnel*

bankrupt and it was not exactly fun to earn a living by backing a loser. His boss Szymanski begged him to stay, and offered him the position of divisional manager for IT. The job appealed to computer freak Bauer: in this position he was able to build a new IT platform and install a new merchandise information system. On top of this, there was a posh company car. He agreed to sign a contract for another two years.

At the end of 1992, he once more wanted to pack the job in. Szymanski had just gone to Escada in Switzerland and was pushing Bauer to follow suit. Bauer thought about it. Then the new CEO Niels Stenhoj persuaded him to stay in a discussion at the ISPO. "The company has a huge chance of survival," Bauer said to Stenhoj. "Unfortunately, no one can see it." It all seemed so easy: Puma was making 30 million marks from foreign licence holders. If the other areas did not go into the red, the firm would soon be in profit again. The simple analysis convinced Stenhoj. He appointed Bauer Group Head of Management Accounting. What Bauer did not know was that Stenhoj was already well on the way to being thrown out again.

When Jochen Zeitz took the boss's seat he extended Bauer's range of competencies again: as well as controlling and IT, he was now responsible for human resources. Not exactly a job to make you popular. In 1993, when the mass redundancies began, Bauer found a note lodged behind the windscreen wiper on his company car one evening: "Don't ever show your face again in Herzogenaurach at night!"

### Katharina Wojaczek, the understanding adversary

In 1978, money was tight for the Wojaczek family in Herzogenaurach. Katharina Wojaczek's husband had just started studying for a degree and their one-year-old was developing a keen appetite. The mother needed to earn some extra money. "I went to Puma first of all, which was the thing to do," she recalls. Armin Dassler made recruiting new members of staff a matter for top management. Likeability was one of his most important quality criteria. His first question was: "Do any of your relatives work at Adidas?" If the answer had been yes, all visions of a job would have been over right there and then. The patriarch peppered the young woman with questions for ten minutes and then said: "OK, you can start next month in reception." She sat behind the counter in the old reception hall, which was later converted into the canteen. She was proud of her new job. "Puma must be doing very well," she thought, and most of the staff shared the same view. The mere fact that Pelé – the personality that outshone all others and all else – was under contract spoke for itself. Katharina Wojaczek knew nothing at this point of the burgeoning economic tragedy behind the scenes.

*Katharina Wojaczek, head of the Works Council*

The Works Council in those days lived out a pitiful existence on the fringe of events. A lady from accounts who had a part-time job handled all the interests of the white-collar and blue-collar workers. There was no question of works agreements between management and labour in this family company. The employees' weakness rankled with the lady in reception. At her previous company, Silvana, an American firm based in Herzogenaurach, she had witnessed for herself just how influential a well-organized workforce can be. In 1983 she decided to take the matter into her own hands and joined the Works Council. Three years later she was elected chairwoman. To this day, Puma has not cut any salaries even in the hardest times. Many employees say that is mainly to her credit.

The more difficult the years became, the more work landed on her desk. In 1986, the banks had given potential investor Cosa Liebermann their agreement that an acquisition of shares by the company could be accompanied by radical job cuts. The Supervisory Board and the employees' representatives had already approved the massive retrenchment, and protracted negotiations on socially compatible redundancy plans and termination agreements were looming. At least 30 per cent of the employees were to go, the production facilities were to be cut back by 60 per cent and the majority of the warehouses were to be closed. All ideas for restructuring ultimately ended in failure because the executive personnel responsible for their implementation never remained in office for very long. Only Katharina Wojaczek stayed and was able to relax.

She did not really notice her new colleague Jochen Zeitz at first. Very soon, however, she began to develop a firm prejudice against the man in the marketing department. Offended employees had told her that Zeitz was behaving with brazen unconventionality and ignoring the unwritten rules of the company. They felt they were no longer being taken seriously in their work and were being disregarded. "Snob," they would call him – he would snootily parade his time and experience in the USA in front of them. Katharina Wojaczek showed professional understanding for the complaints, but at the same time she was also impressed by the fact that Zeitz was so open. Now she wanted to form her own picture of the new Vice President Marketing and Sales as soon as possible.

The first personal contact between them occurred at a meeting of the Works Council personnel committee. "Let's have a chat afterwards," said the chairwoman. At the end of the meeting, they sat down together for a lengthy discussion and took a long hard look into each other's eyes and souls. She liked one of the young man's qualities even at that meeting: Zeitz challenged things – even when his superior managers had made the decisions. This kind of approach was completely new in the history of the patriarch-led Puma.

At the end of the discussion, Katharina Wojaczek had to laugh. How wrong she had been about Zeitz before their first meeting! She had thought of him as a tough guy, unapproachable and frosty. She emerged from the meeting with her opinions transformed: "He is an absolute visionary, he gets on with things and finishes them," she says today, as though he were more the Messiah than her ex officio adversary. He starts many of his sentences "I would like …," "My aim is to …," or similarly. Right from the start she particularly liked the fact that he had a helicopter view of the company's situation and could process the information. For her taste, his predecessors had messed around too much with small sections of the company and at some point lost track of the way they fitted together. Zeitz never left anyone out, he listened, analyzed and acted. "Give him a chance," the head of the Works Council told employees following the private meeting. "He has been fair right up to this day," she says. Previously, that was a rarity in the House of Puma.

Assessing her many years in office, Katharina Wojaczek has had to come into conflict far more often with the trade union officials than with the Board. The pragmatism with which she supported Puma's restructuring left a nasty taste in the mouths of the ideologists. Time and again trade union emissaries tried to get her into line. In early 2007, after 20 years in office, she left the Supervisory Board where she had been a labour representative.

## 2.3 Mission: Impossible

### The restructuring phase: "just out of kindergarten", the big clearout, the underdog and an impossible freak

Some managers have a natural talent for trusting their own point of view. Jochen Zeitz is one of them. Had he relied on the judgment of outsiders, his self-confidence would probably have hit rock bottom within a matter of days after taking up his new position. In those days, pouring scorn on Puma was one of competitors' favourite exercises. The products with the big cat logo were best suited to "dads, whose favourite sporting activity is watching it on TV with a beer in hand," mocked one Nike manager. He wasn't far wrong: the Puma warehouse still held over a million plastic flip-flops with a 19-mark price tag. The press's reaction to the appointment of an unknown was correspondingly sharp. Headlines ranged from amazement to derision. Not only was the company appointing its fourth CEO in the space of two years, the chosen candidate was barely out of short trousers, listened to hip hop in his blue BMW 525i and tuned into MTV in the evenings. The serious Sunday paper *Welt am Sonntag* dubbed Zeitz "the baby of the family of Germany's CEOs". The *Speigel* mocked: "an ambitious kid with a predilection for teen music is the new hope to rescue sleepy, traditional Puma."

The *Spiegel* reporter gleefully committed to paper a scene he had observed during a visit to Herzogenaurach: "His broad shoulders virtually fill the doorway. Jochen Zeitz leans menacingly into the office. With his right hand in his trouser pocket and his left clasping a fat file, he rattles off instructions to an employee. His opposite number has no chance to argue: 'All clear?' Zeitz asks. Although it sounds like a question, it is actually a statement. Two and a half minutes have passed and the brief conference is over. 'Turnover!' Zeitz barks as he leaves, his smile is supposed to indicate that he enjoys his work."

Not even the venerable *Financial Times* greeted the new CEO with open arms, even though Zeitz had always asserted that the Anglo-Saxons had no problem with young executives. This was the very reason why he had previously gone to work for Colgate in New York. But the *FT* thought differently: at the age of just 30, he was some years younger than many of the athletes that Puma sponsored. Compared to the average CEO in German companies, he was "just out of kindergarten".

The man with the broad shoulders seemed unimpressed. Anyone who broached the subject of his lack of professional experience to him was met with a quote from German satirist Kurt Tucholsky: "Experience means nothing. You can spend 20 years doing something wrong." He looked into the cameras with increasing self-confidence. With his smooth side-parting and gently knowing smile, he resembled Roger Moore, alias James Bond in *Moonraker*, as he disposes of "Jaws". When an editor from the German newspaper *Zeit* asked how he had impressed the principal shareholder, he replied: "They wanted a sporting goods expert at the head of Puma who could bring skills from the international branded goods industry to the table. They wanted someone tough and dynamic, who was ideally also familiar with Puma. There was, so Mr Ohlsson told me, only one person who fitted the bill."

In the early years, Zeitz was rarely available to talk to the media – he preferred to speak when there was something to celebrate. He had no time left over for media work. His working day began at eight in the morning and finished at ten in the evening. Evenings at Lo Stivale, an Italian restaurant in Herzogenaurach, became a thing of the past. He carried what he needed with him in his head, he did not keep an appointments diary. At lunch he ate a strawberry yoghurt at his desk or had pasta delivered. He put on the pounds because of his lack of exercise, soon weighing in at almost two hundred pounds. In his first television interview, he appeared as a chubby-cheeked young executive. Weekends off were gone forever – something which troubled his wife Birgit in particular and earned him a guilty conscience. "On Saturdays and Sundays, I brood over global decisions," he said. In order to keep up a reasonable level of physical fitness and be able to cope with his important tasks, he jogged through Herzogenaurach and worked out on the weights bench at his modest-sized home in Nuremberg.

## House of horror

The detailed audit of the company's current situation that he carried out with the help of his trusted colleagues in his first few weeks as CEO produced catastrophic results. The team went through the company with a fine tooth comb, subjected contracts to close scrutiny, examined manufacturing costs and analyzed the international business. Zeitz summarized the results and possible countermeasures in a thick stack of charts, which he presented to the principal shareholder Aritmos in Sweden on 18 June. The title page bore a quotation from American President Franklin D. Roosevelt: "Never before have we had so little time in which to do so much." The kill-or-cure remedy, he told the shareholders frankly, would eat up a heap of money. Profits could not be expected again until 1995. Despite such prospects, the Swedes were unanimous in their belief that the premature praise they had bestowed on Zeitz was justified. Puma was to become a desirable European sports brand, that was the message of his presentation and it carried weight. Excellent quality leisure items with a contemporary design would be developed from the pure sports products. Nothing would be left to chance any more, all marketing campaigns would be subject to his planning and his control. Proventus allowed him to close 1993 with 63 million marks of debt, and announced that it would put another ten million marks into the company at the end of the year.

Zeitz made vigorous attempts to shake the bureaucratic mentality out of his employees' heads. He encouraged an entrepreneurial spirit and gave everyone autonomy within the scope of his or her capabilities. He wanted to awaken innovativeness and decisiveness. People who, in the past, had entrenched themselves behind closed doors and pointed to their colleagues when mistakes were made, were now required to attend regular meetings in order to deal with problems. Departmental thinking was prohibited with immediate effect. The change, wrote Zeitz, will take place "within the whole company, quickly, 100 percent and without compromise".

He did not even hold back in the face of long-serving employees in their mid-fifties. "I have emerged victorious from all previous battles," he boasted self-confidently to the business magazine *Capital*. The high turnover of management staff in the last few years left him equally unimpressed. "I'm not interested in whether or not this is an ejector seat. I wanted responsibility, the really big challenge!" Just a few months after taking over this responsibility, he sensed the first results of his hard work: "Finally, we've got something like a team spirit. They have all understood that there's no time for intrigues or politics and that the only way we can do this is together."

Zeitz expected a great deal from his employees. He challenged or simply wiped out almost everything that Puma employees had held dear. Promising business areas and subsidiaries were converted into profit centres. If it benefited workflow organization, groups that had shared offices from time immemorial were broken up. Even the salary structures were reorganized: in future, an employee's performance would determine how much was in his or her account at the end of the year. Once a month, the management staff would get together and take stock. Managers from all sorts of different departments sat opposite one another. No longer would anyone be able to wriggle out of responsibility if business was not going well.

The human resources department was charged with the hardest job of all. To get costs under control in the long term, a total of 750 jobs had to go – almost half of the workforce. Zeitz personally undertook half of the personnel interviews as well as the closure of the last production plant in Herzogenaurach. One day he found a card in his post, apparently from German terrorist group the Red Army Faction. "RAF, you will shortly be liquidated," the message ran. Zeitz the Bold did not take the matter particularly seriously. However, the new Bavarian Minister of the Interior, Günther Beckstein, gave him police protection – he was no longer to park his car on the street or go shopping on foot. "You can forget that," Zeitz said fearlessly. He did not tell his wife about the incident until six years later.

It was not uncommon for the survivors of the job cuts to plunge into deep crisis because their working environment had changed so radically. In some sales departments, seven or eight people had sat and worked together over the years – now just 1.5 jobs remained. Saddened but convinced of the need for all the interventions, Works Council chairwoman Katharina Wojaczek moved through the offices, called small groups together and talked to them about the "clearout". She did not dare to call an employees' meeting. At earlier crisis meetings, brooms and shoes had already flown at the podium. The anger of the employees was now at its height and she feared that things would get out of control. She argued as though she herself belonged to the management. The economic situation, she said, offered the Works Council no alternative but to agree to the dismissals for business reasons.

The bitter partings were sweetened generously. Those affected received severance pay of one to two months' salary for each year of employment. On top of this there were extra payments for cases of social hardship. In addition, the Board also made contact with Schäffler, a manufacturer of rolling bearings, and other companies in the region to recommend its own people for new jobs. Most of those who were fired eventually found employment in other firms. Seventy of them went to Adidas. Despite the deep cuts, nobody in the small town of Herzogenaurach declined into poverty. The Board and Works Council can only take part of the credit for this. The departure was made easy for many because the social welfare legislation of the Kohl government acted as a soft cushion. Older employees in particular – those over the age of 50 – allowed themselves to sink comfortably into that cushion almost of their own free will. They took their severance pay – quite a few of the production workers had been with Puma for over 30 years – and made their way immediately to the unemployment office. There, they received unemployment pay for three years and still-generous unemployment benefit thereafter through to retirement, without the severance pay being taken into account. For ten years and more, many ex-Puma employees enjoyed this combination of transfer benefit and severance pay. It was virtually impossible to slip into the ultimate subsistence level of benefit. Recipients of the much lower benefits of today, following the "Hartz IV" reform of the German benefits system, would probably have been very happy to have been thrown out by Zeitz.

Laws are not everything, was the conclusion Katharina Wojaczek took away with her from the comprehensive restructuring. "Such decisions," she said, "have to be made at the company level." Unbureaucratically and quickly between the employer and employees. With equal rights and with the aim of making progress together. Time and again, union officials arrived on her doorstep and criticized her unconventional collaboration with the Board. She is not the type who bows down at the feet of ideologies – she is herself a union member.

The months of corporate restructuring were among the hardest

*Brand reinforcement: Linford Christie with tattoo, 1994*

of the then 30-year-old Jochen Zeitz's life. You need to be blessed with a magnificent constitution and a serenity of spirit to withstand such a mental strain. The pressure was stepped up further by the fact that Herzogenaurach was so small. Lesser worries than these had seen the Dasslers seek comfort from the whisky shelves of the bar next to the Board office. How was Zeitz able to cope with the difficult progression through the established institutions in such a cool, some say ice-cold, manner? There is much to suggest that he was driven by a touch of youthful recklessness. He paid no heed to the insults, disparaging comments and scorn of disappointed employees and angry citizens. He went his own way. And he saw this new direction as having three phases. In phase one, the years from 1993 to 1997, he first wanted to complete the restructuring and reduce the company's debts. In phase two, between 1998 and 2001, he planned to invest heavily in marketing, product development and infrastructure and to give Puma a new brand identity that would combine lifestyle and fashion. Finally, for phase three, scheduled to start in 2002, he promised to make Puma the hottest brand in its sector and to convert this potential into profitable growth.

Managers at rival companies were quite taken aback at the military precision of the Puma boss's approach. They were not unforthcoming with malicious comments about him, either. Insiders report that corks popped at Adidas, because they were certain that the young maniac had finally sealed the fate of their unloved neighbour. Themselves driven by quarterly reporting and at pains to keep up their share prices, they found it presumptuous and foolish to plan beyond the next one or two financial years.

### A strict savings plan

The job cuts alone were not enough to save Puma. In addition, fixed costs needed to be lowered by around 40 percent. A thick red pen scored through budgets in all areas. Development and sourcing bled the most with reductions of 44.4 percent, followed by distribution, which went down by 41.3 percent, marketing at minus 30.7 percent and administration at minus 30 percent. The General Manager level, whose members had collectively pocketed over a million marks in salary, was completely abolished.

The management developed a truly draconian 100-point savings plan. In actual fact, the members of the Board had only come up with 97 items – they manufactured another three because 100 sounded snappier than 97. To name a few examples: six of the eight warehouses were closed, cleaners were no longer permitted to clean every day, two of the five company drivers were dismissed, the number of photocopiers was reduced, instead of faxes staff were required to send e-mails, local beauties replaced expensive catwalk professionals as models in front of the camera, the size of the Puma stand at the ISPO was halved (Puma later cancelled its attendance at the trade fair entirely, despite strong protests from the dealers and the trade fair organizers), national and international marketing were merged, and events were to be held in the company's own rooms rather than in expensive hotels.

Comfortable business class flights were also forbidden: in the spring Zeitz endured a 30-hour flight to Peking via Tokyo and back in tourist class – "that was the toughest trip of its kind I ever experienced," he admitted. The vehicle fleet was also vigorously thinned out: instead of 141 cars only 80 were leased. In future, anyone who needed a company car got one that was a class smaller than what they were used to. According to the articles of association, the CEO would have been entitled to a 7-series BMW – however, he continued to drive his 5-series until sometime later the car manufacturer presented him with a 740i free of charge for promotional reasons.

If the economy drive was to be successful, the subsidiaries and licence holders would have to play their part. Zeitz knew that without them all efforts would be in vain. He made it a matter for top management to bring them into line, and rushed around from airport to airport. The first thing he did was to replace the heads of the organizations: almost every subsidiary got a new managing director. He ordered the Spanish subsidiary to be closed and, instead, granted a licence.

He also made a clean sweep in the areas of development and sourcing to ensure on-the-dot delivery and achieve a sustainable increase in margins. In the past, the representatives of both functions had been happy to put the blame on one another if a product was not launched in time or if quality was below standard. The new boss merged the two areas and placed them in the hands of his trusted colleague Martin Gänsler. His first job was to reveal how much the manufacturing of a product could be allowed to cost in the future, down to the second decimal place. In previous years, the controllers had not even noticed if the company was suffering losses on an item due to poor terms and conditions. The new costing produced stretch targets: from that point on, the "King Pro" shoe, for example, had to be sourced 30.7 percent more cheaply and the "World Tech Top" shoe at as much as 48.6 percent less. Accordingly, factories in low-wage countries were placed under contract and existing agreements renegotiated. In 1993, 60 percent of all Puma products still originated in Europe, with 40 percent originating in Asia.

In addition, the branches were no longer allowed to do their own thing. As of now, worldwide marketing concepts were to apply and all Puma managers were obliged to adhere to them. "Look big and be different," Zeitz wrote into their performance specifications. In future, no manager should as much as dream of sponsoring a fun run in a provincial backwater that the outside world had never heard of. The product range was radically streamlined and minority sports no longer fitted into the scheme of things. Football, running, basketball, indoor sports and a little tennis – for the time being, there would be no new additions. The "Puma World Team" – an invention of the PR strategist Zeitz – acted as ambassadors for the advertising message. This "team" included handpicked stars such as Lothar Matthäus and the "Fantastic Four" – track and field athletes and Olympic gold medallists Heike Drechsler, Colin Jackson, Linford Christie and Merlene Ottey. To get young people hooked on the brand, Zeitz, together with Helmut Fischer, came up with the "Street Soccer Cup", a worldwide football tournament in whose first year around 40,000 children aged between 10 and 16 played football against one another at 300 events for a place in the final in Berlin. The idea was not entirely new: Adidas had previously enjoyed huge success with a comparable concept – a basketball event called "Streetball".

The tone in the company was no longer set by grey-haired men in dark suits, but young professionals such as Head Textiles Designer Amy Garbers. Zeitz had poached her from Reebok. With her baseball cap turned back-to-front, the mini-skirted 28-year-old raced through the corridors and spurred on her colleagues. Jon Edgar, the Australian who had originally been in charge of cricket shoes for Puma, took care of the latest sneakers. His eyes were trained on the West Coast of the United States, the source of all innovations. Here, new trends sometimes emerged out of nothing – triggered by music bands, free climbers, tri-athletes or bungee jumpers. "Our business is like surfing," Zeitz taught. "If you start with the wave, you'll make it. If you catch the wave too early, you'll capsize. And if you catch the wave too late, you will gradually sink." The next wave at this time was "retro". It was started in Seattle by rap musicians and brought vintage styles from the 60s and 70s back onto the shelves. "Suedes" – suede trainers like those celebrated by Elvis Presley in "Blue Suede Shoes" – were particularly fashionable. In the first year after the rebirth of the "Suedes", Puma sold two million pairs in the USA. And there was clothing to match.

Zeitz was absolutely euphoric when he discovered pop superstar Madonna on the cover of an American music magazine: she had had three-inch heels crafted onto her Puma suedes, the "Originals". "We'll copy them," Zeitz decided and had them sold as "Limited Edition" shoes in the trendiest shops such as "Wood you" in Munich and "Delirium" in Hamburg. The idea was a complete success, even though, at the end of the day, the shoes did not even constitute one percent of sales. Less is more – the strategy paid off. Some products simply had to be difficult to get hold of. Zeitz wanted Puma items to be desirable. However, he still did not see the leaping big cat as a fashion and sportlifestyle label at this point. His somewhat stiff definition read: "Puma is an international performance sports brand, offering high-quality sports footwear, textiles and accessories with an optimum price-performance ratio." Leisure apparel was still taboo in the market of sports goods manufacturers.

However, he evidently had some inkling of the direction the journey could take. At the beginning of 1995, a man by the name of Lamine Kouyaté made headlines under his pseudonym Xuly Bët. The Paris-based West African designer had cut up old Puma training jackets, like those worn by footballer Lothar Matthäus and Werder Bremen goalkeeper Oliver Reck, and re-stitched them into garish outfits. He produced cropped tops from goalkeepers' jerseys and tight hot pants from comfortable football shorts. He slapped on the Puma label and sold the items in leading clothes shops. Zeitz found out about this "rag designer" through a copy of *Elle*

*Street soccer tournament,*
*1996*

magazine shown to him by a female colleague. Rather than warning the avant-garde designer off, however, he sent him an invitation to Herzogenaurach so that he could congratulate him on his work and cooperate with him. On the one hand, he knew that a man with a fashion range like this to his name, with articles priced at 180 marks and upwards, was one of the trendsetters that Puma urgently needed for its brand image. On the other hand, for the reasons mentioned, he toned down publicity about the collaboration: "We are a sports brand and want to stay that way."

### The power of the underdog

For more than 40 years, Puma founder Rudolf Dassler and his successors had tried to catch up with or even overtake Adidas in terms of sales. Striving for volume was the only valid guiding principle for the day-to-day business. Whatever the cost, revenues were required in order to stay at the very top of the sports goods market. That was why the Dasslers had been prepared to sacrifice the former good image of the Puma brand on the bargain counters of discount stores. At that time, nobody hit on the idea that "small, but perfectly formed" could be more successful than sheer mass. Yet a glance at other industries would have supplied enough justification to end this directionless and masochistic chase. Even now, German automotive industry players are still showing the way when it comes to successful market positioning: although

Volkswagen does the bulk business, Porsche is significantly more desirable among car fanatics, and more profitable.

The idea of being more Porsche than Volkswagen was buzzing around the heads of the Puma managers right from phase one, when restructuring was on the agenda. What choice did they have? They had neither sufficient sales nor a well-filled war chest to enable them to play in the premier league. Zeitz, therefore, industriously propagated the role for Puma that he himself had defined: David, taking on the Goliaths of the industry. Nike, Adidas and Reebok kept Puma under observation, but the firm had no further significance for them. There were no points of contact, nobody felt any desire to meet with Zeitz or his colleagues. At most, recognition took the form of mocking words about the minnow from Herzogenaurach.

Zeitz soon realized that the position of underdog is not the worst in the world when it comes to image-building. Sports psychologists are aware of the public's automatic tendency to side with the weaker player: when, for example, record champions like football club Bayern Munich take to the pitch against a less successful team, the spectators' reflex action is to support the opponents – apart, of course, from the Bayern fans. Zeitz, too, cherished the hope that if he took his own, out-of-the-ordinary direction, Puma could become the champion of people's hearts even if it was not the champion of sales. So as to be different, he closed cooperative deals with companies and organizations who bore the image of rebellious, fun-loving underdogs. He sponsored the Berlin Love Parade, which was regarded as an anti-establishment event. He supported the Skateboarding World Cup in Münster. He cooperated with the music channel VIVA, whose boss, Dieter Gorny, was attempting to attack the all-powerful market leader MTV. And he supported the non-conformist-styled street soccer events in which youngsters were supposed to feel like street footballers on the way to becoming superstars. He was also increasingly choosy about the stars he contracted: "A lot of world sports stars are fantastic athletes but not a good fit with the company," he explained to *kicker* magazine. "We are trying to find athletes who identify with the brand and the company."

He had to get in touch with the opinion leaders, who were primarily young people. Compared with other sports goods manufacturers, who invested around five percent of their turnover in advertising, in the year after the restructuring Puma was already investing eight percent. Customers' brand loyalty was not an issue at that time. "Today it's this brand, tomorrow it's another," explained marketing man Zeitz to *Sports Live* magazine in October 1995. "You have to be seen by consumers as belonging to this collection of brands so that, either today or tomorrow, they will buy your products. That's why we are always having to readjust, particularly for young people. Young people are not only the main consumers, they are also opinion leaders for the older generation."

For a company like Puma, advertising and sports promotion have the same status as research and development in a high-tech company. Even by 1993, it was impossible for any competitor to achieve differentiation purely on the basis of new materials or improved manufacturing quality. All suppliers were working to the same high standard by then, and sometimes had their goods made in the same factories – in this respect, they were in the same position as detergent manufacturers. This made it all the more important for Zeitz to create an image for the brand as quickly as possible. As he saw it, Adidas stood for reliability, Nike for freedom and victory at any price – and Puma should stand for rebellion. Even in later years, his advertisements were not about going faster, higher or further – instead, he preferred to put Jamaican athletes or African footballers, who stood for a life between reggae and revolution, in front of the camera.

Historically, Puma itself was never rebellious but strictly followed the rules of marketing. Jochen Zeitz controlled a powerful marketing machine with the *Brand Manual* as its operating handbook. The brand projected the zest for life of people to whom happiness meant just a few dollars a day to live on, onto customers who needed shoes and clothes costing 100 dollars and more to achieve that same happiness. The goods with the big cat logo, produced cheaply in Turkey or Vietnam, had very little more in common with the struggle for liberty than a punk frock from a high-end boutique had with the Sex Pistols' orgies. Time and again, however, the Franconians broke the rules of the sporting establishment, by introducing coloured football boots, for example. Rebellion "lite", you might say. The image transfer worked particularly well as a result.

### Raging flames

The rigid retrenchment policy and new self-esteem at Puma led to an unexpected upturn for all concerned: the share price, which had fallen from 1,480 to 15 marks between 1986 and 1993, rallied a little. However, the actual act of liberation took place in 1994: one year earlier than planned, the group generated a profit of around 30 million marks. The company had now managed to wipe off a good portion of its bank debts and was no longer trapped in the talons of the bank pool. Don't forget, in 1990 the company had still been 180 million marks in debt, including a debtor warrant bond. The puma was perhaps not yet ready for the big leap, but the seven lean years of heavy cash bleeding appeared to be over. Nevertheless, being frugal, Zeitz ensured that tightening up and cutting back continued to be part of the daily routine. Nothing has changed in this respect right up to the present day: Zeitz and his deputy, Martin Gänsler, still check every application for a plane journey personally.

Nevertheless, detailed checks alone could not put the company back on a permanently even keel. Fires were raging in all corners of the company and all around the globe. Zeitz visited the source of each blaze personally to help with the fire-fighting. Puma items were produced in 20 countries and sold in 80. In 1995, Zeitz spent exactly 180 nights in his own bed in Nuremberg, as his wife, Birgit, painstakingly recorded. On the others, he was somewhere on the road, Hong Kong, Boston, Buenos Aires, Tokyo or Dubai. He visited customers, manufacturers, licence-holders and sales partners to convince them of Puma's new way. All this bustling around enabled him, almost *en passant*, to establish the first virtual company worthy of the name on German soil. During these months, only 180 people, including the porter, still worked at the Group headquarters in Herzogenaurach. With ultra-modern means of communication, this small workforce ran the large factory and earned revenues for the year of no less than 1.3 billion marks, licence business included. Zeitz had ruthlessly outsourced every service that external suppliers could offer better and more cheaply. Basically, only development, marketing and distribution were still done in-house; production and logistics had been taken over by partner companies. Instead of Puma working out transport routes for itself, the British forwarder P&O now collected the goods from its Chinese factory, completed customs formalities in the port of Shekou in southern China and shipped them via Hong Kong to Europe. Back in Franconia, facilities were soon in place to trace the whereabouts of goods on-line at any time of the day or night. The effect was that in 1996 customers received 84 percent of ordered items on time. Three years previously, this figure had been less than 50 percent.

The break-up of hidebound structures was working so well and outsourcing in many areas was so much cheaper than in-house performance, that in the years that followed Zeitz departed entirely from the traditional management teaching which stated that a Group must and can best be controlled from a single headquarters. On the contrary, the importance of the traditional company headquarters in Herzogenaurach dwindled rapidly. The CEO spread Puma's core competences across the entire world, taking them wherever he found them. The marketing and development of sportlifestyle products are still managed from Boston, USA, today. The "World Cat" team in Hong Kong is responsible for sourcing and for monitoring manufacturers. Only the administration and some of the product development have remained in Bavaria. Here, too, there have been a lot of changes: job descriptions no longer determine who works where and when, the work involved in a project decides such issues. Apart from the top management, there are no more rigid organization charts, and there is a flat hierarchy.

Germany was not so important as a market any more either, as a glance at its market share of 11 percent revealed. In the "pile high, sell cheap" era it had been 30 percent. The management was not at all satisfied with this and gave orders that the lost ground had to be made up. However, without massive growth in the USA, the motherland of all sneakers, which generated half of the worldwide sales of these products, no prizes could be won in the long term. Here, Puma's share of the market was still miniscule at less than one percent – in total, 72 percent of Puma's revenues originated from Europe. Zeitz had, therefore, already pressed for the company to repurchase the trademark overseas and take control – this happened in mid-1995. With a new sole called "Cell Technology", company strategists attempted to reconquer shelf space in the mighty American sports retail chains. The sole contained transparent cells filled with air that absorbed the impact when the wearer was running. Puma wanted to score another hit.

### Tony Bertone, the marketing freak

Sometimes chance plays a part in helping people to achieve their aims. In 1994, at a sales conference on Hilton Head in South Carolina, one of the best-known holiday islands in North America, Zeitz became acquainted with a young man with a goatee beard named Antonio Bertone. He had previously worked as a consultant for Converse and was there to give a presentation to the Puma sales team on youth trends. Bertone, in his early 20s and a streetwise type, appeared before the suits in his skateboard gear and talked away – nervously and unconventionally, but with analytical depth. "He's great," thought Zeitz, "he has understood who our customers are." He ran into him again later at Miami airport. "I thought your presentation was fantastic," said Zeitz. "I thought so too," replied Bertone without a trace of respect. He was no less sure of himself than the Puma boss. They drank a diet Coke together and got on well. Bertone then boarded Business Class. When he saw that Zeitz was sitting behind with the tourists, he tried to change his booking likewise – fearing for his job. Zeitz laughed and wished him a good flight.

The son of an Italian emigrant, born in 1973 near Boston, Bertone's marketing knowledge was drawn from real life. At the age of eleven, he had had his left ear pierced and put in a ring from a chewing gum machine to demonstrate his nonconformism. He plaited his hair and

*Tony Bertone (at left) with Jochen Zeitz*

annoyed his teachers. He knew what he wanted to do for a living: he would become a professional skateboarder. He had started skateboarding at the age of ten. At 14 he began organizing gigs and took on the management of a punk rock band. In 1990, aged 17, he left high school and started work in an offbeat store run by a friend. Besides trainers, the store sold printed T-shirts, records, musical instruments, badges and posters. After a few days, the friend did not show up again and Bertone took over the business. He worked hard and slept in the back room – however, he was unable to prevent the shop from going bankrupt two years later.

"It was an expensive, but valuable lesson," is his take on it today. After a brief interim phase as a car park attendant, he signed up with another way-out emporium, the well-known hip meeting place "Alston Beat". Here, he developed his feel for what urban young people wanted. They wanted the Puma "Clyde", for example, a former basketball shoe that the rebellious hip hop group Beastie Boys paraded at their concerts, because to them this shoe was not as commercial as Converse products, among others. Bertone witnessed and kindled a downright mania for the "Clyde" shoe. He sold so many pairs that his boss offered to open a store of his own for him.

In 1992, Bertone got into conversation with a leading employee from Converse. He offered him a contract as a "streetwear" consultant. Tony was delighted. His job was to tell the managers what was happening on the street – something he had only been able to dream about until now. However, his hopes of finding a permanent position at the sportswear company quickly faded. His contact made it clear to him that he was a bit too way-out for that. Following this disappointment, Bertone phoned the Puma marketing department. He introduced himself as a consultant for Converse who would much rather work for Puma.

Puma invited him to the branch in Brockton. There, he met the top boss Bill Kirkendall and told him his story. Kirkendall was astonished and smiled. He found the 22-year-old's impudence refreshing. His insight into the potential of a market that was determined by skateboarders, BMX bikers and street kids impressed him. Bertone was given a contract as a permanent freelance consultant and was permitted to fly with them for the first time to the sales meeting.

Just a few days after Zeitz had bought back the US trademark rights, he appointed the young maniac of Miami airport Product Manager on the American team for the newly established Lifestyle category. In this role, he absorbed the young generation's attitude to life and translated it into sportlifestyle branded products. Now skaters and break-dancers appeared in the promotional videos in place of footballers and track and field athletes. Externally, the CEO retained full responsibility for marketing, but Bertone's influence on his way of thinking and on the processes in the company grew day by day. No marketing campaign went public without being given the nod by the brand manager and lifestyle custodian in person. In the years that followed, the former freak developed a level of professionalism needed in the world of big business. Without the guiding hand of the CEO, however, he would not have survived a week in the group. "Nutcase" was the most benign name given to the new colleague. When Zeitz returned from America with the edict: "Let's make shoes for the street," even very close confidants declared him to be "brainwashed" and bayed for

Bertone's blood. In Franconia, practically no one believed in the American way. "Where are we supposed to sell street shoes?" asked the sales people. The traditional sales channel via sports retailers did indeed prove to be unsuitable. In the first Puma shop in Los Angeles, however, the shoes became an absolute bestseller overnight.

## 2.4  Welcome to Hollywood

### The new shareholder Monarchy/Regency: a "Pretty Woman", a visit to a strip club and a loopy boss

One evening in the middle of August 1996, Zeitz's phone rang. Mikael Kamras, the boss of principal shareholder Proventus, was on the line. The Swedes – in line with their own investment strategy – had parted via Aritmos with a large part of their Puma shares at three times their original purchase price, retaining just 25 percent. Kamras said he was in contact with a film manager who was interested in Puma. "Why not?" Zeitz thought to himself. He wanted to get into the US market. He himself was not in touch with any leading figures from the movie world. The Franconians had always tried to place products in the media somehow, but had met with little success. "Let's talk to them," said Zeitz without taking much time to think about it. America was important.

The mystery film manager was called Arnon Milchan. He came from the aristocracy of Tel Aviv. He had attended elite schools in Switzerland and England and had a burning passion for sport. He loved football and tennis. In 1970 he had met a "very clever and smart man" by the name of Shimon Peres, who wanted to set up a political party. Milchan became its financial manager and a good friend of the Israeli prime minister to be. Money worries were long since a thing of the past for this charming 52-year-old. At an early age, his father had left him 60,000 dollars and a more or less operational import and export business. Milchan, who had a degree in biochemistry, built up his own chemical company and invented a nutrient that quadrupled citrus production. Years later, in addition to chemicals, he sold fabrics and "anything that could fly". According to research carried out by the CBS show *60 Minutes*, he also advised the Israeli government on weapons issues. He denies that he was ever an arms dealer, on the side of the law or otherwise.

As well as sport, Milchan loved movies. In the early 1980s he had been involved in a minor TV production called *Masada* as a

*Zeitz with Arnon Milchan and Israeli prime minister Shimon Peres*

co-producer. Through this series, he came to the attention of film producer Elliot Kastner (*Farewell, My Lovely*). Kastner arranged to have dinner with Milchan on Sunset Boulevard and brought along a charming companion: Elizabeth Taylor. Kastner secured the rising entrepreneur an entry to the Hollywood studios. Some years later, Milchan set up his own production company, which spawned the leading film production and distribution company Monarch/ Regency in 1991. Shareholders included the late Australian media entrepreneur Kerry Packer, the Anglo-Australian tycoon Rupert Murdoch and even the German film and television baron Leo Kirch. Milchan soon climbed to the top level of the industry. In 1990, he landed his biggest coup with the film *Pretty Woman*. Seven years later, the industry voted him Producer of the Year – his rise to the ranks of the film nobility was ensured.

In 1996, Milchan had the idea of expanding his business into the sports sector. The strategy was not a new one: nearly all the world's leading media entrepreneurs were buying broadcasting rights to attractive sports events or shares in football teams at the time. Leo Kirch – together with Swiss agency ISL, which had originally been founded by Adidas boss Horst Dassler – had just acquired the global TV rights (excluding the USA) to the 2002 and 2006 football World Cups at a cost of around 1.7 billion euros. Rupert Murdoch was digging away at Manchester United, and sold the television rights to the English football leagues in order to increase the value of his pay TV company BSkyB. Milchan was looking for the third way: he thought it made sense to buy into a sports equipment company and give sales of his sports products a hefty boost with skilful product placement in his own films. His first thoughts turned to Adidas, which had recovered quickly from its crisis. Following a football match, the film producer held a discreet meeting with Adidas boss Robert Louis-Drefyus. It soon became clear to him that the price would be high – too high.

## A hot tip

A few days later his investment banker, Richard Kelly of Chase Manhattan, called him and urged him to consider Puma. Major shareholder Proventus had already reduced its engagement via the stock exchange from 85 to 25 percent, and now wanted to part with its remaining stake, as Kelly knew. Milchan and his banker got on a plane to Stockholm. They met Proventus founder Robert Weil and his top manager Mikael Kamras at an office in the city centre. It was love at first sight – though from the business, not the personal point of view. They agreed to pursue the matter further after just a few minutes, the parties later reported.

Milchan moved fast. He was eager to meet Zeitz and arranged an appointment in Herzogenaurach. When the private jet landed at Nuremberg airport, the Puma driver was waiting to take him and adviser Kelly, who was accompanying him, on board his white VW Passat estate car. Milchan turned his nose up: his only experience of such small vehicles was from advertisements. The developments of 1960s terraced houses on the road into Herzogenaurach also appeared comical to this city-dweller. The driver could hear the visitor repeatedly using the "F word", and thought to himself that the signs were not good.

Zeitz was well-prepared for the meeting. He was aware that Milchan could lay on the charm, but was a wolf in sheep's clothing. They shook hands in the conference room. Milchan was amazed at how youthful the Puma boss was. Zeitz presented apologies for the absence of Kamras, who would be delayed by half an hour. After the initial warm-up the film producer straightened his silk shirt, smoothed down his jacket and launched into the presentation of his company. He showed videos of his cinema films and reported on his many successes. Next, he outlined his visions of the union between two such different partners and presented concrete examples of how Puma products could be displayed to effect on the big screen. Meanwhile, the Proventus manager had arrived.

Zeitz liked the warmth and confidence that Milchan radiated, and talked about his own business and the phase two efforts, especially on the US market. Finally, the man from Hollywood stood up and shook hands with Zeitz and Kamras: "I'll buy the package," he said. "Puma will be my new *Pretty Woman*." He did not say for definite whether he would buy 12 percent or the entire 25 percent. Milchan loved movie-style exits. "How much money do you need?" he trumpeted over dinner at the Hotel Herzogspark, and toasted the planned deal with a glass of fine French red wine.

The gentlemen agreed to work out the details at their next meeting. Milchan sent his toughest negotiator, co-founder and CEO of Regency David Matalon, to this event in Franconia. This overweight, delightful and sincere man had known him since they were both youngsters. Their parents had been friends. They had gone to the same boarding school in London and subsequently lost touch. After twelve years, they had a joyful reunion in the lobby of London's Savoy Hotel. Matalon was by then the boss and co-founder of production company Tri-Star Pictures and was in charge of the branch offices of Columbia Pictures in various countries. His old friend persuaded him to join Regency as head strategist and manager of operations.

Although Matalon had promised his boss he would take a look at the Puma organization, in reality, he was bound and determined to overturn the deal. "Arnon has 100 ideas a day, and time and again I have to slow him down, otherwise it all ends in chaos," he said. Purchasing a more or less dead brand from some provincial German dump seemed to him a weird thing for a Hollywood company to do. A film company investing in a German sports equipment firm: "Crazy!" And yet within a few minutes of the start of the secret meeting at the Grand Hotel in Nuremberg he began to sit up and listen. Zeitz entranced him with his ideas for sport and entertainment. He had no intention of dressing stars to begin with – in the first instance he wanted to place his brand at key locations in production, with the make-up artists and wardrobe staff. "No problem," said Matalon. The Puma CEO's explanations of the potential power of the brand convinced him. Since the chemistry was right too, the pair agreed to finalize the purchase within the next few weeks. Zeitz kept his shareholders informed of the current situation. He didn't mention a word to his colleagues in the company.

A few weeks later Zeitz, Kamras and Milchan met at Milchan's country estate in Montfort-l'Amaury, south-west of Paris, which he used as a second home on his trips to Europe. The palatial residence was surrounded by a vast park with its own tennis court, and huge oil paintings by Russian artists adorned the walls in every room. The innumerable photographs in the corridors showed the *Pretty Woman* producer posing with actors such as Leonardo DiCaprio or Kim Basinger. The adjacent property belonged to French president Jacques Chirac – Milchan later bought it off him.

Milchan conducted a guided tour and then invited his guest into his drawing room. Matalon, who had a meeting he couldn't postpone and was therefore still in Beverly Hills, was hooked up via a phone link. "Let's talk about the price," said Milchan. "What is there to negotiate?" wondered Zeitz. The Americans wanted to pay a market price, not the share price. They discussed put and call options. At some point they found a common denominator, and Regency took a 12.5 percent stake in Puma. Proventus later exercised the put option for the other 12.5 percent. In the ensuing period Regency gradually built up its stake to 40 percent when prices were low.

### Goodbye Germany!

"Come over to Hollywood and take a look at the industry," Matalon had called to the Puma boss on his departure from their Nuremberg meeting. Zeitz not only accepted Regency's invitation, but also decided to relocate to the USA lock, stock and barrel for a few years at least, until operations were up and running there. He did not return to Germany until 2001. The USA was not a country that could be managed by remote control – Zeitz knew this from his time at Colgate. Orders from the Old World to the New went largely unheard. The German automotive industry had already found out at heavy cost how unproductive it was not to have your own people on the ground. America decides and the rest follow is how the common perception goes. You have to go there, you have to do it yourself, Zeitz told himself. Particularly since Puma was bringing in eight million dollars in losses on a turnover of 20 million dollars overseas.

Half Herzogenaurach advised him not to make the move, including the Supervisory Board: "Get yourself a good general manager. You are putting your career on the line if it goes wrong," they advised. Even personnel head Bauer, his confidant, said: "You can't do this!" But Zeitz did do it, and his wife Birgit stood by him. They took an apartment in Boston on the Charles River, a few blocks away from trendy Newbury Street, and spent seven months

*The Puma boss in the USA*

of the year there. They kept their home in Nuremberg. This was the start of a tough time for Birgit Zeitz in particular. There was not much private life and no social network in Boston. Anyone who does not keep up their contacts in America – an impossibility with the constant travelling – is swiftly dismissed as uninteresting.

At the parent firm on the Aurach river there were fears of a cultural revolution and the loss of the location. "Herzogenaurach is staying," affirmed Zeitz – no one was prepared to believe him. From that point on, he managed Franconia from Boston. The time difference meant he often started work in the early hours. By that time, however, the Internet and e-mail were available.

The warnings and moaning got on his nerves. In his eyes, they seemed provincial. Would no one fully understand the company's new way? Didn't the fact that young colleagues were arriving in Herzogenaurach in droves from Sweden, England, Asia, Australia and the USA help prove that Puma Germany was now just one department in a global concern? Hadn't English been the company language pretty much from day one? Wasn't there now the Internet, e-mail, mobile phones and other modern means of communication, making the geographical location of decision-making irrelevant?

The Puma branch in the USA was provincial too, but more than that, it was dangerous. Thus far the company had occupied a shabby rented floor in Brockton, Massachusetts, directly opposite the social welfare office. The decayed town half an hour's drive south of Boston had been home to a flourishing shoe industry before manufacturers discovered Asia. Unemployment then escalated, and now street law ruled. The offices belonged to Etonic-Tretorn, a subsidiary of Puma shareholder Aritmos. They were asking a lot of their employees: it was not unusual for bullets to ring round their heads as they left the building. And anyone finishing work late at night had to be accompanied to his or her car by a security guard. "We have to get out of this place," Zeitz thought. He took a map and worked out where most of the employees lived. The location: Westford, Massachusetts. He did not have enough money yet for a place in sophisticated downtown Boston, so Puma moved to a country town 40 kilometres away. Here, Zeitz found an old factory building which he had restored and on which he concluded a long-term lease. The lease is still current today, although Puma also had to rent a neighbouring building due to its strong growth, and has relocated its international business to the inner-city Boston Design Center. Only the US business has remained in Westford.

Every sports equipment manufacturer knew that the US was where the trends were set. Buyers from Europe regularly jetted in to run an eye over what was new on the shelves. No US dealer would ever have dreamed of crossing the pond in the other direction for the same purpose. The Puma scouts made one discovery in particular: their brand was non-existent over there. To change this situation, Zeitz parted with the German agencies and relocated all marketing operations to Boston, to the horror of the Franconians. He had faith in Tony Bertone's abilities and his own experience, gathered as a student and trainee at Colgate in New York. So much self-confidence almost bordered on an overestimation of his own abilities: after all, he had only lived in the USA for two and a half years.

In his first few weeks in Herzogenaurach, Zeitz had already noticed how much ignorance the Puma staff brought to their encounters with Americans. At initial meetings between the Germans and the Americans the two sides barely understood one another. It was not so much an issue of language as of business culture. While the US managers' approach demonstrated a lot of professional friendliness and motivation, the Germans were matter-of-fact and offered frank criticism. Conversely, the Germans assumed that the results of meetings were binding, while the Americans saw agreements as open arrangements.

Turning around the US business was anything but child's play. "We started from a base that was way below zero," said Zeitz. Puma not only lacked a brand image, it was also unable to pay particularly high salaries to secure the services of top-level personnel. In Boston at this time you could walk around for days before seeing a consumer with worn Puma Clydes on their feet – and you might not see one at all. Zeitz booked a headhunter on a general contract who would try to attract staff using Puma's Hollywood connection and the firm's dazzling potential. However, the headhunter found hardly any top people. Who would want to come to Boston to a semi-moribund medium-sized company? The elite went to the big shots of the IT and Internet industries in Silicon Valley and had no

*The classic Puma Clyde*

desire to sell shoes in Massachusetts. Internet firms were springing up all over, even around Puma's new headquarters, and offering their employees fabulous salaries. Zeitz appointed each member of staff in person; initially he accepted third-raters, gradually replacing them with second-rate and finally first-rate candidates. He always acted rationally, especially when it came to the workforce, and had little time for sentimentality. The transformation process lasted for two years, during which up to 60 percent of the personnel left the company. Zeitz was at war with himself: had he not already gone through all that with the restructuring four years earlier in Herzogenaurach? Did he have to put himself through it all over again? Fire and hire? The hangover from those days in the early 1990s, when he had anaesthetized his frustration by downing tequila with his colleagues Martin Gänsler and Ulrich Heyd, returned to haunt him. "Why have I done this to myself?" he wondered on occasion.

### Tinseltown in action

Zeitz made repeated trips to the West Coast, the Mecca of the film producers. He wanted to get a picture for himself of how he could use Hollywood for his company's purposes. He had declared Regency a matter for top management because of its particularly go-getting management style, and no one but him was allowed to get into contact with the new shareholder. Regency managers' judgment on the quality of the film material alone was not enough for him. He advertised to dealers using the Hollywood connection, to give the brand a bit of sex appeal.

Zeitz soon paid his first visit to the Regency headquarters, which were located on the premises of Warner Bros. After a quick drink, company boss Milchan proclaimed: "I will introduce you to the Hollywood bosses!" He meant the five big talent agencies, such as William Morris Agency and United Talent Agency (UTA), who had the stars under contract. He kept his word and took Zeitz on a road show. Zeitz shook hands with the Warner bosses, too, including the legendary Terry Semel, the former Chairman and CEO of Yahoo! He kept close tabs on what the film people had to offer. The answer was, not much. They promised a lot, the big entry into Hollywood, dollar signs twinkling in their eyes, expecting deals worth millions. "And who will be wearing our stuff?" Zeitz kept asking. "We can't force anyone," replied the agents. He soon realized that Tinseltown people were no better at working miracles than anyone else.

Nevertheless, Milchan said: "Great! Let's do it." Zeitz sounded a note of caution: "Slow down!" He had to keep on retracting the Regency manager's big, bold promises, without jeopardizing his reputation. Zeitz was still unfamiliar with the rules of Hollywood: talk a lot without saying anything, and accomplish a lot with a full wad. He preferred a slightly over-cautious approach. When it came to sponsorships, his ideas on how much to invest often differed completely from Milchan's. For example, the film boss wanted to pay five million for an actor to be seen wearing his Puma sneakers for a few seconds – Zeitz preferred to look for a solution to get the actor to wear the shoes voluntarily. The constant squabbling became too tiring for him in the long run. The Puma man decided to do the second round of the road show without Milchan.

Zeitz also discovered that Hollywood loves to party. Once a year, the film stars' managers sent out invitations to big parties in their private homes in Beverly Hills. Anyone and everyone involved in making the huge wheel of the film industry keep on turning came together at these events. "You have to go," said Milchan, and Zeitz, who always felt a little ill at ease at such events, followed his advice. He got to know Arnold Schwarzenegger, Wesley Snipes, Christopher Lambert, Kim Basinger and Robert De Niro. They called him "the Puma guy". His first one-on-one discussion was with Schwarzenegger, who had his office in Los Angeles directly above his own restaurant "Schatzi on Main". "Jochen," he sighed, "I am too old for this young business. But let's have a schnapps together at least." He had created a mock-up of a small Black Forest house in the room for drinking occasions. Then he opened a bottle of corn schnapps between life-size Terminator figures and an imitation crocodile. It was lunchtime, Zeitz was suffering from jetlag and was about to set off again for Boston. He had a drink nevertheless, for friendship's sake. It nearly turned his stomach.

Because the employees of Tinseltown did not really know the Puma name, Zeitz sent small gift parcels of Puma products to their homes. The stars did not respond to the goodies very often. Jodie Foster, who had just finished filming *Contact*, thanked him prettily. But the nicest letter of all came from Dustin Hoffman, via Milchan: "Thank you for the parcel though I'm really a bit too unathletic for this business." Milchan took increasing pleasure in sending out big packs crammed full of Puma footwear and clothing. Zeitz kept having to put the brakes on his missionary zeal. Such lavish favours did not come cheap. The contents of each pack cost the company between 500 and 600 dollars. When the film manager even wanted to send plump five-footer Danny DeVito shoes and shirts, it was the last straw: "Hold it, Arnon, it's still my money, you know!" Following a tough verbal wrangle they agreed that in future Regency would finance the packs given to friends who were irrelevant to the business.

The battle of the big packs made it clear to Zeitz that it would be careless to rely solely on Regency for US marketing. He wanted to put out feelers right across Hollywood. He therefore opened his own office, Puma West, in a former private house just ten minutes away from the Warner Studios, to establish contacts with actors who were not part of the Regency empire. The new boss of the US Apparel division, whom Zeitz had appointed and who flatly refused to move to Boston, would also be head of PR.

In July 1998 moviegoers all over the world experienced the first-ever Puma product placement in a Hollywood movie when a pair of Puma sneakers appeared in the film *City of Angels*. The film's story is easily summarized: a patient of doctor Maggie Rice, played by Meg Ryan, dies on the operating table and this drives her to despair. Angel Zeth (Nicolas Cage), who collects the dead man, shows compassion for Maggie. When he appears to her they fall in love. Zeth has to make a decision: remain immortal and an angel or become mortal and the man at Maggie's side. It was a tearjerker whose soundtrack didn't exactly match the image that Zeitz wanted the Puma brand to represent. The musicians Regency had engaged were the great stage acts of yesterday: U2, Jimi Hendrix, Peter Gabriel, Eric Clapton, John Lee Hooker. The freshest talent was Alanis Morissette, who contributed her track "Uninvited". The leaping puma was visible on Meg Ryan's feet for two seconds. Zeitz exploited this fleeting moment of joy *ad nauseam*, showing the scene to partners and customers over and over again, in slow motion.

In September 1997, about six months after the start of their relationship, Regency and Puma staged a big welcome party for the film industry in Los Angeles. They wanted to introduce themselves to the film producers and sports equipment dealers as a strong doubles partnership. A short time before, Milchan had decided to switch studios. Regency's partner was no longer Warner Bros., but Rupert Murdoch's 20th Century Fox, who for the past few years had been cleaning up in the cinemas with hits such as *Die Hard, Home Alone, Speed, Independence Day* and *Titanic*. Milchan had had a celebrity video filmed especially for the day, in which his stars said a few words to him and Puma at no charge. The leading Hollywood figures spoke with professional passion to the camera, from Al Pacino to Robert De Niro. Fox boss Peter Chernin passed on regards from Murdoch. Zeitz presented his business ideas for Puma. The dealers present applauded enthusiastically. Zeitz felt as if he was growing wings. It was a bit like that day in London when he was moved to tears.

In the evening, a glittering party night began against a background of film scenery. It formed the prelude to phase two in Zeitz's five-year economic plan. The greetings from the film stars had also left an impression on him, yet he did not believe that such messages alone could give a lasting boost to the US business. Nevertheless, the dealers were showing genuine interest in Puma for the very first time. It was now a question of linking sport, fashion, entertainment and lifestyle

*Sponsored film: City of Angels*

skilfully using marketing resources. In the ensuing period, he invited the company's most important customers to every Regency film première. In 1999, when the bruiser film *Fight Club* opened featuring Edward Norton and Brad Pitt in the leading roles, the launch party was held in Las Vegas. The climax of the evening saw the entry into the ring of American boxer Oscar de la Hoya, who held the world super featherweight title and was sponsored by Puma. Then Zeitz, his wife Birgit, Brad Pitt and Ed Norton, followed by an entourage of party-goers, did the rounds of the gambling city's low dives. They watched the gambling millionaires earning their money and finally ended up in a strip and table dance club. The excursion was a total hit for Puma: from that day onwards, Pitt and Norton voluntarily wore the clothes with the cat emblem.

In the cinema, too, Puma made a celebrity showing again that

*Birgit Zeitz, Brad Pitt and Matalon's wife Danielle in Las Vegas, 1997*

year: Ben Stiller and Cameron Diaz donned Puma sneakers for the box-office hit *There's Something About Mary*.

## 2.5 Independence Day

### Who will buy Puma? Irritating analysts, sleepless in Sydney and a shoemaker who really wanted more

Zeitz could not conceal a certain satisfaction once he had announced phase two of his economic plan, which he called "the Road to Excellence". The Puma had been declared dead, but he had been able to help it back on its paws and report record sales quarter on quarter. Yet Zeitz still had some bitter pills to swallow. By comparison with the sales, profits were not exactly particularly high, partly, of course, because Puma was making investments again, and its share price was dropping – much more steeply than those of its competitors. The consumer slump in North America and the Asian crisis were preying on investors' nerves. After years of vigorous growth, the Asian countries had unexpectedly fallen into deep recession in 1997. The capital markets reacted violently. Puma shares, too, were caught in the rolling avalanche. Market experts didn't yet have much faith in the Franconian paper.

Zeitz was irritated by the analysts' constant carping. Although they had praise for the turnaround, they were still unwilling to believe in a future for Puma. What's more, they did not follow the logic of his argument that the success of the brand depended on up-front investments. And major shareholder Regency was putting pressure on him to bump up those investments. Zeitz had been toying for some time with the idea of what it would be like to take the group off the stock exchange and reprivatize it. If the new sole owner really believed in Puma, he reckoned, then much more aggressive investments could be made in the brand than at present, when they were drawn from the meagre profit. Milchan was keen on the idea of buying the whole thing. Nevertheless, it was clear to everyone that reprivatization would be an impossibility unless all the Regency investors were on board.

In the spring of 1997, Milchan arranged a private meeting with Zeitz at the house of Regency's major shareholder, Kerry Packer. The Australian, then 60 years old, a self-made billionaire to trade and the richest man on the continent, owned a large part of the country's TV broadcasting companies and print media through his company Publishing and Broadcasting Ltd. In addition, he held shares in Rupert Murdoch's empire. Six foot four inches tall and broad to match, he loved sports and played cricket and polo. And he loved gambling too: he once made headlines by blowing 20 million dollars in a single evening in the casino at Caesars Palace Hotel in Las Vegas. Milchan hoped he would love Puma just as passionately, once he had met Zeitz.

Zeitz boarded the plane determined to make the idea of reprivatization palatable to Packer. First, he and Milchan met one of Packer's managers, a man named Warwick Mitchell. By pure coincidence, his father had managed Puma Australia back in the days of Armin Dassler. The men discussed what dress code would be suitable for the meeting with Packer – at Zeitz's meetings with the top guns of Anglo-American industry, he almost invariably appeared overdressed. They agreed on "smart casual". An open-necked shirt, light jacket and casual trousers. They also talked about suitable subjects for small talk with Packer. A good topic seemed to be the Australian football team Sydney Swans. Puma wanted to sign up the team, whose famous goal-getter Tony Lockett already wore the big cat logo. Mitchell recommended a discussion of the team and its performance. Packer, he said, was a fan of the Swans and Lockett was his celebrated hero.

That evening, they waited on the terrace of a huge property high above Sydney Harbour for the arrival of their host. Suddenly, the man with the figure of a butcher stood before them and extended his paw to Zeitz. The pressure of his fingers made the

*Mogul Kerry Packer*

German's knees buckle. Packer wore a crumpled shirt, as though he had just been mowing the lawn. He started off with a barrage of jokes about Regency: "What rubbish did I invest in there?" then laughed till the walls shook. He loved horsing around and drawing attention to himself. Zeitz talked about Puma's achievements and the brilliant Tony Lockett. Packer frowned: "What a god-awful player! Much too slow and fat. Just forget him!" Mitchell tried to correct him – in vain. When Milchan finally presented the media mogul with the idea of reprivatization, he slapped his thigh again: "Great idea, then we can just change Regency's name to Puma."

After the informal chat and an opulent dinner, they made a spontaneous trip down to Sydney's city centre. They drank wine in a street café until three in the morning, and talked about everything and nothing. Packer revealed intimate details from his professional and private life. He described how he had suffered a heart attack in 1990 at a polo match and lay there for six minutes with no pulse. "Let me tell you something," he turned to his listeners, "when you die, there is nothing f•••ing there. So enjoy life." Then he pumped the Puma boss, wanting to know every detail about the company. Zeitz developed a strong liking for the entertaining rough diamond.

Despite the warmth of this convivial gathering, and the further negotiations they had, Packer showed only a limited interest in taking over Puma. He made his decision dependent on whether his rival Murdoch, who also held shares in Regency, would go along with it. So Milchan and Zeitz set off for Los Angeles, to persuade the most powerful media czar in the world, the ruler of News Corporation, to join in. Zeitz knew that Murdoch, who owned the Hollywood film studio 20th Century Fox and the US TV network Fox Television, was a wolf in sheep's clothing too, not exactly easy to deal with. Because of his tough management style, the Australian-born mogul bore the dubious reputation of a ruthless patriarch. He owned many other holdings in film and television companies, newspaper and book publishers, and had even bought a baseball team, the Los Angeles Dodgers. It was not uncommon for him to intervene in editorial policy to promulgate his political convictions.

Zeitz asked his US managing director Jim Gorman and his second man Jay Piccola to accompany him to Murdoch's. They agreed to meet at 3.15 pm in the lobby of the Loews Santa Monica Hotel. The Americans arrived in leisure wear. They had a drink and got into the car. En route, Milchan told the driver to make a brief stop. He got out, took a silk shirt, jacket and tie from the boot and changed his entire outfit. Upon arrival at Fox, they were shown to the conference room. First of all, they were welcomed by Peter Chernin, the CEO of the Fox Group. He was followed by David Hill, head of Fox Sports. Finally, they met Murdoch in his office. He wore a grey suit and made a worldly-wise and charming impression on the visitors. After they had all introduced themselves, the talk went back and forth. For more than half an hour, they talked about the strengths and potential of the sportlifestyle brand in conjunction with Fox. Suddenly, Murdoch spoke up: "Why don't you sell the shoes in Wal-Mart?" Zeitz restrained himself with an effort. He had worked for years to liberate Puma from the bargain counters. And now he was supposed to sell the products through the biggest discounter in the world? Had Murdoch failed to grasp anything at all?

Another half hour later, the group broke up. Chernin promised that his strategic planners from Harvard would examine Puma and review the possibility of an investment. They did – and rejected the takeover. Puma would be lucky to survive another one or two years, the strategists told their boss. Murdoch didn't want to know – and that meant that Packer's decision was also taken. Nevertheless, the bull from Sydney bought more than five percent of Puma shares and sent his son James to join the Supervisory Board. He also allowed Regency to top up its shares in the Franconian company to 40 percent.

Zeitz benefited from his new found friend Packer on another occasion – though only for a few hours: in 1999, at the Film Festival in Cannes, Packer offered him the chance to hold an important business meeting on his ship in Monte Carlo. The Puma boss wanted to sign up American basketball player Kevin Garnett, and could use an impressive setting. Packer had had a former German ice-breaker converted into a luxury yacht, complete with helicopter pad, at a cost of 20 million euros. Zeitz and Garnett's agent were impressed – but no deal was struck. The star would have burst every budget in sight. Maybe the setting was a bit too opulent, after all.

By now, another engagement was proving much more successful. Puma managers had spent months thinking about ways and means of getting the brand into the National Football League (NFL), the American football professional league. It seemed plain enough that the company could not afford direct entry as an outfitter; the sums that were normally poured into the teams by Nike, Reebok and Starter were too high. In addition, the brand did not yet shine brightly enough to sweep powerful competitors out of its way. In the summer of 1998, Zeitz therefore cleverly found a means of access to NFL by the back door: he bought a 25 percent share of TKS Acquisition Inc. of Indianapolis for the sum of around 20 million marks. The company had been set up specifically to take over the US sports equipment group Logo Athletic, which at that time numbered among the leading licensees of American sports leagues such as the National Football League (NFL), Major League Baseball, the National Basketball Association and the National Hockey League. The coup was a success: soon, the Puma logo leapt on four, ultimately on as many as 13, NFL team shirts. Even the finalists in Superbowl 2000, the St Louis Rams and Tennessee Titans, wore the big cat on their vests. The annual costs to Puma: around four million dollars. For direct sponsorship of the teams, the company would probably have had to shell out 25 to 30 million dollars per season.

### Visit to the luxury shoemaker

Regency's investment bankers continued their search for an investor. Rumours circulating around the companies today say sales talks had actually already taken place with fashion company Gucci, which now belongs to Puma's major shareholder PPR. No one at Puma is willing to confirm this rumour, or even to comment on it.

At the beginning of 2000, the bankers came on another dream candidate: Diego Della Valle, owner and manager of the Milanese footwear and clothing firm Tod's. He was tempted. The Puma story was a good fit with his company, which holds the Hogan and Fay (textiles) labels in addition to Tod's. He contacted Regency and asked for an appointment. In the spring of 2001, Della Valle, Zeitz, Milchan and Matalon met for a business dinner at a classy Italian restaurant in Boston. The party was very relaxed, particularly when it turned out that Milchan's daughter lived in the same building as Della Valle's son Emanuele in New York. The Puma representatives found it much easier to persuade their listener this time around: awareness of the brand had risen significantly, even in Milan young people wore the big cat label. And Della Valle already held 4.9 percent of the Franconian group, and had done so for some time. The Italian's interest in increasing his stake grew visibly. He visited Puma USA's premises and talked to the unorthodox staff there. Everything seemed to be going fine – apart from the share price: it bounded upwards in great leaps during that period, and quadrupled within the shortest possible time. Puma became really expensive.

To Della Valle, money counted for more than hope. So he sold his Puma holding and cashed in, instead of increasing his holding. Zeitz was happy enough at the outcome, despite his admiration for Tod's. The Italian had told them during the discussions that if he increased his engagement he would want to take control of operations, an aim little to the taste of either Regency or Zeitz. The two managers are still business mates. "Shame it didn't work out," says Della Valle every time they meet.

In the years since then, Zeitz has wondered quite a few times whether he wouldn't have had the opportunity to buy Puma himself. However, the banks would have been very unlikely to give a 34-year-old a big enough loan, and private equity investors, who now control funds in double-digit billions, were not around at the time. By the time the talks with Tod's were over, Puma's rising share price had charged it up with enough power to make serious investments on its own.

A further event brought the company a financial injection that was as unexpected as it was powerful: an arbitration decision. In August 1998, Puma had signed up the then 22-year-old US basketball player Vince Carter for 150,000 dollars a year – a bargain that would run for five years, as it turned out. In the same year, Carter had been "drafted", as inclusion in the selection process for the best talents in the National Basketball Association is known. Every basketball player dreams of participating in the NBA draft. Shortly afterwards, Carter was elected Rookie of the Year for the 1998/99 season at the Toronto Raptors. Suddenly he was a superstar, and was soon hot gossip in the media as the new Michael Jordan.

So much fame went to the head of his manager William "Tank"

Black in particular. The shady agent, who was sentenced to six years in jail in 2001 for fraud and money laundering, suddenly announced in November 1999 that his protégé's feet hurt in the Puma shoes – and promptly broke off the contract. In actual fact, Black wanted to negotiate a new million-dollar contract with Nike. Zeitz rejected the penalty payment on offer and insisted that the contract be fulfilled. He had had a handwritten addendum included in the contract with Carter providing that disputes would be settled by arbitration, not before a judge and jury. Zeitz appointed the famous law firm of Oberstein, Kibre & Horwitz of Los Angeles as his attorney, which cost Puma several hundreds of thousands of dollars in fees. It didn't matter, after all, the stake was much higher. Puma was demanding satisfaction in double-digit millions – though nobody dreamed it would get that much money. In several sessions of the arbitration panel, all parties concerned had to give evidence, including Zeitz and marketing chief Tony Bertone. The other party also brought witnesses who fed the arbitrator all kinds of fairy stories.

The arbitration decision surprised even the Puma managers: the contract between Puma and basketball player Vince Carter was to be terminated in return for damages of 13.5 million dollars. In addition, Carter was ordered not to conclude any endorsement contracts for footwear or apparel with a competitor without Puma's consent for a period of three years. Black's threat to go into personal insolvency and get out of the payment that way fell sadly flat: Carter would have had to go on playing for Puma. That, of course, was not a good basis for business. So in the next few days, Zeitz negotiated some kind of severance payment on a terrible phone line from Namibia with sports agent Mark Steinberg of the US talent giant IMG, which was to take on Carter as soon as he was playing for Nike. Puma then invested this sum profitably in building its own new Puma shops for North America. And that was how Nike came to donate a large sum in sponsorship money to its competitor's expansion.

## 2.6 What Women Want

*Puma goes girlie: a momentous phone call from the white villa, a colourful tennis star and African football stars in bright colours*

All was well with Puma. Business was running smoothly again, with both company performance and the share price on the rise.

The designers and product managers in the USA focused on the areas of running, Heritage, cross-training and sportlifestyle, while Herzogenaurach managed the football, tennis, indoor and outdoor sports, training gear and textile sectors. In nearby Schlüsselfeld, Puma opened a new distribution centre with a fully automated high-bay racking warehouse to cope with the ever-increasing traffic. Pure fashion was still the last thing on anybody's mind.

One afternoon in early 1998, the phone rang at the Puma headquarters in Herzogenaurach. The caller was from the Jil Sander fashion house. It seemed that the designer wanted to order Puma football boots with studs for her upcoming fashion show. Jil Sander had discovered the good old "King" Pelé football boot and found the look perfect. Zeitz and his deputy Gänsler were thrilled at the idea of Puma featuring in the top class of the fashion world. This was the icing on the cake. This time, however, Bertone was not in favour: "You're kidding!" he said. The lifestyle freak simply couldn't connect with the elegance of the German haute couturier. Zeitz and Gänsler were undeterred. They initially planned to produce a special "King" model featuring a textured sole to prevent the models slipping and breaking bones on the runway. Then they pushed their thinking a step further. Why shouldn't some of the Jil Sander glamour rub off on Puma? In fact, wouldn't it be much better to jointly design a special Jil Sander shoe with the Puma label? In a straw poll among Puma managers, two-thirds of those asked rejected the idea. However, Puma not being a popular democracy, Zeitz's and Gänsler's votes constituted a sufficient majority to seal the relationship with Jil Sander. Gänsler took charge of the project and went to Hamburg for an initial meeting in the austere surroundings of the fashion house's administrative headquarters. Zeitz kept out of the matter and, to this day, has not met Jil Sander in person.

This initial visit was primarily to get acquainted. Gänsler was introduced to second-level managers and chatted with them about ways and means. The final decision on a collaborative venture was to be taken at the second meeting, when Ms Sander herself would be present. Three weeks before this meeting, Gänsler happened to run into Ulf Santjer of Puma's marketing department in the corridor. The two men got talking about the forthcoming meeting with the doyenne of fashion. Santjer is originally from Dithmarschen, an area in the northern German state of Schleswig-Holstein, and this is still where his heart is – just like Jil Sander's. She was born Heidemarie Jiline Sander in 1943 in the tiny Dithmarschen town of Wesselburen, and is still very attached to the area. "Do you know where the name Jil actually comes from?" Santjer asked the Puma director, and proceeded to tell him about the fashion designer's background. "When you're making your presentation, don't forget you are talking to a dyed-in-the-wool Dithmarschen girl. It might not be amiss to say a few words in the local language," he added jokingly. Gänsler took his decision within seconds: "You're coming with me to Hamburg, and you're going to do the marketing presentation yourself." Santjer was surprised, but pleased to have the chance to meet Jil Sander. In the days after this conversation he put all his energies into the marketing presentation, working in collaboration with Gänsler. The presentation would highlight Puma's presence at the 1998 World Cup in France extensively. Puma had kitted out its World Cup players with coloured football boots for the first time ever. Santjer therefore included a spectacular World Cup photo of Cameroon captain Rigobert Song wearing a yellow Puma "King" on his left foot and a red one on his right. The message was "Let's bring more fashion and more colour into the game."

Gänsler, designer-in chief Eyan Allen and Santjer set off for Hamburg a well-prepared team. Their destination was the two white villas on the Aussenalster lake which make up Jil Sander's head office and home. They were amazed at the sheer simplicity of their surroundings, a look which even extended to the toilets. They were received at the entrance by tall, slim, black-clad women with hands encased in white gloves, who led them into the meeting room. At first glance, Gänsler could only see one man in the assembled company, a delivery-van driver. Then when Jil Sander glided into the room the chief executive of her company shot out of his chair and kissed her hand in greeting. The designer didn't make things easy for the visitors from Puma. She conducted the negotiations in a chilly manner. Once he had overcome his initial nerves, Santjer's presentation flowed effortlessly. The one question was: how would the couturier react to the subject of football? Would she reject it out of hand, switch off or listen attentively? Ms Sander initially sat almost expressionless. When the subject of football arose, however, she asked specific questions about the design and the fashion aspects of shirts, and when Santjer told a story from the Cameroonian team's quarters at the World Cup, the hint of a smile appeared on her face for the first time. It was a start.

In fact, that day saw the inception of a lucrative collaboration which was to continue for many years and which formed a major part of the foundations underpinning the long and steady rise of Puma as a sports-fashion-lifestyle company. People were amazed. Who would ever have imagined that shoes of the former cheap Puma brand would one day be going over the counter for 300 dollars a pair in the US and 400 dollars a pair in Japan? Demand for the Sander-Puma shoe exploded. Many prospective customers had to go on waiting lists even before the launch date arrived.

Even Puma's directors were amazed by their brand's potential. The alliance with Jil Sander gave them courage. More and more often, they were emboldened to think outside the box that had been restricted to such narrow dimensions throughout their company's 50-year history. But this didn't mean that the champagne flowed straight away. Puma has always been characterized by rationality and economy, and it is not the company's way to indulge in self-congratulation. However, when a press release made the news of Puma's alliance with Jil Sander public, the corks popped again at Adidas on the opposite bank of the Aurach. The company was quite convinced that Puma had now gone down the wrong track for good and all, and would soon vanish from the market entirely.

Puma managers, however, took quite a different view, and they were vindicated during the weeks that followed. The sportlifestyle segment enjoyed excellent sales in the USA and was driving the development of its own image. In addition, the alliance with Jil Sander proved to be an opinion-former. It would not be historically true to say that Zeitz had predicted this development with keen acumen, or even deliberately steered towards it. On the contrary, much of the success had come about after erratic stabbing in the dark, and chance, too, played its part. Regency's investment in the company, the phone call from Jil Sander's headquarters, the meeting with Tony Bertone and many other things could never really have been planned. But Zeitz had demonstrated a feeling for the spirit of the times and all his hard work had brought him the good fortune he deserved.

There was now no further doubt in Zeitz's mind: the traditional sports equipment firm with its legendary founder Rudolf Dassler was history. In future, the company would belong among the hot manufacturers of sportlifestyle and fashion products. This intellectual decision cost Zeitz many a sleepless night. Still not enough of his colleagues had confidence in his way. From that time on, he avoided calling Puma a "firm" or "company", referring to it only as "the brand". There was a message behind this. Puma

*Puma goes girlie: 2006 model*

was no longer to be one firm among many, but was to be unique, a sought-after label, different. He constantly impressed on his staff: "If every mountain is white, then we are blue." No longer would comfort, fit and production quality be the desirable features of the products with the big cat logo. Their future appeal would lie in the emotions that logo evoked in the customer. This could be fostered with marketing tools. Customers had to be attracted and enthralled in the way that companies such as Gucci, Porsche and Marlboro had been demonstrating for years. Whenever a new product was launched, whenever an advertising campaign was conducted, whenever a new contract partner was signed up, Puma managers had to ensure that the emotional, rational and cultural association with the defined brand image was preserved. It was of the utmost importance never to disappoint customers. A brand is only ever as good as it is perceived to be.

The big Los Angeles show presentation with the greetings from big-screen stars was run in shortened form in the other countries where Puma had a presence. That was when Zeitz had first formulated his vision of Puma as a sportslifestyle brand, and he wanted everyone to be aware of where the company was now headed. He made the unpolished tramp Bertone international marketing manager, with a direct reporting line to the board. The whole organization was aghast, Martin Gänsler included.

### Skin-tight tops and short skirts

It was impossible for Puma to keep up with its competitors in sponsoring top athletes. For example, in 1997, his penultimate year with the Chicago Bulls, US basketball star Michael Jordan earned 30 million dollars, most of which was paid by Nike in the form of sponsorship money. The likes of Lothar Matthäus and Rudi Völler, whom Puma was paying at the time, were small fry in comparison. One day, a man named Richard Williams phoned the talent agency International Management Group (IMG). He said he had two daughters, Serena and Venus, who would very soon be ranked the tennis number one and two in the world, and he was looking for a financial backer. IMG founder Mark Hume McCormack did not do business on the basis of dreams, and said no. A few days later, McCormack mentioned his dubious caller to Regency CEO David Matalon. Matalon got on the phone to Zeitz straight away. "I know the Williams girls, Arnon thinks they're fantastic. Take a look at them." At the end of 1997, Serena Williams wasn't on people's radar – she was ranked number 99 in the world. Nevertheless, Zeitz asked marketing manager Tony Bertone to fly to Los Angeles and go with Arnon Milchan to meet the two black sisters. Bertone reported back "The father's a bit of a nut, but the girls have got something." Richard Williams had asked for 20 million dollars for a three-year term, without giving any guarantee of performance, and Milchan's response had once more been a resounding "No problem," even though Zeitz had not yet approved the amount.

Zeitz and Bertone put the ideas together: an African-American woman in the white sport, wearing coloured clothing – it could be a hit, even if the player never made the world number one spot. They made arrangements to hold further negotiations at the end of the year, this time at the Williamses' family home in West Palm Beach in Florida. Zeitz was accompanied by his wife and an expert,

*Tennis star Serena Williams*

tennis agent Ken Meyerson. It was one of the toughest negotiations that Zeitz would ever enter into. The visitors had to remove their shoes before entering the house and were not offered so much as a glass of water all the time they were there. Richard Williams, a strict Jehovah's Witness, is well known for his strange escapades during negotiations. Serena and Venus huddled in an armchair and did not utter a word.

Weeks later, the parties finally agreed on a five-year contract for Serena, guaranteeing payments of up to 12.5 million dollars even if she just got into the top ten. The hard work had paid off. Over the next few years, the top athlete with the curvaceous figure won every Grand Slam tournament in her brightly coloured, tailor-made cat suits and reached the number-one spot in the world rankings. Zeitz and his wife were watching from the grandstand at the final of the 1999 US Open when Serena, wearing a skimpy one piece, wiped her opponent Martina Hingis off the court 6–3, 7–6, and raised her tennis racket to the skies in a gesture of triumph. That day, she finally made the breakthrough to superstardom. At the Australian Open the following year, she stepped onto the

Centre Court sporting her own collection for the first time – a bright red mini-skirt and a skin-tight top bearing the Puma logo. That she went out in the second round didn't matter – photographers had taken thousands of pictures of her and they went all round the world. Puma had once again struck a massive PR hit in the world of tennis, 13 years after the company's first spectacular coup with Boris Becker. Serena Williams turned the Centre Court into a catwalk – the perfect setting to advertise Puma products. Back in Herzogenaurach, nobody was contemplating a return to making tennis rackets.

With Serena Williams, and also Anna Kournikova, who was under contract with Adidas at the time, the personality of the player now took centre stage in the tennis world. Gone were the days of the cool serving and volleying fighting machines. The athletes' new-found fashion-consciousness was also becoming prominent in other disciplines. In particular, footballers like Italy's Paolo Maldini, Britain's David Beckham and Portugal's Luís Figo became perfect advertisements for the fashion industry. When the time came to extend the five-year contract, Serena's father Richard set extremely high stakes. Negotiations dragged on like a never-ending tiebreak – and Serena continued to play in Puma outfits free of charge. In the end, negotiations broke down on Williams' high demands. This did not worry Zeitz. He wanted out in any case; the engagement was long past its peak.

The new Puma chic now began to attract the attention of other fashion houses besides Jil Sander. Puma's board entered into discussions, but turned down even some very big names. One of the rejects was French fashion designer Jean-Paul Gaultier, who took the inspiration for a lot of his creations from everyday wear and pop culture. Zeitz found his style over-elaborate. On the other hand, Britain's "Queen of Punk", Vivienne Westwood, was later welcomed aboard, as was Japan's Yasuhiro Mihara. French designer Philippe Starck and Alexander McQueen, the Brit with the bad-boy image, turned their talents on for Puma too. Californian supermodel Christy Turlington launched an intellectualized line called "Nuala" (natural – universal – altruistic – limitless – authentic) followed by "Mahanuala" (movement affords higher aspirations), a variation on the original collection.

Puma had discovered women and sensed a huge business opportunity. The designers worked on clothing for "mind-and-body" forms of exercise such as tai chi and yoga. Puma also tried to take the lead in the rope-skipping movement, a new fitness trend which had started in the Netherlands and was spreading. Coloured skipping ropes, music CDs and exercise videos were set to guarantee good revenues. Puma's campaign was fronted by Fikriye (or "Vicky") Selen, a European Championship boxing runner-up. Her beautiful face smiled out of 35,000 posters from Flensburg in the far north of Germany all the way to Lake Constance in the far south.

In 2001, Madonna's management team made a call to Puma's Product Placement Office in LA. The pop diva had found a sneaker from Puma's latest collection attractive. The shoe, called "Mostro", had been created by Tony Bertone and looked like a contemporary version of 1970s running spikes. It had a hook and loop fastening and was fashioned in the camouflage colours of Vietnam soldiers. Staff sent the singer 19 pairs in white. The pack cost the company no more than a few hundred dollars, including postage, but the advertising impact was worth millions. Madonna wore the shoes for her concerts and every Madonna fan recognized them in photos in the glossies. The "Mostro" sold brilliantly, so much so that Puma could hardly keep up with deliveries.

Female customers were the discovery of the year 2001 – although women had been wearing Puma for years. This does not mean, however, that Zeitz neglected what the men wanted. On the contrary, in fact. He increased Puma's engagement in the tough male sports. In that same year, he signed a contract with rebel Eddie Jordan's Formula 1 racing stable and had sports fashion clothing developed for Jordan's team. His colleague Martin Gänsler, a motorsport enthusiast, led the project. The "Speed Cat" shoe was Gänsler's idea, and a total sales hit. Jordan's drivers had already worn Puma shoes back in the 1970s. Zeitz described motorsport as "fast, dynamic, and kind of aggressive" – exactly as Puma itself should be. The 2001 contract between Zeitz and Jordan extended the partnership by a further three years. It wasn't long before another four Formula 1 teams placed orders for the high-fashion functional wear from Herzogenaurach: Sauber, Minardi, Toyota and Jaguar. BMW Williams followed later. Puma's new motorsport department also sponsored freestyle motocross champion Travis Pastrana and started backing the World Rally Championship (WRC).

### Footballers from Cameroon

The market for sports clothing pure and simple was proving more difficult than the sportlifestyle and fashion business. Sports retailers were interested in tough products for wear in the stadia rather than the new, chic designer lines. Puma did not have much of a chance in track and field athletics with the marketing budget available, which was modest despite sales of more than a billion marks. Management therefore turned its attention to football, where the company was still credited with some remaining expertise. Zeitz and Horst Widmann put their heads together to work out how they could achieve a lot without spending much. They would not have been able to afford Brazil, Italy, France, or even the German national team had the sponsorship rights been on the market. The best route, therefore, seemed to be to work with the underdog image again.

Just as the directors were thinking along these lines, one-time Adidas networker Horst Widmann joined them. He had good connections with Africa. "Are you familiar with Cameroon?" he asked. This West African coastal nation's team had worked its way up to become a formidable opponent in major tournaments. Cameroon's star player was Roger Milla, who had been voted the Old Continent's best player as far back as 1976. In the 1990 World Cup in Italy, he had risen to the ranks of a football legend when, almost single-handedly, he carried his country as far as the quarter finals with his goal-scoring. He celebrated every ball that went into the net with a makossa dance by the corner flag. Nevertheless, so far no outfitter or sponsor had shown any interest in Cameroon.

Puma had already played the colour card before with one African-American athlete, Serena Williams. Why shouldn't it work with football as well? Zeitz wondered. Zeitz was an Africa-lover himself and was familiar with Cameroon's joie-de-vivre, its live-and-let-live attitude to life. It fits our brand, he decided, and without further ado gave Widmann instructions to initiate negotiations with Cameroon's national football association. Puma's foreign minister booked a flight to take him to the Cameroonian port city of Duala via Paris. From there, he was driven to the capital, Yaounde, the headquarters of the Fédération Camerounaise de Football. The journey took him some 300 kilometres through the jungle, straight ahead all the way, on one of the most dangerous roads in the world. Two days later, the car sped back along the motorway, heading for the airport. Widmann sat in the passenger seat and was on top of the world: he had a contract in his hand

*The Cameroon team in
sleeveless shirts*

luggage giving Puma the right to kit out the Cameroon team for
around 700,000 dollars a year. Suddenly, there was a mighty bang
right beside him and the windscreen shattered. In overtaking, the
driver had failed to see an oncoming vehicle and, in frantic
attempts to get back into his own lane, had grazed a lorry carrying
timber logs. The negotiator stood there at the roadside, badly
shaken up. An hour later, he was picked up by a high-ranking football official and taken right to the door of the plane, bypassing all
official checks. "Typical Cameroon," remarked Widmann.

With the "indomitable lions", as the Cameroonians were
known, Puma launched its first attack on the sporting establishment and a guerrilla marketing approach aimed at getting the
company's name into the news. The Franconians kitted the team
out with coloured football boots and with sleeveless shirts to help
them cool off more efficiently. They were delighted, as was Win-
fried Schäfer, a former German national league trainer and now
Cameroon's new national coach. Widmann had helped him on his
way to the African job in mid-September 2001. On 10 February
2002, the sleeveless Cameroonians beat the Senegalese 3–2 after a
penalty shoot-out in the African Cup final. The domineering grey-
beards of FIFA were furious about the team's going its own way and
banned the fashionable outfits for that summer's World Cup in
Japan and South Korea. Quick to react, Puma added net sleeves to
the jerseys, in black to blend in with the players' dark skin. The
petty quarrel over the sleeveless shirts dominated the news and

Puma's name was mentioned again and again. When Cameroon came up against Germany on 11 June, Puma's CEO found his loyalties divided for the first time. Cameroon played magically – and Germany won 2–0.

## 2.7 The Incredibles

*Puma rolls up the market: the wrath of the department store managers, farewell to the major shareholder and a new, wonderful solitude*

For many years, market researchers had been conducting regular surveys of the Puma brand among the population at large. The results were mostly disappointing: in consumers' eyes, the quality of the products was not as high as the management believed. Cheap, male-oriented and lacking a distinct image – this was how the brand was seen. In 2001 their opinion changed: suddenly Puma was desirable – and feminine. The label stood for sport, lifestyle and fashion and was purchased by trendsetters. Puma's "Sprint" and "Mostro" models stood side by side on the shelves with Manolo Blahnik stilettos. All of a sudden, Prada clothes and Puma shoes could be worn together. The products were selling faster and faster, and Zeitz wanted to take advantage of this explosion. He had been charming the stock market with annual sales growth well in excess of 20 percent for three years now. In 2001 alone the company's share price rose by 168 percent – it was the fastest-growing stock in the DAX-100. Following the drastic remedy administered to the firm eight years previously, over 2,000 employees were now working for Puma again worldwide, and some had even become rich as a result of the sharp upturn in the share price. It was now time for the company to really start earning money. Zeitz launched phase three of his economic plan. "Puma is a film that will run forever," he promised in the stock market journal *Das Wertpapier*.

Competitors and financial experts took him seriously. The object of ridicule had bounced back to become a respected sports brand again. "Nobody is laughing anymore and many people admire him. Analysts and shareholders because of the excellent share price, consultants because of his rigorous strategy and employees because of his down-to-earth management style," was the gushing praise from *manager magazin*. Margins on the mass market were traditionally low, and this prompted Zeitz to set his sights high: Puma was to become the most desirable sports brand in the world – and consequently the most expensive. Not the biggest, however: Adidas and Nike, with sales of 6.1 and 10.6 billion euros respectively, enjoyed an unassailable lead. Reebok (3.4 billion euros), Amer Sports (1.1 billion euros) and Fila (1 billion euros) also ranked above Puma.

At a trade fair in Atlanta, the CEO informed Joachim Schröder, who was then head of sports for the Karstadt department store chain and one of his largest customers, that he would no longer be able to purchase some of the company's products. The department store's assortment, he said, was not in keeping with Puma's high-priced Lifestyle category products, which already accounted for a quarter of the group's revenues. The manager, a formidable power in the market, was dumbstruck. Then he let fly with an annihilating tirade for all bystanders to hear, and never spoke a word to Zeitz again. The purchasers from Kaufhof, another department store chain, made their irritation clear as well.

The Puma chief also had to turn leading American chain Foot Locker down on some products. It was positioned in the low-price sector but was keen to purchase the cool styles in large volumes. He had invited his US manager Jay Piccola to attend the meeting in New York. They met for a preliminary discussion in a fast-food pizzeria and looked at a selection of shoes from the latest collection that would continue to be sold by the store. Twenty minutes later they were confronting CEO Matthew Serra. On the table by the wall of the meeting room, sandwiches on paper plates and tubs of coleslaw had been laid out as a business lunch. "These are cool," was Serra's comment on the shoes. "Is that everything you've got?" "Of course," replied Zeitz. "What about the Mostro?" asked Serra. This was the high-end shoe that Madonna wore. Zeitz said nothing. "Never in my life have I had to try so hard not to sell a product," he recalls.

At the other end of the price scale he expanded Puma's own sales channels. In Los Angeles, San Francisco, Tokyo, Paris and New York he opened exclusive Puma stores, so-called "concept stores". Eight others were to be added in the coming months, including outlets in Frankfurt and Moscow. Fashionable stores such as Thomas i Punkt in Hamburg, Harrods in London and Henri Bendel in New York cosied up to the big cat with increasing frequency. Once again, Zeitz was constantly on the move. "I don't have time for children, not even for a dog," he told *Bunte* magazine. "What would be the point in having children anyway if they never saw their father?" his wife Birgit commented.

If you've got cool products, you need a cool advertising agency. Brand manager Tony Bertone parted company with market giant McCann-Erickson, which had performed solidly over the years, and signed up with Steven Grasse, the 30-year-old founder of hip agency Gyro from Philadelphia. He didn't even really know what Puma was, but was looking after MTV, which ensured that he was admired by Puma's managers. The agency's employees exactly matched Puma's target group.

### Farewell to the major investor

The good business feeling at Puma's headquarters was in stark contrast to the state of mind of the general population. Since 11 September 2001, when planes hijacked by al-Qaeda terrorists were flown into the towers of the World Trade Center in New York claiming 2,600 lives, people had been living in fear and uncertainty, especially in Western nations. The attack had left Zeitz, too, in a profound state of shock. The day before, he had visited a business partner on the 114th floor of the building and admired the breathtaking view. He could then do nothing but watch as the towers collapsed after the attacks. Later he found the name of his business partner in the records of mobile phone calls made by people saying goodbye to their partners.

Regency also began to think deep thoughts during this period. Puma had been part of its portfolio for six years and the sharp rise in its share price had put a big smile on the faces of the film people. However, the shareholding was now worth almost more than their entire media empire. Principal shareholder Kerry Packer therefore told Arnon Milchan to sell the Puma shares. There were two options: either he would find another major investor to take over the entire package, or the shares would be offered to institutional investors via an intermediary and the stock exchange. Nobody was keen to go down the first route, following the failed attempts with Tod's. They therefore went for option two. Zeitz, who heard about the intended sale at the end of November 2002 from Regency CEO David Matalon, could only welcome the step: following a successful placement, for the first time there would no longer be a major shareholder among the company's owners.

The preparations for the big deal were made with the utmost discretion. Nothing was disclosed either to the Supervisory Board or to other members of the Puma Board. During the Christmas holidays, which Zeitz spent with his wife in Florida, the Chairman of the Puma Board met his friend Christian Meissner. He was a managing director of the investment bank Goldman Sachs and headed the European investment department. They had a leisurely and undisturbed discussion of the opportunities and risks associated with such transactions. On the stock exchange Puma was still a "small cap", a second-line stock without a high trading volume, even though its shares were being purchased with increasing frequency. However, the risks were great. In particular, Meissner warned about the unpredictability of the new "hedge funds", which – unlike traditional equity funds – played around with a company's share price to their own advantage. The two managers decided first of all to enjoy their holiday and then to arrange a meeting with Regency.

### Bad news

On 9 January 2003 there was an unexpected development: Puma's share price crashed from 68 to 59 euros. What had happened? A hot-headed young analyst from Brooklyn had made his way around the sports shoe stores in his region and carried out some field research. An ordinary retailer told him about the difficulties he was having selling Puma products. He had managed to sell only nine pairs, compared to 55 pairs the year before; the brand was simply no longer in demand. The analyst did some sums and arrived at a downturn in sales of 80 percent. He immediately downgraded the share to "sell". This man's shopping trip turned out to be an expensive one for the Franconian firm: it wiped 60 million euros off its market capitalization at a stroke.

Zeitz, who was still in Florida, heard about the crash from an American fund manager. She called him up as he was about to go for dinner. "Mr Zeitz, I've received a devastating report by an independent market research institute," she said. This gave Zeitz a jolt, and he wanted to know details. He quickly realized that quite a few rumours were circulating in the market. "You'd be better off believing our figures than any dubious market studies," was his advice to the financial expert. A few hours later, Regency head Matalon also got in touch: "What's up?" he wanted to know.

Somehow this all seemed familiar to Zeitz. Once before, six months earlier, Puma's shares had fallen from 74 to 47 euros, completely out of the blue. On that occasion, an analyst from the bank HSBC Trinkaus & Burkhardt had used the depressed economic sentiment resulting from the terrorist attack as a reason to issue a

*Jogging as a way to combat stress*

recommendation to sell. Zeitz had not revised his forecast for the current quarter in any way. However, the market was volatile, a new Gulf War was looming and a sense of fear had gripped stock exchange operators. Shortly afterwards the rumour even circulated that one of Puma's largest shareholders had pulled out due to fears of a slide in the share price.

The parties concerned continued to prepare rationally and calmly for Regency's withdrawal. In January 2003, Jochen Zeitz, Goldman Sachs banker Christian Meissner and David Matalon, who had flown in on his company jet, convened in a conference room at the Grand Hotel in Nuremberg for their first joint meeting. Goldman Sachs was no stranger to Puma, the bank had already worked for Proventus in 1996. Matalon stated a clear price for his company's 40 percent stake: 80 euros per share – at least. He continued to believe in the Puma way and was not prepared to bail out for less. There was just one thing: in the strained political climate, nobody could foresee how much the shares would actually make on the market.

The three men then discussed the next steps. As is usually the case with such deals, they spoke openly. Goldman Sachs was to buy all of the shares and act as intermediary, which meant that the shares would be parked with the bank and sold on to institutional investors as quickly as possible. The fees that Meissner was demanding were high – after all, the risk to Goldman Sachs was not exactly small. Two years previously the bank had been left with a package of shares in French media group Vivendi on its hands, because they had been completely overvalued. A handshake set the seal on their collaboration. Zeitz was pleased that Meissner, his confidant, would be taking care of the transactions. As CEO, he was not allowed to intervene himself.

On 20 March 2003, American President George W. Bush gave the order to attack Iraq. There was no way for Puma's managers to assess the impact that the war would have on business. A few ships that were importing footballs from the production locations in Afghanistan and Pakistan had to be diverted. There was little movement on the stock exchange.

Zeitz decided that it was business as usual. In May he travelled to the UK and USA to sell his strategy for the coming years to bank analysts and potential investors. His company was only listed on the German stock exchanges, and that alone meant that the Anglo-Saxons paid little attention to it. Hardly anyone had Puma on their radar. Even Goldman Sachs analyst Margaret Mager, who took care of the sports equipment sector, had not looked at the German firm for six years and had only re-admitted it to her portfolio a few weeks previously. When he was late for a meeting in San Antonio, one of the participants bit his nose off: "What's up, don't you have your company jet under control?" Zeitz pulled his economy class ticket out of his case and held it in front of the fund manager's nose. "I'm sorry," he said, "my company jet is an economy class seat, and unfortunately it was delayed."

In spite of all the bad news being broadcast on German television, Puma's business results soared. While many competitors were suffering from the fact that consumer fears were driving them to save more, this trend appeared to pass Puma by. The presentations by the company's chief had an effect: within a few days its shares reached a new all-time high of 97.50 euros. Regency managers Milchan and Matalon immediately got in touch with Meissner and urged him to set the sale in motion. Zeitz, too, received a phone call – from the representative of a British hedge fund: according to him, rumours abounded that Regency would soon be placing its shares. "You'll have to ask Regency about that," was the stock response from the company's boss.

On Tuesday, 26 May 2003, Goldman Sachs and Regency took the decision to settle the deal on the following Monday, 2 June. The bank wanted to take the package after the close of trading on the Friday and promote it to the first institutional investors over the weekend. It all went very quickly. Goldman Sachs immediately demanded a due diligence declaration, a kind of written assurance that, in business terms, Puma was not hiding any skeletons in its cupboard. Unfortunately, head of finance Dieter Bock, who was responsible for investor relations, had just flown off to the Maldives on his summer holidays. Zeitz called him and arranged a time for a telephone discussion with the Goldman Sachs headquarters in Frankfurt. The call lasted for three hours – then the preparations were complete.

### The day of reckoning

On Friday 30 May, at 8.00 pm, 6,706,960 Puma shares, 42.3 percent of the company's share capital, changed hands. The seven-page contract was signed within the space of an hour by Monarchy/Regency and Goldman Sachs. The Americans suddenly had 576 million euros more in their company coffers and had earned around 400 million euros on the bottom line from their involvement with Puma. Four days later the money was in their account.

Now the transfer had to be sold in the right way to potential investors and the public. During this period Meissner was in London, the Regency managers were staying in Malibu, Zeitz was sitting at his desk in his Boston apartment, finance chief Bock was in the Maldives and Ulf Santjer, Head of Communications, was in his Herzogenaurach office at Würzburger Strasse 13. Outside, the sun was blazing and the hottest summer in a century, which saw temperatures soar above 35 degrees Celsius, was driving people into the shade of the beer gardens along the Aurach river. Employees from the investment bank spent the whole of the following day calling up their best clients all over the globe, from their offices and from home. The strategy was to keep selling small blocks of shares.

They met with no shortage of interest. The power of the brand made itself felt and an increasing number of analysts had changed their recommendation to "buy". Puma had grown into an attractive stock that was a match for cult brands like Porsche. This was due not just to its good performance figures, but also to Jochen Zeitz, who, in the eyes of stock exchange operators, had developed from the company boss who was "just out of kindergarten" into a credible top manager.

At around 11.00 pm on the evening of Sunday 1 June, Meissner reported to Matalon that his colleagues had already stirred up interest in roughly a third of the volume. The next day the book-building procedure got under way, in which investors were given the opportunity to state the number of shares they were interested in taking and their maximum price. The issue price was calculated on the basis of the interest shown in subscribing. In consultation with Zeitz, Santjer drew up an ad-hoc announcement, which had to be sent to the major news departments before the start of trading, to notify all investors of the development. They also discussed different communication strategies for the possible sales scenarios.

Zeitz remained in his Boston office, keeping himself awake with coffee. He was supposed to be available for interviews from 8.00 am Central European Time onwards – 2.00 am in Boston. At 7.43 am the ad-hoc announcement ran across the ticker. Minutes later the first financial analyst got in touch. An interview marathon began. Santjer put the most important media representatives through to Zeitz in Boston.

Within six and a half hours almost seven million Puma shares had found new owners. The members of the Supervisory Board and the members of the Puma Board were equally surprised by the speed with which this took place. Nobody had expected it. Thore Ohlsson, Deputy Chairman of the Supervisory Board, watched the sale unfold on his laptop in his office in Falsterbo on the southern coast of Sweden. In the afternoon he received an e-mail from Zeitz: "I'm writing to let you know that the transaction has been concluded successfully. Regards, JZ." Minutes later Santjer issued the official press release:

"PUMA AG Rudolf Dassler Sport informs that Monarchy Regency has sold its shareholdings in PUMA to a broad base of institutional investors in a successful transaction completed today. Since its foundation in 1948 it is the first time that PUMA AG will operate without a majority shareholder. This transaction will enable PUMA to significantly broaden its international shareholder base, as well as increasing the company's free float to 100 percent and enhancing its attractiveness to the global capital market."

## A time of relief

By this time Zeitz had already given 16 interviews and taken more than 60 calls. He did not feel tired, however. Adrenaline was coursing through his veins. What a deal! Everything had gone extremely well. The press evaluated Regency's withdrawal with critical detachment, but on the whole as a positive development for Puma. Again and again the question cropped up of whether the Americans had perhaps pulled out because the incredible Puma story was gradually coming to an end. Zeitz pointed to the fact that the company had just concluded the best quarter in its history, and put forward the opposing evidence that the film production company had committed contractually to a close collaboration with his firm for a further five years. There was no reason, he said, to change the strategy.

## 2.8 The Empire Strikes Back

### *Puma attacks the big guys: fashionable Latin lovers, Schumi's shoes and more trouble with FIFA*

Puma's CEO was happy with the new situation: he no longer had a principal shareholder keeping tabs on what he was doing. And Zeitz was happy with himself, as well. Despite all the doubts of the analysts and the journalists that the media had forced on his attention over the past years, his shareholders, great and small, had always been able to make money. The equity ratio was now a reassuring 55 percent, and even the financial results, which had been negative for years, had now gone from red to black. The gross margin was at the top of the industry league table at 47.5 percent – the company was really making a profit. Puma was desirable, designers were constantly knocking on the door, seeking to work with the Franconians. The glossy magazines showcased its products. This was a major thorn in the side of the Adidas managers: Puma had grown into a formidable opponent. Again and again, they tried to put analysts and journalists off their little ex-brother.

But the facts spoke for themselves. The hot summer of 2003 had evidently whetted people's appetite for Puma products. Despite persistently and generally slack consumer spending and a "cheap is cool" mentality among customers, Zeitz upped his profit forecast for the third time in a row. Now that he was expecting an increase of 60 rather than 50 percent, sales were to go up by 30 percent. "The numbers are better than I expected myself," he admitted to analysts. The share price leapt the 100-euro hurdle for the first time ever, a dynamic that carried it way ahead of rival Adidas.

It seemed to be just a matter of time before Puma would enter the upper house of the stock exchange – DAX. Zeitz had already collected numerous awards for his business achievements – now he was even elected "Entrepreneur of the Year" by *Horizont* marketing magazine. After years of hard work, his company was suddenly playing in a different league. It had left Adidas and Nike far behind in the established sportlifestyle market segment. And it had advanced into market regions never previously visited by a sports gear manufacturer: into the high-class boutiques of the most famous couturiers. With such surprising developments, it was no wonder the editors of *Vogue* and *Elle* were now just as interested in Puma as reporters from *Sport Bild* or *kicker*. The new customers who looked for Puma clothes for the office or evenings out were not restricted to women. For business travellers, for example, there was a "96-hour trolley" with a price tag of 3,900 euros: The all-round no-worries package consisted of 26 individual items including non-iron shirts, crease-resistant trousers and high-quality accessories.

Zeitz, whose background had never really brought him into contact with fashion, was now mingling with the haute-couture players. On 12 January 2004, he was stuck in traffic in a Milan taxi. Employees of the local public transport services were on strike again – in the middle of the famous fashion week. Nervously, he jigged his legs and kept reaching for the phone. Time was running away with him, the fashion show at "Superstudio Piu", Puma's first real catwalk presentation, was due to start shortly. The show collection had been designed by Puma's new creative director Neil Barrett. The British couturier had come to Herzogenaurach the previous autumn, having previously worked for Gucci and Prada. The collection, from football shirts to evening wear, was called "Italia" – no surprises there – and was based on the Italian national football team strip.

Puma had signed a contract with the *Azzurri* the year before. Zeitz had been a supporter of the southern squad since his days as a student in Florence. At that time, he had followed the victory of the Italians over Germany in the World Cup in Spain, and sucked up the sheer enthusiasm of the fans like a sponge. He had evidently been able to communicate this rapture credibly to Franco Carraro, then President of the Italian football federation FIGC.

Naturally, a popular national player was to appear on the catwalk in the fashion show: Gianluigi Buffon, the Italian goalkeeper with the deep blue eyes, Latin lover smile and the intricately styled "Undone" hairdo. The applause after the show was deafening. The fashion journalists appeared impressed. And the

*Zeitz (at right) with Neil Barrett*

football fans were absolutely wild about the tailored vests worn by their hero of the pitch.

On 29 March, Zeitz returned once more to Italy. This time, the taxi took him to the Meazza Stadium, where he was to present the Italian team's new outfit to the public. This, too, was the product of Neil Barrett's tailoring and cutting. He called his style the "layered look". His inspiration was the equipment of the Roman gladiators. The shoulders resembled those of armour, because the material used had a metallic glimmer. From the front, the socks looked like antique, bound leg protectors. And the names and player numbers appeared in a classical Roman script. At the photo shoot with the team, coach Trapattoni waved his arms wildly in front of the photographers: "Presidente! Come here!" Then he put Zeitz in the middle: the team photo showed a smiling Zeitz surrounded by players.

### It's always best to check

Zeitz still considered brand management a matter for top-level attention – even though business was booming. One morning in April 2004, he raced through the streets of Munich's arts and entertainment district Schwabing in black "Hammer" sneakers, a shoe from an in-house collection. Red traffic lights couldn't stop him. Rain fell in torrents on his head from the black clouds overhead – that didn't worry him either. His black Puma coat flapped in the spring wind, underwear with the Puma logo kept him warm. Three men gasped and panted in his train: Martin Gänsler, Puma's number two man, Sales Manager Christian Wiesender and Fashion Managing Director Neil Beeson. The Puma CEO had a challenging programme for the day: he had two dozen boutiques on his call schedule. He wanted to scrutinize every single one minutely, go round all the shelves to check whether the Puma products were in the right place and ask the sales staff how his products were going. He called the mini marathon a "store check". He still loves this kind of check-up operation to this day, and always schedules one wherever he goes.

In this spring of 2004, the world was just beginning to recover from the bursting of the Internet bubble and the terror attacks of 11 September 2001. The old principles of globalization still applied. Zeitz liked one of them in particular: the best opportunities in the market don't go to the biggest players, but to the fastest. "Speed equals success," was his reckoning. For that reason alone, apart from anything else, he never let up in his role of indefatigable pacemaker. The day before, he had hammered the message home to 500 Puma executives from all over the world, who had gathered in the Steigenberger Hotel Frankfurter Hof for the annual sales conference: "We have to get even faster!" Faster? Puzzlement put a frown on the foreheads of quite a few. Hadn't sales risen six-fold since 1993, from 210 million to almost 1.3 billion euros? Hadn't the pre-tax results shot up from a loss of 35 million euros to a gain of 264 million? But yesterday's performance was of no interest to Zeitz. His global market share in sports apparel was just one percent, in sports footwear 5.3 percent. So there was still a lot up for grabs. He always looks forward. Quite a few Puma employees considered that unfair.

Zeitz had had himself driven to Munich in a 279-horse power company Mercedes S 430 and had spent almost the entire time en route making phone calls or answering e-mails on his Palm Treo smart phone. As soon as he was back outside an outlet after a store check, he reached into his pocket for his mobile office, fingers flying on the keypad like those of an addict on a gambling machine, impatient, as though constantly expecting urgent news. Nothing goes fast enough for him, not even keyboarding: "It's a pity I don't have three hands." Wonder gadgets like the Treo hadn't been in the shops for long, but Zeitz had one. Of course. After all, he was an early adopter, one of the technology-loving opinion leaders, and worked in a virtual company that would collapse like a house of cards without modern communication media. Tireless managers like him feel naked without round-the-clock accessibility. The whole company was now dependent on the achievements of tele-communications. Even on these store check trips, Zeitz used the time difference and communicated day and night – apart from a maximum of six hours' sleeping time – with his 3,200 employees at the corporate centres of Herzogenaurach, Boston and Hong Kong – generally in the mother tongue of the person he was calling. As a rule, he never takes more than two hours to answer an e-mail.

### More trouble with FIFA

Zeitz was now able to focus on the company's internal problems. Externally, he no longer had to produce headlines to get the firm's strategic direction into the heads of customers and shareholders. The sales and profit figures as well as the sponsorship contract part-ners spoke for themselves. However, he wanted to maintain the image of the underdog, little David who defeated Goliath with his own weapons. So the new battle with the all-powerful football gods of FIFA that loomed on the horizon fitted in well with his plans. It caused a lot of trouble, but also generated a huge amount of publicity and newspaper reports. Zeitz could be sure that popular feeling would be on Puma's side in this duel.

Once more, it was about Cameroon, and once more it was about clothing. The row was sparked off by the African Cup of Nations in February 2004. On that occasion, Cameroon's national team did not go out on the pitch in shirt and shorts, but in a one-piece kit known as the Cameroon UniQT. It was part of the new Puma marketing strategy. The shorts were sewn to the skin-tight shirt, emphasizing the Africans' athletic physique. Marks of lion claws were stitched in over the stomach muscles, in reference to the team's nickname: the indomitable lions. Horst Widmann, Puma's foreign minister, had presented the new outfit to deputy general secretary Jérôme Champagne at FIFA's headquarters a year before the African Cup. He had agreed to the new style. But Widmann had made a mistake: no one had put the decision on record. The Puma manager had depended on the fact that the right-hand man of FIFA boss Joseph Blatter was trustworthy and had the power to make the decision.

Shortly before the tournament began, Blatter suddenly con-tacted Widmann in his hotel room. The two had known each other for 30 years and were on first-name terms. Widmann remembers the FIFA President storming at him: "What kind of a circus are you running, this kit is prohibited!" Widmann immediately suspected that Adidas was putting on pressure in the background – good relations between Adidas and the global football association had grown since the Dassler era; the sports equipment manufacturer even sponsored FIFA. Blatter didn't want to know about the meeting with Champagne and the fact that he had given the okay. Widmann grabbed his mobile phone and called Champagne immediately. Champagne confirmed the background. Blatter declared out of hand that Champagne had had no authority. The FIFA boss wasn't exactly in the picture; he presumed Puma wanted to re-introduce the sleeveless shirts that had shocked him so much in 2002. Widmann offered to obtain an outfit from the Cameroon team by the next morning and to present it for his opinion. Blatter agreed. Next day, Widmann appeared in FIFA's hotel room at nine o'clock on the dot, the kit under his arm. Everyone was prepared for a debate, except for Blatter – who was conspicuous by his absence. Instead, Urs Linsi, the general secretary, led the discussion. He himself wasn't all that sure what the objection to the outfit was. "You will hear from us," he said, and departed the scene. That afternoon, the judgment of big chief Blatter was conveyed to Widmann: "This kit is not allowed."

Widmann was furious and changed tack. FIFA, he argued, was not actually responsible for the African Cup. He turned instead to the African football association, the Confédération Africaine de Football (CAF), and asked for their permission to use the strip. Its president, Cameroonian Issa Hayatou, had been a friend of Widmann's for years. Hayatou listened to his explanation of the case, took the matter very seriously indeed, studied the regulations and consulted with his lawyers for two solid hours. "No worries," he then decided. "You can play."

He had made the reckoning without host Blatter. The FIFA boss did not give up and demanded replacement kit. Puma was unable to deliver it in the short time. The world association granted a reprieve for the first three games, Widmann confirmed in writing that new outfits would be obtained within two weeks. Before the fourth game, the Cameroon team received an official letter from FIFA: they were forbidden to continue to play in the strip, and would otherwise be subject to disciplinary action. However, Widmann did not yet have the new gear, and the Cameroonians continued to play in the one-piece outfit. Blatter went berserk. FIFA deducted six points from the Cameroonians' World Cup qualification campaign and imposed a fine of 200,000 Swiss francs.

Widmann vented his outrage in public: "It is a matter of plain fact that Adidas has been favoured one-sidedly over the past 30 years. It's totally arbitrary." He was particularly annoyed by the fact that for years FIFA had judged the three Adidas strips on the players' shirts to be a design element, not a logo. In Widmann's opinion, that gave Puma's rival many times more advertising space than any other competitor. In addition, he scented a personal vengeance campaign by the FIFA boss against Hayatou, who was considered a severe critic of Blatter's and had stood against him unsuccessfully in the Presidency election of 2002.

Cameroon's trainer Winnie Schäfer was seething as well: "When we lions are cornered, we bite back." How was he to qualify for the next World Cup, coming from six points behind? At a press conference in Cameroon, at which Widmann turned up prepared to take all the blame on his own broad shoulders to calm the situation down, he was nearly thrown to the lions himself. "I don't know yet how I'll do it, but I'll get your six points back for you," he vowed in conclusion. The audience was silent. Puma then started a global PR campaign against FIFA.

Puma paid the fine and started court action against FIFA, claiming damages of two million euros. For the first time ever, a sports equipment manufacturer went up against the most important sports association in the world. At the same time, Puma's in-house lawyers offered FIFA an out-of-court settlement. The Swiss did not accept the deal – their lawyers disputed more or less everything that Puma was putting forward. On 6 April, the proceedings started at the Nuremberg-Fürth district court. In the end, the third chamber found against the football association, on the grounds of an infringement of the law on monopolies. For Blatter, the world had turned upside down.

On 10 September 2005, Widmann went to Marrakech for the 55th FIFA Congress. Attendance at these generally annual sessions is considered mandatory for all representatives of the industry, because all those who have anything to say in the world of football meet and network there. Franz Beckenbauer had announced that he would celebrate his 60th birthday in Marrakech, Morocco's "Pearl of the South". Widmann had asked FIFA through his secretary's office where he could get a hotel room. To his surprise, the association readily obtained accommodation for him in the main hotel where all the FIFA officials were housed. When he checked in, the receptionist explained to him that the room was reserved in FIFA's name, and he would not have to worry about the costs. Widmann was astonished. Hardly had he got to the room and put his case down, when there was a knock at the door. It was Blatter. "Mr Widmann, I have to talk to you," he said. First-name terms had long since been withdrawn. He asked whether the offer of an out-of-court settlement was still open. "We don't want a fight," replied Widmann, "We were only standing up for ourselves." Blatter was under severe pressure, official enquiries were being made as to how the row had started, and he had to make an official report on the subject at the Congress the next day. He therefore pushed for a speedy settlement.

"Let's call a meeting right now," Widmann suggested. However, Blatter's diary was overflowing, so they agreed on the following morning at seven o'clock. The meeting place was Blatter's suite. When Widmann arrived there bright and early, Blatter was once more absent. In his place was general secretary Linsi, who immediately started to tear him to shreds because of the court case. Widmann was just about to break off the discussion when Blatter came in and Linsi promptly fell silent. The tug of war commenced – in spite of the fact that the legal representatives of the combatants had already negotiated a compromise weeks ago: the six points to be given back, the entire fine to be donated to social purposes in Cameroon, and Puma to have the chance to buy admission tickets for World Cup 2006 in Germany – which up to then it had not had the right to do, because the company was not registered as a main sponsor. Blatter had rejected the proposals at the time. Now Widmann put in a higher bid and demanded VIP tickets for the World Cup in addition, so as to pamper the friends and business partners of his company. At the end of an hour, the settlement was reached and the wishes of the Puma negotiator fulfilled. "FIFA was extremely just and fair towards us afterwards," says Widmann.

The fight with FIFA had cost the big cat a lot of energy – and brought it a huge amount of publicity. In view of the positive press and the announcements of solidarity from the sporting world, its victory over the powerful association has to be considered complete. FIFA's opinion on the matter remains a mystery; the association failed to respond to the author's request for comments. Puma's managers had made a full frontal onslaught on the tyrannical Blatter – no manufacturer of sporting goods had ever dared to do that before. Puma reinforced its reputation as a rebel by this act of resistance.

### *Fit as a training shoe*

At the start of 2004, the Puma was bursting with energy. Its share price was experiencing the more or less vertical take-off it had enjoyed at the height of the new economic boom. By market capitalization, the company was now the third largest sports equipment group in the world after Nike and Adidas. Nevertheless, the critics' voices were not silenced. They warned that the group was overly dependent on trends and constant innovations. In addition to that, they claimed the customer base was too young and did not have a scrap of loyalty. Morgan Stanley even downgraded the share to "neutral" at the end of February. The reason it gave was that there was practically no more room left for positive surprises. Nils Lesser of HSBC Trinkaus & Burkhardt warned of a possible "collapse of the new market segment". In actual fact, the warnings were not entirely unfounded: today's cool can be tomorrow's totally uncool – Puma's competitors Converse, Fila and L.A. Gear had suffered this painful experience and their significance in the market had plummeted.

The clever ones among the staff who were blessed with share options cashed them in. Zeitz was one of the intelligent early birds: on 1 September 2003 he swapped a package of his options for 66,707 Puma shares at a price per share of 24.61 euros. The very same day, he sold them again for the price on the day of 101.58 euros per share. He took a profit of 5.1 million euros. That wasn't bad on top of his annual salary of over two million euros. "Shareholders will not grudge the Puma chief the money, since he has made the share price rise to arguably record-breaking levels," was the sympathetic view of *Spiegel* magazine. Nevertheless, his co-owners did show some signs of irritation. At the annual press conference for the year 2003, Zeitz announced a moderate increase in dividend from 55 to 70 cents per share, although sales had gone up by 40 percent and net profit by 111 percent. He pointed to the steep rises in the share price, from which the shareholders also benefited.

In April, Puma stock went over the 200 euro mark for the first time. And Jochen Zeitz received a new five-year contract, up to 2009, from the Supervisory Board before renewal was due. The 41-year-old still showed no signs of fatigue, although with 14 years' tenure he could already claim the status of an old retainer who, in earlier days, would long since have been presented with a golden watch by his boss. But that year and those that followed promised further rich pickings: The European Football Championship in

Portugal was coming up, in which Puma would be on the field with Italy, Switzerland, the Czech Republic and Bulgaria, as well as the summer Olympics in Athens, at which the Franconians had a wide range of athletes from all over the world under contract, in particular 15 members of the Jamaican team. Now the company had to plough a ton of money into advertising, to get as much of a return as possible. The annual marketing budget had reached a dizzying 180 million euros, amounting to around 14 percent of consolidated sales.

Although the proud *azzurri* in their gladiator shirts failed to survive the group stage at the European Championship and the Jamaicans with their reggae vibe just managed to win 34th place in the Olympic medal table, Zeitz declared himself satisfied with both tournaments. The deals with the sports and fashion retailers had been completed long before the opening ceremonies began. The third quarter of 2004 proved to be the strongest in the history of the company. But the analysts expressed disappointment – they had expected more. Despite their dissatisfaction, all the signs pointed to Puma's soon moving up into DAX, where tourism company TUI was faltering and looked like dropping out. In the end, a sudden upturn in the travel company's share price prevented the swapover. Zeitz took it calmly: he would rather be a heavyweight in MDAX than a lightweight in DAX.

On 8 September, the press office announced that the Franconians would be outfitting the Ferrari Formula 1 team from 1 January 2005 onwards, and would offer a merchandising collection. The bestseller was to be the "Future Cat", a red and white racing boot with the Ferrari and Puma logos. The new German-Italian relationship was just the kind of thing Zeitz liked: the most successful racing stable of all times with its superstar Michael Schumacher, who had swept the board with one world championship title after another since the year 2000, was being backed by Puma, not Adidas or Nike. After signing up the Italian football federation, Zeitz (with coaching by Martin Gänsler) had successfully brought off his second coup in the absolute top ranks of the sporting world. Once more, his language skills expedited matters: he had negotiated the contract with Formula 1 team boss Jean Todt in French and with the Italian managers in Italian, which earned him a sizeable bouquet of laurels before the deal even started. Success brings happiness. "I feel younger than ever," he told the *New York Times*. The professional world approved of his élan: he received another title, this time "Strategist of the Year", funded by the *Financial*

*Zeitz (second from left) with Formula 1 manager Flavio Briatore at the first Formula 1 Grand Prix in China*

*Times Deutschland* together with management consultancy Bain & Company and the WHU school of management. The reason given in the eulogy was that he had "performed a minor miracle and made Puma into a trendy brand".

Zeitz also felt a sense of satisfaction when he read an interview with Herbert Hainer, CEO of his Herzogenaurach competitor. The Adidas boss had said then that profitability would have priority over sales growth in his company. In other words: Hainer had temporarily given up his attempt to catch up Nike by means of more and ever more million-euro deals. This was a strategy of intelligent restraint that Zeitz had been demonstrating for years, by putting an end to his team's constant focus on the eternal opponent across the Aurach. Zeitz's comment on the Adidas chief's announcement at the time: "It is quite amazing that our most outspoken past critics are now copying us. To me, that is confirmation of the way we have gone. Nothing more."

## 2.9 The China Connection

### The ups and downs of being desirable: eternal scepticism, the Chancellor show and a visit to a counterfeiter's factory

At the beginning of 2005, many analysts once more viewed the whole company as problematic, with a lot of fixing required. After the record year which had witnessed such major sporting events as Euro 2004 and the Olympics, their expectations were completely exaggerated. It became difficult for Zeitz to trigger price hopes in the market and to keep the shareholders happy. He put forward a comparatively modest forecast and predicted an increase in both sales and net earnings of five to ten percent (in the previous year, the figures had been 20.1 percent for sales and 43.5 percent for profit). The dynamics slackened off – and the share price tumbled. By February it had lost ten percent, while the MDAX increased by 6.5 percent. It is the fate of the serial winner for commentators to talk it into crisis if one victory is not quite as glorious as the last. Zeitz took up the cudgels: he still saw inexhaustible potential for the brand, he said.

Undeniably, the market was becoming increasingly tight for Puma. On the other hand, its increased product offering was expanding the potential customer base. All Puma's rivals, including Nike, Adidas, Fila, Reebok, Dunlop, Converse and Gola, now operated in the sportlifestyle segment with designer footwear. The skating brand Vans had hired Marc Jacobs, the most influential American fashion designer, who worked for Louis Vuitton. Reebok had engaged the talents of English fashion superstar Paul Smith and the super-cool British designer Kim Jones was creating lifestyle shoes for English sports goods manufacturer Umbro. On the other side, the fashion houses were edging closer and closer to Puma – Prada, Gucci, Ralph Lauren, Helmut Lang, Hogan, Tod's, Tommy Hilfiger, Dsquared, Boss, Diesel and Byblos, in particular. Dolce & Gabbana had brought a sneaker onto the market as early as 2002. The Italian clothing company Ermenegildo Zegna offered its own leisure sports line under the name "Z", which included white sneakers with green stripes, and Lacoste launched retro tennis shoes on the market for upwards of 150 euros which were suitable for neither grass nor clay.

A lot of fixing was, indeed, going on at the Puma headquarters in Herzogenaurach during these weeks – quite literally. Saws screeched and hammer drills clattered on all sides. Due to the company's rapid growth, the old beige and green building on Würzburger Strasse, which radiated all the charm of a 1970s comprehensive school, was bursting at the seams. The Board had, therefore, decided to invest ten million euros in the site and to incorporate a new, five-storey office complex with a floor space of 7,000 m². The glass front of this building was intended to reflect the new chic of the sportlifestyle and fashion group, and Zeitz's

*Puma headquarters with new building (at centre)*

Puma red was to dominate the reception hall. The only room to remain dust free during these weeks was the showroom, in which Puma was presenting its 2005/2006 winter collection.

Finally, the company boss was able to move out of the Dassler family's old-fashioned, mahogany-panelled office. It was converted into a fitness centre for the workforce and packed full of running machines, steppers, cross trainers and strength machines. *Mens sana in corpore sano*: once a week, the staff now had access to a trainer and physiotherapist. The Puma CEO's new office was filled with light and fitted out with a modern chrome look.

Zeitz likes to concentrate on his work at all times and has no desire to be distracted by side issues. He refused all invitations to appear on talk shows such as *Christiansen* – there were plenty of opportunities now that the Puma was ready for its big leap – and was still only rarely seen at parties. Most of all, however, he dreaded politics in all its forms. When the German Chancellor Gerhard Schröder had invited him to Berlin the year before to discuss with other executives how the football World Cup could be pushed further, he declined and sent his right-hand man Horst Widmann to the capital instead. Schröder's parting shot was: "Give my regards to the boss, it would be nice to see him sometime too." "Well, come and visit us, then," replied the Puma foreign minister. "Okay, I'll do that," promised Schröder.

## *Visit from Berlin*

On 10 March 2005, the day of the official opening of the new company headquarters, the Chancellor flew into Herzogenaurach in a Eurocopter "Puma" helicopter. His visit to the company that was so rich in tradition meant more to him than just an official engagement. As he repeatedly stressed, sport – and football in particular – had played an important part in his life right from his childhood as the son of a war widow. It was on the football pitch next to the temporary accommodation in Bexten, Lower Saxony, where the Schröders lived for a time that "Acker" ("Slogger"), as the other players called him, found respect and admiration and developed "self-confidence for my own journey through life".

At Puma, the preparations for the Chancellor's visit ran strictly to protocol. Time and again, Head of Communications Ulf Santjer was on the phone to government spokesman Béla Anda to get the obligatory details. Three days before the visit, the security forces from Berlin had arrived and had their dogs sniff round every corner of the building to track down any hidden explosives. Puma became a high-security zone. The risk in provincial Franconia was low – apart from the fury of the Adidas managers, who were unable to comprehend why the German Chancellor should visit the hated small ex-brother and not the big company that kitted out the German national football team.

In the red entrance hall of the new wing, the reception committee had taken their positions: Hans Lang, the mayor of Herzogenaurach, Eberhard Irlinger, District Administrator, Christa Matschl, CSU member of the Bavarian parliament and, of course, Jochen Zeitz. The man who shies away so much from the company of politicians was unable to hide a shake of his head: how the local dignitaries basked in the shade of the Chancellor, despite not being members of the same party! The mayor, Hans Lang, in particular, was a friend of Adidas and had very little to do with Puma. Together with Schröder and government spokesman Anda, the party climbed the steps and disappeared into a meeting room where there were open sandwiches and coffee, which the distinguished guest sipped at. Helmut Fischer, the Head of Advertising for Germany, recorded virtually every second of the meeting with his digital camera. The Chancellor knew the Puma story astonishingly well and wanted to know how it was possible to manufacture goods in Asia and create jobs in Germany. After a quarter of an hour, they moved into the assembly hall where the Puma employees were already waiting in keen anticipation. Zeitz gave a brief welcoming speech, then

*Visit to Herzogenaurach by the German Chancellor, Gerhard Schröder*

Schröder said a few words, followed by the District Administrator and, finally, the mayor launched into a long-winded speech about Herzogenaurach, everything and nothing.

Visibly bored, the Chancellor leapt to his feet: "So, now let's go and see what goes on here," he said. The fisher of men was very much in the mood for a major charm offensive. "When I look at your team – I see you're not as young as you were," he called to 41-year-old Zeitz and flashed his teeth. The team roared – one nil to Schröder. He shook hands with everybody, mingled with the employees and had his photograph taken with them. Great things were being achieved here, he flattered them, "not somewhere or other in the world, but here in the business location of Germany".

The group then began a tour of the company. They started at the very top of the building in the Apparel department. From there, they made their way down to Product Development where the Chancellor looked over the shoulders of the young women working there and was interested in all the things they could do with their notebooks, drawings and fabric samples. They then called in briefly on the footwear department to take a look at the latest achievements in the areas of football and motorsport. Finally, the group headed to the Order Centre, where the Puma boss presented the statesman with a Cameroon national football shirt, complete with the key player's number ten on the back. There had to be a political gag in there too: the colours of Cameroon are red and green – just like those of the government coalition at that time.

The Chancellor stayed for a good hour. As he left, he turned to Zeitz: "Come to Berlin and meet me there." Six weeks later, Zeitz took up his invitation. He had to go to the capital anyway to present the new World Cup collection in a disused suburban railway station at Potsdamer Platz. Football legend Pelé had come to the event as the star guest. "Why don't we take him with us to the Chancellor's office?" thought Zeitz. Despite the presence of Pelé, the meeting turned out to be considerably less relaxed than in Herzogenaurach. This time, Puma was nothing more than one appointment in the German Chancellor's jam-packed agenda. Schröder had put a vote of confidence to parliament, unsurprisingly lost it, and his mind was now in the middle of an election campaign. There was polite conversation in his office over a cup of coffee. When the photographer wanted to take a photograph, Schröder hid his cigar. Sport and smoke do not mix.

As they shook hands in farewell, the Chancellor invited the Puma boss to accompany him on one of his next trips abroad. "Asia would be good," said Zeitz – he often had business to attend to there anyway. It was not to be. Soon, there was a new Chancellor by the name of Angela Merkel. Nevertheless, the visit turned out to be worthwhile: the red-green coalition and the subsequent Grand Coalition supported him, for example, in fending off Chinese customs restrictions. The new government even honoured Schröder's offer for Zeitz to join a trip. In 2006, he flew to China with the new Chancellor and 25 business representatives, including Deutsche Bahn CEO Hartmut Mehdorn and Heinrich von Pierer who, at that time, was Chairman of the Supervisory Board at Siemens. He got on best with the young Klaus Kleinfeld, the former CEO of Siemens. However, despite good discussions, he made a vow upon his return: never again! He had seldom felt so out of place as he did among the wheelings and dealings and occasional apparent obsequiousness of the economic decision-makers.

Being Chancellor, he says, would not be his thing. Despite some autocratic traits, Zeitz acts too openly to be able to engage in trench warfare. What information do I have to spread and when? Who do I have to get rid of at what point in time? He cannot stand questions like that. He loves stress – but only the positive kind. Politics, he says, would most likely cause him negative stress. And that would ruin his chances of success in it.

### The devil wears Puma

Sometimes, however, even Jochen Zeitz needs politics to be able to perform his job without hindrance. Take the case of the battle against brand piracy, for example, fought by Merkel for German industry in China.

A day like any other in mid-2004. In Jingjiang, the centre of the textile and footwear industry, 1,000 kilometres south-east of Beijing, a handful of English gentlemen passed through the gate of a shoe factory belonging to one Mr Ding. The visitors passed themselves off as business people who were interested in the goods of the well-known manufacturer. Mr Ding gave them a warm, business-like welcome and conducted them through the long halls. As if fascinated, the visitors followed the work of the people and machines busily and steadily producing the latest generation of Puma shoes. Excellent quality models, professionally made. The men gaped in astonishment. Mr Ding must have invested a great deal of money into the moulds.

What the proud Chinese factory owner did not know was that the business people were in fact detectives from an English private investigation company who had been engaged by Puma to track down plagiarists. Mr Ding was without a doubt one such counterfeiter, and of the most brazen variety. When the Britons came back some weeks later together with officials from the Chinese Administration of Industry and Commerce (AIC) to raid the counterfeiter's lair, they were not allowed in. Very wisely, Mr Ding had had his factory built on military land. The area was surrounded with heavily armed soldiers who started to play menacingly with the triggers of their weapons whenever a stranger approached. Despite an official order, the detectives continued to be denied access. They could only watch as, in the distance, giant cardboard boxes were loaded onto transporters and taken deep into the military grounds – there was nothing they could do. The soldiers became increasingly restless and threatened to shoot. The delegation retreated, "totally frustrated", as Puma's chief lawyer Jochen Lederhilger remembers. In the days that followed the investigators turned to higher authorities. As always, they were assured that the authorities were outraged and that they would take care of it. As always, nothing happened.

Globalization opens up great opportunities for impudent characters like Mr Ding. Businesses all over the world suffer as a result. The Organization for Economic Cooperation and Development (OECD) assumes that two percent of world trade involved counterfeit goods in 2006. Sales of 136 billion euros were achieved in this year with such goods, whether chainsaws, brake pads or medicines. Up to two-thirds of all imitation goods originate from Chinese factories like Mr Ding's. Considered in absolute terms, this is not an alarming figure. However, the trend is increasing sharply – a fact that is borne out by surveys among customs officials from over 50 nations. The OECD is less concerned about the odd jogger breaking his or her leg wearing dodgy Puma sneakers than the fact that foodstuffs and medicines from the counterfeit factories could cause serious health damage.

As a result, owning a desirable brand has a bitter side. Bargain counters at the weekly bazaar in Manavgat on the Turkish Adriatic, or the Vietnamese markets on the Czech border with Germany, are overflowing with imitation products which holidaymakers and bargain-hunters alike are only too happy to snap up. As each new wave of tourists washes into the holiday resorts along the Mediterranean coast, it is generally just a matter of days before all the children are kitted out in the latest football shirts – fakes, of course. You can't really blame people, as the goods are of increasingly high quality and are even sold in apparently reputable shops. This is a concern for other companies as well as Puma: the stitching, printing and details of the imitations are so sophisticated that even company employees have problems identifying them as such. Once, even forgery-proof security tags were found in the counterfeit shoes. They were, Puma lawyers suspect, stolen from partner factories or sold on the quiet by corrupt employees. Sometimes suppliers actually report that tags have been stolen. The Puma managers are then a bit doubtful, but they send out new ones as quickly as possible so as not to impede production. As Puma is still growing rapidly, there is virtually no hope of stopping employees with criminal leanings from accepting bribes and sending production data by e-mail to brand pirates. Puma lawyers claim that the factories of the company's own trading partners in China, Thailand, Turkey, Russia and the Ukraine are not the source of the problem. This is hard for outsiders to believe. However, the "S.A.F.E." team (Social Accountability and Fundamental Environmental Standards) regularly sends inspectors to the manufacturers and checks to make sure that nobody is overproducing.

Puma is fighting the battle against the plagiarists with increasing vigour. The first imitation products surfaced in the early 1990s as things started to go better again for the brand and its image improved. In 2006, over two million fake Puma items, primarily

*Puma bag – object of the counterfeiter's desire*

footwear, were seized across the world. Although brand piracy is forbidden in China and the central government is doing a great deal to put a stop to the manufacturers of imitation goods, it is not really possible to keep tabs on a population of 1.4 billion. To compound the problem, the piracy is supported by many governors, particularly those in the southern regions, which pocket quite a bit of the income from the counterfeiter's factories: no point in appealing to their sense of justice!

You could argue that the Puma managers should be rather proud of the omnipresence of the counterfeit goods, as the number of trademark infringements is a reflection of the awareness of the brand. However, Puma's Intellectual Property department, which deals with brand piracy, takes a merciless line. If customs officers find suspect goods anywhere at a border, the officials inform Herzogenaurach immediately. Puma's lawyers have filed global "border seizure requests" for this purpose. The customs investigators have a CD-ROM listing the security features of Puma products and a route list detailing the usual distribution channels. If they harbour any suspicions of having counterfeit products on their hands, they call Puma direct or hold back the goods so that they can clarify the facts. If their suspicions prove to be correct, the find is destroyed on the spot. Puma shareholders take limited pleasure in this rigorous action: after all, the costs of the disposal have to be borne by the holder of the right, that is to say, Puma.

### Forbidden cargo

The brand pirates are becoming ever more industrious – and the bills for disposal ever higher for Puma. In August 2006, customs employees at the port of Hamburg discovered 117 containers holding fake trainers – mainly Nike – plus watches, clothes and toys. The officials of the mighty international port had never before landed such a coup. They estimated the market value of the products at 383 million euros. Five of the 117 containers were each stuffed full with 14,000 pairs of Puma shoes – mostly imitations of the bestsellers "Speed Cat" and "Future Cat". The originals as sold in the shops cost 100 euros, the fake products would have been peddled for 20 euros at the Asian markets of the Czech Republic and elsewhere. In November, the goods, which originated almost without exception from China, were shredded and incinerated in spectacular fashion. Each container cost approximately 3,000 euros to dispose of, so that Puma got a bill for 15,000 euros. A large proportion of the plastic from which the shoes were once made can now be found mixed into the surfaces of many sports facilities.

Zeitz maintains that the best way to tackle the problem is at the root. That is why his company finances a tight-knit network of law firms and security services spanning 60 countries around the globe which cooperate with the managers of the company's subsidiaries and distribution partners. The investigators get their information from customs, the industrial police, reputable sports goods dealers or Puma representatives who, through their travels, know the market in detail. Eventually, all the information ends up bundled in Herzogenaurach. Tracing the origin of the products is becoming increasingly difficult. The brand pirates are constantly coming up with new detours to disguise their trade routes. A large proportion of the merchandise is now transported via Dubai, for example. Turkey, Thailand, the Philippines, Poland, the Czech Republic, Hungary, Slovakia, South America and South Africa are considered to be the main markets for selling black-market goods. There is little the lawyers from Herzogenaurach can do to prevent it. They are virtually always defeated by corruption and leaks. Take the events of 2006 in the Bulgarian holiday resort of Sandanski near Sofia, for example: a raid had been planned there to arrest a gang of counterfeiters. Annoyingly, precisely on the day of the operation, there was no longer a single counterfeit item to be found.

In isolated cases, imitations even turn up in German chain stores. In 2005, phantom shoppers from Puma discovered excellently manufactured imitations at wholesaler *Selgros*. They originated, as it turned out, from Mr Ding's factory. *Selgros* is not a direct customer of Puma and – presumably in complete innocence – had used a Dutch dealer on the grey market.

Locating the bad apples and removing them from the loop is among the foremost tasks of Neil Narriman, Brand Protection Manager at Puma. There are shoes and shirts lying about all over his small office that have come from the counterfeit factories in Asia, including a brown and white "Future Cat" motorsport shoe from the containers found in Hamburg port. A package has just arrived containing suspect shoes from the Bavarian customs office in Furth im Wald on the Czech border. They are counterfeits once again, 14,000 of them, found in a container shortly before Christmas 2006. Narriman types the address *www.chaussures-sports.net* into his Internet browser. A page opens through which any interested customer can order copies of products by well-known branded manufacturers. The website operator makes it easy for his customers. The offer can be called up in eight different languages. However, a search for the originator's details is fruitless. Whether you are looking for Puma, Nike, Airmax or Gucci, they are virtually all there at a third of the original price. Narriman knows that any order placed here will land in some Chinese factory or other. He does not hold out any hope of arresting the provider of the online shop, hiding somewhere out there behind bogus addresses in cyberspace. There is often nothing more behind such links than one or two men and a computer, and Chinese law, for example, does not permit action to be taken against counterfeiters if counterfeit goods are not physically present. In any case, if a company manages to have an Internet shop closed down using legal remedies, it will appear again shortly afterwards under a new address.

Puma stands more of a chance with eBay, the number one spot for turning over fake Puma products. In the room next to Narriman's office, a work experience girl spends her days rummaging among the auction house's never-ending offers. She discovers a new case of brand piracy practically every day. Narriman estimates that 90 percent of all Puma products sold or auctioned are fakes and eBay makes money on every item sold through its fees. Puma's lawyers accuse eBay of doing far too little to prevent illegal sales. The auction site maintains, however, that such extensive checks are not reasonable. Why, then, is it possible, wonders the Puma legal expert, to check for child pornography or extreme right-wing content?

## 2.10 These Wilder Years

***The Tchibo heirs come on board: awkward individuals, potato soup instead of dividends, a black Wednesday and a nasty knock on the head***

On the evening of 10 May 2005, business journalists in the main newspaper offices were going about their normal routine. The day appeared to be over, when suddenly a message flashed over the news ticker. It read as follows: "Sportlifestyle company Puma AG today announced that Mayfair Vermögensverwaltungsgesellschaft mbH has taken a stake of 16.91 percent in Puma AG Rudolf Dassler Sport. A further 9.78 percent of Puma's shares are being examined for monopoly restrictions." The shares were purchased in several packages on 2 May 2005. Mayfair is the asset management company of the families of Günter and Daniela Herz. Like all Günter Herz company names, the title originates from one of the equestrian fan's current or former horses. "With just over 25 percent, we could hold the majority at a Puma general meeting, because attendance at such events is often not particularly high," said Hinrich Stahl, one of the Mayfair managers.

The journalists rubbed their eyes in disbelief: why on earth would the Herz siblings, two of the wealthy heirs to the family-run coffee business Tchibo, invest around half a billion euros in Puma? The *Handelsblatt* business newspaper hurriedly reported in a preliminary announcement that the former coffee roasters were planning to take over the group. Later, Mayfair director Rainer Kutzner left the question of a majority interest open, telling news agency Reuters: "We have not taken any firm decisions on that as yet." At any rate, according to Kutzner, Mayfair did not want to become involved on the operational side. Until this time the investment fund company Fidelity had been the largest single Puma shareholder, with 4.85 percent at the last count. Jochen Zeitz, who had learned of the investment in a phone call from Herz, announced officially: "We welcome Mayfair as a new shareholder and appreciate the investments made in the company, particularly in relation to Puma's further strategic development." In fact, he, too, was surprised: he had just got accustomed to a pleasant life without a principal shareholder. Mayfair's entry boosted Puma's share price on the stock exchange. The share closed 5.5 percent up, at 192.66 euros.

Günter Herz bore a huge load of expectations on his shoulders. He was born on 22 July 1940, the eldest son of coffee entrepreneur Max Herz and his wife Ingeborg. Max, a worthy citizen of Hamburg, who to this day can still be seen smiling down from a painting hanging in the foyer at Tchibo's headquarters in that city, had completed an apprenticeship in his father's coffee importing company and had later entered the parental business. In addition, he opened a Lotto agency at the end of the 1930s in order to take care of his retirement years. In 1950, he became director of the coffee firm Carl Tchiling-Hiryan GmbH and established the first coffee mail order firm, Tchiling-Bohnen (Tchi-bo). He was also the

*Concept store in London*

originator of the idea of setting up a chain of outlets to provide consumers with the opportunity to try out coffee. Max Herz died in 1965 of a heart attack and left behind a fortune – and a fuzzily worded will and testament. When eldest son Günter and his brother Michael took over the helm, family rows started amongst the total of four brothers, sister Daniela and mother Ingeborg.

Nonetheless, business prospered wonderfully, particularly thanks to Tchibo's popular side-line products, which ranged from asparagus cooking pots to package holidays. In 1974, the Herz clan took a stake in Beiersdorf (Nivea), and in 1980 it took over the cigarettes and drinks group Reemtsma. Nine years later, brother Michael stepped down from management. Günter, descriptions of whom by close friends and confidants range from "easy-going" to "overbearing", was now the sole boss. He expanded Tchibo's operations abroad and bought competitor Eduscho. Soon the family strife reignited all over again. His brothers, who controlled the Supervisory Board, refused to extend his contract beyond 2001. On 10 January 2001, Günter Herz threw in the towel as CEO but continued to keep up the family frictions as a minority shareholder. At the end of June 2001 he caused a scandal: he voted against the annual discharge of the Supervisory Board from accountability for the past year's management activities because he regarded his successor in the office of CEO as a dead loss.

In August 2003, Günter Herz left the family behind once and for all. He sold the Tchibo share package of nearly 40 percent that he held with his sister Daniela to the shareholder group led by his

brother Michael for around four billion euros. The money he pocketed came from the sale of Reemtsma. Since this time, the media
and bankers had speculated on what he would do with all that
cash. In 2006, *manager magazin* estimated the wealth of Günter
and Daniela Herz at around 5.1 billion euros. Rumours surfaced
that the pair wanted to buy tourism group TUI or the private bank
M. M. Warburg. No one had Puma on their list.

## All according to plan

At the time Herz came on board, Zeitz had met virtually all his
forecasts – by hard work, but at times also by outrageous good
fortune. He seemed to have a golden touch, evidenced, for example,
by his signing of tennis queen Serena Williams when she was still
a nobody. Now the Lifestyle and Fashion sectors were posting
excellent sales and even better profits. The brand was desirable, for
some consumers even more so than any other label in the industry.
Even in Herzogenaurach, they gradually appeared to have forgot-
ten that the firm had started out with innovative sports equipment
and this was what had made it big. The celebrated football boots
of Pelé, Eusébio and Maradona were preserved in glass display cabinets, and some saw them as belonging to a past world. It was high
time to score points again in the Performance sector as well, particularly in football. Sufficient investment funds were available for
the company to approach the very great players, and to close quite
a bit of the gap on Adidas and Nike. Especially now, when a genuine
home fixture was imminent: the 2006 World Cup in Germany.

In July 2005, Jochen Zeitz appeared before the press to
announce a new chapter in his economic plan. From 2006 onwards,
he explained, phase four would start: Puma would expand and
close in on the top of the market. "We have ample funds available
to invest in areas that will strengthen the brand and the company,"
he said. He approved 500 million euros up to 2010 for organic or
acquisition-based expansion. The Puma brand, as trademark rights
firm semion brand-broker worked out for business magazine
*Capital*, was now worth in excess of 600 million euros. "The recipe
followed by successful brand creators – irrespective of whether they
are launching new products or reviving classics is this: they communicate a strong image, focus on clearly defined target groups,
carefully foster the product and demand brand loyalty from
employees too," explained *Capital*. Everything was going to plan
– save for the ownership structure.

### *A good investment*

Following their surprising entry in the spring of 2005, the Herz investors were able to increase their Puma stake to over 25 percent in September, giving them a blocking minority. The Hamburgers were suddenly able to dictate to the sports equipment group. With their cloak-and-dagger approach, no Mayfair representatives had asked to inspect the company books beforehand, and no bankers had conducted an audit. How did they know that Puma was a good deal? Did they have hidden sources of information? Or did they just want to avoid causing a stir, in case it drove the share price up ahead of the purchase? Was Herz possibly planning to seize the reins, and plant his own children on the Board? The staff in Herzogenaurach, particularly the labour representatives on the Supervisory Board, were in a state of uncertainty: what exactly did the Tchibo man want?

In January 2006, Mayfair manager Kutzner voyaged to darkest Franconia to meet the labour-side Supervisory Board members Katharina Wojaczek and Erwin Hildel. The meeting was a low-key event in a bare conference room at the company's headquarters. Hildel had merely entered "Meeting" as the reason for reserving the room. Kutzner came across calm and relaxed as he sipped a glass of water and started to explain what Mayfair wanted. The audience found him frank. The plan was to create several pillars for Mayfair's assets, said the Herz representative, and analysis had revealed that Puma would be a good one. The engagement was in place for the medium to long term, and they intended to top up further but not take over the company, he reiterated. They had already demanded and got places on the Supervisory Board weeks earlier. Arnon Milchan and David Matalon, who had represented the previous major shareholder Regency since 1997 and 1999 respectively, resigned their mandates with effect from 9 January 2006. In February, Kutzner assumed his place on the Board as the first emissary of the new owner, and he was followed by his boss Günter Herz on 27 April.

The familiar atmosphere in the supervisory team turned uncomfortable with the arrival of the men from Hamburg. In the years before, there had rarely been any fierce arguments. Borne up by success, management and labour had been on cosy terms for many years. The new men on the scene were not greatly concerned with harmony. In the meetings, they focused intensively on the strategic alignment of the company. Although owners of a public limited company are not allowed to intervene in operations in

Germany, Zeitz kept getting calls from Hamburg, for example when a Herz manager had had a bad experience with the presentation or quality of Puma products when out shopping. Herz managers increasingly asked to be put through to Zeitz, and the irritated Puma CEO swallowed it, though he hated anyone meddling in his affairs. His friend and deputy Martin Gänsler, the man with the Harley and the ponytail, could no longer stand life with the exhausting shirt and tie brigade: he announced his retirement at the end of 2007.

## Grumbling shareholders

It was the 27th of April 2006: the rain beat down on Sigmund-strasse in Nuremberg. Towards midday, the first visitors reluctantly left their vehicles in the car park behind number 220 and turned their collars up against the weather. As every year, they were mostly older people with grey hair and beige jackets – anything but life-style customers. They tiptoed across the sea of puddles to the entrance of the Puma Brand Center, where normally the latest collections were shown to business customers. Just one more hour and there would be cause for celebration: the Puma general meeting was imminent and the CEO had decided to propose a doubling of the dividend.

Once through the security system, most of the guests went straight to the catering room where waiting staff dressed in black and white were serving goulash and potato soup with traditional southern German bread. Some of the shareholders left the crowd for the high tables at the wall bearing the vast Puma logo, and stood silently spooning down the hot food. Others stood bunched in small groups, sipping their coffee. The Puma shareholders are a different bunch to those of energy giant E.ON or VW, for example: they don't bolt down as many snacks as they can just because they are free. They have clearly taken on board the CEO's conviction that rigorous economy – even at the buffet during the general meeting – is a prerequisite for high returns.

Shortly before 1 pm, the room was well filled. Amongst the guests, major investor Günter Herz, his son Christian, daughter Michaela and manager Stahl had taken their seats. Herz's wife was unable to travel due to poor health. Zeitz appeared at the lectern wearing a jacket, black trousers and a white shirt with the two top buttons open. He always communicates effectively, but is not exactly one of the most charismatic of speakers – his words were beamed onto a transparent Plexiglas screen in front of him. He reported that Puma's market value since he had taken office in 1993 had risen by over 4,000 percent and that new orders had been over a billion euros for the first time ever. The Herz legation looked relaxed. After just under half an hour, the CEO finished his speech. The applause was brief. Puma shareholders are spoilt. A representative from the Schutzgemeinschaft der Kapitalanleger (the Association for the Protection of Capital Investors) stepped up to the microphone and objected to the "extremely restrictive dividend policy" of the past years. He was speaking for many co-investors: the small shareholders feared they were getting handed comparatively little of the constantly expanding cream cake.

### Black Wednesday

Most of the growth for the future lay in Africa – Zeitz had realized this even before he had signed up the Cameroon national football team. He could make excellent use of the Africans' national spirit – their joie de vivre – to give an emotional charge to the brand. And if Puma was to make a big impact in phase four, then the World Cup in Germany that year, and above all the following World Cup in 2010 in South Africa, was the best vehicle. It was therefore a no-brainer to get on board as a campaign partner of the PR umbrella organization "United for Africa", which supports more than 30 relief organizations. According to its own information, the organization tries to counteract the image of Africa as the "lost continent" and raise awareness not only of the continent's suffering and poverty, but also of the potential it has to offer. Zeitz was primarily concerned with positioning Puma as a close friend of the continent in public and capitalizing on this position in the long term. Africa was a perfect fit with the company's World Cup campaigns.

The kick-off meeting for the collaboration took place on Wednesday, 5 April 2006, in the Berlin Puma store. Zeitz had spent the night in the extravagant Hotel Lux at Rosa-Luxemburg-Strasse 9. Grand accommodation and simple elegance: the exposed concrete walls were painted Chinese porcelain green, tables and chairs were made of bleached white wood. The CEO, who had grown up in an educated, middle-class parental home far removed from the fashion world, felt at home in this cultivated setting. He had an eye for style in his personal life, too: he and his wife had furnished their home in Nuremberg in Pop Art mode, their holiday home in

Ibiza in Bauhaus style, and their farmhouse in Kenya with Bieder-meier and Louis XVI antiques.

The organizers had signed sunny-tempered Ghanaian Anthony Baffoe to present the event. The man with the shaved head appeared on the catwalk in a white t-shirt bearing an imprint of the African Continent, above which a puma leapt in pursuit of a ball. Baffoe, the clever son of a diplomat from Bad-Godesberg near Bonn, was anything but the downtrodden Black African for whom the donors' hearts beat; however, he was the exact personification of the joie de vivre that Zeitz wanted for his brand image. Baffoe was born in 1965, was only a year younger than Zeitz in fact, and had formerly played for the Puma team 1. FC Köln, amongst others. Moreover, he had had the privilege of playing 16 times in Ghana's national team, where home games would regularly spark off cele-brations that lasted for days, even when the team only scored one goal. Some of his jokes have gone down in the history books, for example when faced with a yellow card from a referee – referees in those days were still dressed in black – he said: "Man, we blacks are meant to stick together!" Thimothée Atouba and Guy Demel had also made the journey, two coloured, highly paid stars of Puma sponsorship partner HSV.

Whilst the journalists enjoyed chocolate-covered skewered fruit, cocktails and Orangina at the counter, Zeitz went and sat down between primetime TV presenter Anne Will and United for Africa director Susanne Anger. He felt relaxed, although talking does not rank amongst his favourite occupations. These days Zeitz has to adopt a political stance – although politics is one of his least popular subjects. "Africa and the Puma brand are perfect partners," he gave as the reason for his company's engagement, and he praised the "enthusiasm, elegance and power" of the African foot-ball players. The journalists wanted to know why Puma was surfing the wave of pity and making a lot out of Africa, but did not manu-facture its products there, which could after all give jobs to people with little or no hope. Zeitz wriggled his way out of the question, saying there were some production facilities but basically "the logistics were too complicated". A coloured representative of "Africa TV" fundamentally challenged the purpose of the action and felt that Puma's input was a pure PR manoeuvre. "Africa is poor, down and out. Donations have been coming in for 300 years and nothing has helped." Zeitz retorted: "We have a positive view of the African continent." The television reporter shook his head in disbelief. "Conditions are extremely hard in the slums, but

*Berlin PR tram with Anne Will, mayor Klaus Wowereit, Zeitz (left to right)*

people still enjoy playing football in the fields," Zeitz said in an endeavour to substantiate his opinion.

In conclusion, a handful of young models presented the Puma Charity limited edition collection. For every item sold in the range, which was available at only ten locations, a stated amount would go as a donation to "United for Africa". In the first year, they collected about 500,000 euros by this means. In addition, the charity double act published a CD of African music and a book entitled "The African Game", which were sold at the Puma concept stores, on a Berlin PR tram, and at Café Moskau on Karl-Marx-Allee 34, Puma's PR headquarters during the World Cup. The company had converted the most well-known gastronomic flagship in the former East Germany into the PR and entertainment centre for the World Cup.

### Italy: a summer's fairytale

On 9 June 2006, the most important home fixture in the history of German football began in the Munich Olympic Stadium: the World Cup. Germany beat Costa Rica 4–2. The sun shone and people rejoiced. At Puma in Herzogenaurach, the celebrations were somewhat muted: it was not the Puma World Cup, even though twelve teams wore the cat on their shirts, but an Adidas one. The rival firm from provincial Franconia was fitting out what turned out to be the world champions of all the host nation's hearts – the German team. Although Puma's Italian partners won the tournament, it was Germany coach Jürgen Klinsmann's team who caused most excitement and got the big headlines on their home turf.

Zeitz was not to be found in the football arenas. He was at home in front of the television. He had decided only to go to the stadium if Germany played Italy, which happened in the semi-final. He reckoned he could not lose: he would win either as a patriot or as a sponsor. "If Italy beat Germany then they have to make world champion too, otherwise I will be really mad," he told his colleagues.

The semi-final tie was set for 4 July in Dortmund. Puma wanted to make the most of every aspect of the event for PR purposes. On the Sunday, 2 July, the Puma management decided to hold a press conference for the following day at the Italian camp in Duisburg. The MSV Duisburg arena had been transformed into "Casa Azzurri" for the World Cup. This was not just where the team trained; it was also the Italian football federation's organization and marketing headquarters. There was just one problem, though: all flights from Nuremberg to the Ruhr had been fully booked for a long time. Zeitz took the decision there and then: "I'll fly myself." He chartered a twin-engine plane and flew himself and his entourage north from the airport in Herzogenaurach the next day, making the return journey the same evening. The following morning he got behind the controls again and landed two hours ahead of the kick-off at Dortmund airport. He had a stroke of luck: he had managed to secure the last slot. Even a government plane from Berlin was refused permission to land. The charged atmosphere later on in the stadium sent repeated shivers down the spine even of this man who was usually ruled by his head rather than his heart. At the end he was sorry for Germany. He felt strangely torn: he had won and lost.

Zeitz did not follow the final in the VIP lounge, but watched the match with his brother Reinhard, his friend the former Porsche boss and management consultant Arno Bohn, and six friends from Italy in the heart of the Italian fans' area. As though the gods themselves had a hand in the game, in a dramatic encounter the "Azzurri" secured the win against the équipe tricolore (an Adidas team) in a penalty shoot-out. Even Zeitz's emotions overflowed when Zinédine Zidane, the superstar of the French team, lost his temper in the 110th minute, "nutted" his opponent Marco Materazzi and was sent off. After the game the Puma boss, his brother and Bohn toured the centre of Berlin with his exhilarated Italian

*The Puma boss in the middle of the dream team (2004)*

pals and partied in wild spirits. Then they had something to eat in the vicinity of the Hackeschen Höfe before driving to Café Moskau. In addition to hip live music, there were six football tables and several big screens inside and out.

Business-wise, Zeitz was ahead of the times. On 15 June, when the game between Germany's group opponents Ecuador and Costa Rica in Hamburg ended 3–0, he flew to South Africa to launch the 2010 World Cup at a press conference. This is "his" World Cup, as it could feature five African Puma teams and is set to open up a brand new source of revenue. Zeitz has estimated that sales in Africa could quadruple in the next five to six years.

## 2.11 Men of Honour

### *Puma and ethics: warm words, clean clothes and an unusual doctor's bill*

The World Cup had an impact. The 2006 financial year broke records again on several counts. With sales of almost 2.4 billion euros, 34 percent up on the previous year, Puma had broken through the two-billion-euro barrier for the first time. On average, each of the company's employees, of which there were now almost 7,000, was generating sales of over 370,000 euros a year. The consolidated profit stood at 366 million euros (it had fallen slightly on the previous year's figure as a result of higher investments) and Puma was now valued at around 4.8 billion euros on the stock exchange – 4,300 percent more than in 1993. Shareholders, too, could rub their hands: with a dividend of 2.50 euros per share, they were participating more than ever before in the company's success.

Puma's managers like to claim that with their company everyone is a winner: employees, who share in the company's success through bonus systems, shareholders, who benefit from the rising share price and the dividend, and customers, who can buy top-quality functional or fashionable clothing at a fair price. They argue that even suppliers in low-wage Asian countries such as China or Vietnam, where the vast majority of the Franconians' products are manufactured, can be counted among the winners: jobs and prosperity are being created there, enabling a stable economy to develop. To support this argument, economic decision-makers at government level put forward the thesis that former low-wage economies, like the former "tiger economies" of South Korea, Hong Kong and Taiwan, have been given the means to catch up with the Western industrialized world.

Worldwide, there must be more than 25,000 people involved in the manufacture of Puma products. For many of them, the prosperity thesis does not apply, because of globalization, which has triggered proliferating competition for labour around the globe. What once worked in isolated, controlled markets, i.e. improving the prosperity of the population by means of a controlled foreign economic policy, is no longer possible in the era of extremely mobile or even virtual companies. Corporate groups are making constant efforts to optimize their value chains. If the underlying conditions are no longer right (which, in the case of Puma, not only includes costs, but also production quality, supplier reliability and social standards), they simply move on to the next wage-dumping country – thus increasing the pressure on local businesses to continue to keep wages down. Christliche Initiative Romero e.V. (CIR) of Münster, a Protestant organization that is primarily concerned with the poor in the factories of Central America, even describes a steady decline in the prosperity of employees in many textile factories, some of which also supply goods to Puma. In 2006, CIR reported that in El Salvador employees are paid a state-set minimum wage of around 119 euros. According to government data, four members of a family would need to work full time in the factory to be able to lead a dignified existence. Annual inflation means that the purchasing power of wages is falling all the time – but this cannot be laid at the door of companies like Puma. In El Salvador the minimum wage in the global-market factories rose overall by a mere five percent between 2000 and 2006. Over the same period, the cost of basic food requirements more than doubled.

We cannot blame globalization for failing to ensure that Western social standards are applied. After all, it is not the primary task of business people to impose such standards. Their remit is to increase their company's profit, in accordance with the laws of economics, to enable them to invest further and create jobs. The rules that govern how caring an entrepreneur is obliged to be towards his workforce and business partners can only be drawn up by politicians. And governments in the low-wage countries of Asia and Eastern Europe have a long way to go – in spite of many warm words. General Motors CEO Rick Wagoner once worked out that every vehicle built in the USA includes 1,500 dollars of social costs which ultimately have to be borne by the customer – a Chinese manufacturer such as Chery Automobile is spared this investment, as the millions of meagrely paid migrant workers from China's hinterland have no lobby to demand the money on their behalf. Differences in the environmental costs involved in production have a similar impact.

In summary: anyone who buys a pair of Adidas, Nike or even Puma shoes that have been manufactured in a low-wage country such as China, Vietnam or Turkey is tacitly accepting these unequal living conditions. The same applies to other consumer goods, such as televisions, toys or cars. The vast majority of the inhabitants of industrial nations have to live with this accusation, and this includes Puma's customers. Swiss author Adolf Muschg summarized in one sentence how consumers, with their "cheap is cool" and value-for-money mentality, are partly responsible for the trend in low-wage countries: "There is nothing more neoliberal than the customer." Had Puma continued to manufacture in Germany, other EU countries or the USA, the company's upturn, which saw sales, profit and the firm's share price rise at dizzying rates, would only have been possible if the products had retailed at roughly four times the price.

Nowadays it is the done thing for any global group to emphasize and praise its efforts to maintain social standards in the various countries in which it operates. In most cases the PR department is responsible for managing and communicating these good deeds. The claim is also set out in Puma's annual report:

Puma is aware of its responsibility as a globally operating company. Environmental responsibility is a major component of the company's development strategy. Puma observes the principles of sustained development in all of its activities in order to satisfy today's demands without impairing the opportunities of future generations. The realization of sustainability is underpinned by a Code of Conduct, which is binding for all producers. Through this code Puma acknowledges ethical and social standards in both the individual and corporate areas.

The company's PR staff proudly report that Puma's "S.A.F.E." team monitors standards and that the group is a member of both the Fair Labor Association (FLA) and the UN Global Compact. Of these, the FLA at least lays down strict requirements with regard to the social quality of production facilities. In actual fact, even the critical, independent CIR does not make any concrete accusations against the Herzogenaurach firm. According to Zeitz, in 2006 more than 300 factories were checked, around two-thirds of all Puma suppliers, and over 90 percent were found to be in order – this means that they were paying at least the state minimum wage to the lowest wage groups, as referred to above in the example of El Salvador. CIR employee Maik Pflaum, however, warns against wrong conclusions: the upstanding flagships among a company's supplier partners should not lead us to assume that the situation is anywhere near as satisfactory at these partners' own suppliers.

## Clean clothes

Puma regularly cooperates with organizations that aim to ensure fair working conditions in the countries of production. However, these collaborations are not always fruitful. On 3 May 2002, a conference got under way in Cologne with the name "Fit for fair". It had been organized by the German "Clean Clothes Campaign" (CCC) and the General Students' Committee (AStA) of the German Sport University in Cologne. Important guests had travelled in from Berlin and Frankfurt: Renate Künast, Federal Minister for Consumer Protection, and Manfred von Richthofen, President of the German Sports Association. They were keen to find out about working conditions in the global sportswear industry. Female employees from Indonesia, Bulgaria and Central America reported on the reality of the inhuman conditions in the factories that supplied sports equipment manufacturers. A representative from Puma was also present in the audience and later on the podium: Dr Reiner Hengstmann, Head of Environmental and Social Affairs. At the end of the second day of the conference, he offered to put a few supplier firms under the microscope in a joint project with CIR experts. At that time there were only eight Puma controllers for 150 suppliers, "and they spend more time in the air than on the ground," Hengstmann had to concede.

It took almost four years and a whole host of meetings for this offer to become reality. On 26 January 2006, Puma and CIR announced their one-year collaboration in a joint press release: this would involve "examining the working conditions at direct and indirect Puma suppliers and implementing and expanding independent monitoring and verification of compliance with social standards. Particular attention will be paid to issues specific to women and the direct involvement of local organizations." The checks would therefore be focusing on discrimination against women, overtime and pay, as well as freedom of association and the implementation of the right to collective bargaining. The CCC's code and Puma's own Code of Conduct would serve as a reference. With the exception of the specific personnel costs for CIR employees, Puma would bear the cost of the project.

CIR insisted on examining factories and their subcontractors in Central America, in particular El Salvador, as this was the region it knew most about and in which its own employees were working. However, it was hard to arrange this. Although Puma initially identified two manufacturers who were suitable and willing to take part, one of them unexpectedly broke off business relations with the sports equipment group. As a result of this development, CIR and Puma started to drift apart. The year of their collaboration was drawing to a close and the second factory – which was essential to enable a comparative study to be performed – had still not been found. CIR pushed for a factory in Mexico. This would have cost Puma only 30,000 euros more. The Board in Herzogenaurach promised to provide two-thirds of the investment and demanded a contribution from the CCC. It also proposed an additional project for production sites in Asia, Eastern Europe or Africa, where it purchased the majority of its goods. In the end the entire project collapsed, with both sides laying the blame at each other's door. The moral of the story is that entrepreneurship and benevolence are not easily reconciled.

## Help to help yourself

Sports equipment manufacturers are much freer with their money when it comes to obtaining advantages from cooperative ventures, as this book has made clear. Small gifts maintain a friendship, while big ones maintain business relationships. Puma's current managers are undoubtedly also aware that in this industry what you can take depends to a great extent on what you have already given – and this does not necessarily mean cash.

Take the example of Cameroon: the more the African football team captivated spectators all over the world, the more it became the focus of Puma's financially powerful rivals. Puma spokesman Horst Widmann – for whom "connections" is a favourite term – therefore went all out right from the start to get the necessary officials on side, in particular Mohamed Iya, the president of Cameroon's football federation. Achieving his goal by handing out envelopes stuffed with cash is not really his thing. Widmann is a master of more subtle ways of winning over business partners. For example, he organized all manner of friendly matches, as a result of which plenty of cash flowed into the coffers of Cameroon's football federation. His commitment secured Iya's trust.

When Iya told him that he was suffering from severe diabetes and only had a year to live, Widmann got this well-to-do head manager of a state-owned company into a specialist German diabetes centre. Soon Iya was on the mend. Puma employees like Widmann because he often helps others selflessly. In this case, however, he was hoping that his efforts would pay off when it came to the pending contract extension. Cameroon had grown into a Puma trademark – losing the team would have been a bitter blow. In November 2006, the poker game got under way in the capital city of Yaounde, with all the big manufacturers around the table. Nike, which aims to be the number one company in football by 2010, immediately staked everything on one card. Puma had become too strong in Africa for the Americans' liking. Nike's negotiators started by bidding three times the sum that Puma had offered for the Cameroon contract, eventually increasing this to six times as much. An expensive game to play, as nowadays whoever is awarded the contract in such negotiations has to hand over a signing bonus immediately. This means that part of the sponsorship has to be paid up front, even if the contract does not take effect for a number of years. Widmann called Zeitz over from Germany to apply some moral pressure. The effort they had made over the years to look after the

Cameroonians ultimately bore fruit: Cameroon were not tempted away and remained with Puma. Widmann gave a satisfied smile, even though the Herzogenaurach firm would now have to dig much deeper into its pockets for the right to kit out the indomitable lions.

### "Barça, Barça, Baaarça"

After football's 2006 World Cup, Puma tried to get a really big fish under contract: FC Barcelona, one of the best teams in the world. The Spaniards, under Dutch trainer Frank Rijkaard, had just won the Spanish title for the first time in a number of years. Nike had been pouring millions into the club for years, but the contract was now running out. When Nike's scouts told their head office in Beaverton, Oregon, about the Herzogenaurach firm's visit to the club's administrative centre, Nike chief Mark Parker got cold feet and suddenly doubled his offer. Zeitz nevertheless believed that he was close to landing the biggest deal in Puma's history. And with good reason: during the briefings, which Zeitz conducted in Spanish, Barcelona's club president Joan Laporta y Estruch claimed that he harboured a grudge against Nike and wanted to switch to Puma at all costs. He even drafted a "letter of intent" for a cooperation. When they said goodbye, he flung his arms around Zeitz and swore everlasting friendship.

In the end, however, money talked. Laporta turned the Puma boss down in two blunt sentences: Nike had submitted the better offer. It was worth over 30 million euros a year. And Laporta needed the money. When he took up his post in 2003, Barcelona were said to have had debts in the region of 180 million euros. He also had a penchant for buying the world's top players for big money: he brought in Ronaldinho from Paris Saint-Germain, Ludovic Giuly from AS Monaco, Samuel Eto'o from Real Mallorca, Mark van Bommel from PSV Eindhoven and Deco from FC Porto.

## 2.12 The Day After Tomorrow

### The future of the big cat: offline in the bush, trouble with the coffee roaster and a welcome fashion house

23 February 2007. Nairobi charter airport, Kenya. It was 9.02 am and a single-engine Piper was taxiing towards the runway. Pilot Derek Sutton, an experienced bush pilot with 20,000 flying hours

under his belt, looked once again at the navigation instrument through his yellow-tinted aviator sunglasses and set the correct course: 230 kilometres due north. In the back pocket of his seat there was a plate-sized wooden cross. Sitting next to him was a man who would have dearly loved to take the controls himself: Jochen Zeitz, himself an amateur pilot of 20 years' standing. He had flown with KLM from Nuremberg via Amsterdam to the Kenyan capital the day before and had spent the night in the chic Serena Hotel. Now, he wanted to get to his farm as quickly as possible and relax for a couple more days, before visiting projects in Uganda with the aid organization "United for Africa", for which Puma collects donations. Rather, he wanted to relax and work as he did so. He can't do one without the other.

The plane took off and broke through the dense yellow fog that wafted over Nairobi. Here, smog is as much a part of life as the air you breathe. The flight would take an hour. The Piper flew over the slums of the capital city, which are inhabited by around one million people. Right behind them, on an area of green, a herd of giraffes filed past. On they flew over the undulating highlands with their extensive tea and coffee plantations. In the distance, the contours of Mount Kenya were visible, its 5,200-metre high glaciers sparkling in the sun. The green of the earth gradually disappeared in the rain shadow of the mountain and, below the Piper, the steppe began. A herd of elephants romped about at a waterhole. "They are on farmland," said Zeitz and pressed his forehead against the side window. He had bought the 200 $km^2$ area of his farm privately two years previously and now managed it.

Pilot Derek circled one more time and touched down gently on the ranch's grass landing strip. The plane rumbled towards the house, which was bedecked with palm branches. Zeitz ate a second breakfast on the covered terrace: tea, sausages and fresh fruit. He did not speak English with the servants, but Swahili. He had studied the language of the local people by listening to a CD on car journeys between his home in Nuremberg and Herzogenaurach and now had a reasonable grasp of it. In this way he hoped to get a little closer to the country, the people and the culture.

For 13 years, he had scoured half of Africa to find a property like the ranch. He had travelled with his wife to Tanzania, Namibia, Zimbabwe, South Africa, Botswana, Cameroon and many other countries, but had not been able to find anything suitable. Then, at the 2005 Australian Grand Prix, Flavio Briatore, the Formula 1 manager, had given him the crucial tip about the farm in Kenya.

*Zeitz on his farm in Kenya: new shirts for the employees*

Zeitz had flown there and, as another party appeared to be ready to sign, closed the deal within 48 hours.

The farm employed 130 Africans. Zeitz worked flat out here, just as if he were going through the lean years at Puma once again. Get out of the red, invest in the brand, then create growth. He had not bought the farm to make money, however. When he took it on, there was a prevailing sense of lethargy, cliquishness and corruption amongst the staff – reminiscent of Herzogenaurach in 1993. He restructured the operation and invested in it. There are plans to build a new school, a new village for the families of the gamekeepers and cowherds, and a research station. In addition, a "Zeitz Foundation for Intercultural Ecosphere Protection" (Zeitz Stiftung für Interkulturellen Ecosphaeren-Schutz) was being set up that he intended to finance and collect donations for himself. In order to lower the costs of his African engagement and to create new jobs, he is also planning a luxury camp for safari tourists. It should cost up to 700 dollars to spend a night under canvas there – as soon as the site is finished.

The ranch is a gift of creation. Virtually nowhere else in Kenya has such a plentiful stock of giraffes, elephants, buffaloes and other wild animals as this stretch of land. Zeitz enjoyed this abundance – despite all the problems that the land brought with it. Driving his Toyota Land Cruiser over the bumpy natural tracks, he did not have to be on the look out for long before spotting wild animals.

*Waiting for elephants at the waterhole*

A paradise, but with a snag for managers like the Puma boss: there were only a few places with mobile phone reception. Every few minutes he would try to call up e-mails on his BlackBerry – to no avail. A wireless network was only just in the process of being set up. He was only able to find a connection to the world in his emergency office in the manager's house, which was two kilometres away from the main house. There he was able to log onto the World Wide Web via satellite. Even when spending his weekends or holidays there amidst the lions and leopards, he never lost sight of the Puma. He had created a virtual company that functioned fully at all times, regardless of where in the world the CEO happened to be.

Observers of Zeitz in Africa soon realized how he had managed to achieve one of the most glittering corporate growth stories of the post-war period in Germany: his achievement awoke a passion within him to take on apparently hopeless projects, to get them back on their feet and re-establish them. It didn't matter to him if the projects – like the farm – were over 6,000 kilometres away from his home. The same drive had led him as a young CEO to leave the company headquarters in Herzogenaurach for five years in the mid-1990s in order to take a personal hand in focusing his company on the American market 6,000 kilometres away in Boston. Zeitz created virtual working environments as if it were the most natural thing in the world. It did not bother him if he had to make decisions without being physically present. Nothing gave him a greater kick than success. The loyalty of the Puma employees towards their top boss was almost uncanny.

We have already seen how Zeitz's way of working is in many ways reminiscent of the methods employed by the former national football coach Jürgen Klinsmann, who, during the preparations for the 2006 World Cup in Germany, slaughtered sacred cows by the dozen in order to get his own way. Zeitz had not formed alliances with anyone either, be they employees, association members or competitors. The guiding principle for his decisions was always his rationality. And if he did make a decision on gut instinct, he would then check it using the instruments of reason.

Keeping an eye on everything, always being ready to attack and defend – these are skills that he has perfected over the years. When he meets new people or enters unknown realms, his eyes work like scanners recording data and sending it to the brain where it is quickly processed and classified. He hones this ability at home with his fitness and boxing coach. "Jochen, where's the remote control?" he calls to him unexpectedly in the middle of a sparring session. The Puma boss then has to locate the device in a flash without dropping his guard.

Back to Kenya. The weekend on the farm flew by. On Monday, Zeitz had to move on to Uganda. There, he met representatives of the "United for Africa" aid alliance. He wanted to take a look at relief projects for which Puma had collected money during the World Cup. The contrast with Kenya was striking: foul-smelling refugee camps in the war-torn area of Kitgum, poverty-stricken villages in Gulu and aged leprosy sufferers in Combra. "Dreadful!" Zeitz often sighed during the visits. And he wracked his brain for explanations of and solutions to this incomprehensible misery.

In the middle of the jungle, a different Puma boss was revealed: the man behind the tireless manager who sells things that, actually, nobody really needs. He philosophized about life and joked around with his travelling companions. He listened in horror to the child soldiers as they told how they had been forced to kill their own parents. Affectionately, he ruffled the hair of the orphans in their blue school uniforms who clung to his arm. As he left the leprosy station, he put a CD of spirituals on the car stereo and turned it up: "Oh happy day"! In the evening in the bush plane, which bore the inscription "To the Glory of the Lord" and brought the group to a simple hotel in Gulu, he read Sigmund Freud's work *Moses and Monotheism*. He worked through the pages underlining

*Group photo with women in Uganda*

passages like a student. He wanted to find out whether religion was just an obsessional neurosis, as the founder of psychoanalysis claimed, or whether a God was responsible for everything.

In the middle of nowhere in Uganda, where people have to survive on just half a dollar a day, his mobile phone showed it had a full signal. He was, however, only able to use the telephone, not to receive e-mails. His fingers flew over the buttons, his legs once again jigging vigorously. Three days without incoming mail – he had never been cut off from his virtual mail box for so long. In his hotel room in Gulu, where, because of a three-day power cut, a generator rattled in the back yard, he learned from the television that the stock market had slumped due to bad news from China. Zeitz grabbed his BlackBerry and phoned Germany. He bought more Puma shares for the company. His belief in the company is stubborn.

### Out with the coffee roaster

Perhaps Zeitz was so thoughtful and detached during this period because life as the Puma boss was not proving to be much fun. His relationship with the principal shareholder Herz had never been particularly warm, even though he valued and respected the Hamburg man's business achievements. The team from Hamburg had come on too strong after joining Puma and immediately burned their bridges with a number of managers. The worlds of Mayfair and Puma were simply too different. Outwardly, Zeitz never let any of this show. Under no circumstances did he want to start a conflict. Only his closest associates at Puma noticed that something was not right. For two whole years he swallowed his frustration so as not to trigger any public controversy, and worked together with the team from Hamburg as well as he could, hoping for an eventual solution to the smouldering problem. However, the northern entrepreneur and his men were intervening in the day-to-day business of Puma with increasing frequency. According to enquiries made by *manager magazine*, they had driven away deputy CEO Martin Gänsler by doing so. Too often Herz's representatives let it be known that Mr Herz was not satisfied with this, that or the other. The Puma world lost its relaxed atmosphere and Supervisory Board meetings became agony. Herz put forward his arguments using a retailer's logic and tried to steer the company's development in a direction that was acceptable to him. Despite all their differences, Zeitz endeavoured to draw something positive from the constellation. When he decided, for example, to get involved in sailing as a sponsor, it was passionate sailor Herz who established the necessary contacts with the cup management of the "Volvo Ocean Race", the toughest world regatta, which is held every three years. In Zeitz's opinion the sport was perfectly suited to Puma's brand image. He positioned the race as the rebellious antithesis to the "elitist America's Cup", as he called the annual top yachting competition in which the teams have budgets of 100 million dollars and more.

However, the pressure that was building up between the Puma management team and the Hamburg visitors was growing all the time. Zeitz's contract as CEO still had until April 2009 to run. Normally, when all was well, the contract was extended two years before it expired – at the latest, therefore, in April 2007. Zeitz hesitated. Should he really sign again under these circumstances? It was clear that inwardly he did not believe in long-term success with Herz as a shareholder. But in the eyes of the Hamburg clan, Zeitz was Puma and Puma was Zeitz. In the long history of the company, he, and only he, had succeeded in achieving such high profit rates for the shareholders. Did they want to take the risk of having to continue without Zeitz? And what would be the alternative? To sell the share package again?

Zeitz reckoned that if he were to present Günther Herz with a buyer interested in his Puma shares and he could profit handsomely from it, perhaps he might take the opportunity and go. The Puma boss already had a suitable candidate in mind. Since 2004, when he was wanted as the head of Gucci, he had kept in touch with François-Henri Pinault, the boss of the financially strong French group PPR, which was looking for new global brands with potential. Such an investor was the ideal partner for Zeitz: Pinault was multilingual, had an affinity for the Internet and was equipped with the best distribution channels in the world of luxury goods. Not a tie-wearer who did not understand Puma's corporate culture and saw the emotional world of sportlifestyle and fashion items as being no different from that of coffee beans or espresso machines.

*Puma boat for the Volvo Ocean Race*

For a long time, François-Henri Pinault, born on 28 May 1962 in Brittany, had had to live in the shadow of his famous father, François Pinault, who had forged the luxury goods and trading group in the 1980s and '90s with strong hands. His son grew up in Rennes with his mother, whose marriage to François Pinault had failed, and joined his father's company after studying business management. There followed a permanent war between the generations. In 2005, François-Henri was permitted to take over the helm alone. His father delivered the news to him over a glass of Château Latour, one of France's finest red wines, from the company's own vineyard near Bordeaux. With the Gucci, Yves Saint Laurent and Stella McCartney brands as well as the Conforama (furniture), Fnac (media) and Redcats (home shopping and e-commerce) chain stores, PPR generated sales of around 18 billion euros in 2006.

### Rich kid

Suddenly, François-Henri, the "fils de papa", as the French call a son born to rich parents, was in the public eye – at first not so much because of his entrepreneurial success but rather courtesy of his relationship with smouldering Mexican actress Salma Hayek, who had become famous with roles in films such as *Frida* and *Wild Wild West*, and also as the advertising face of cosmetics group

Avon. The captain of industry and the film diva – a match made in heaven for Hollywood reporters and the popular press. Shortly before the takeover of Puma, the couple had divulged the story of how they had met and fallen in love, a romance in Venice, to colourful French magazine *Paris Match*. It had also been announced that "FHP", as he is referred to in Parisian high society, and his fiancée were expecting a baby. François-Henri already had two children from his first marriage. According to friends, he preferred a life of harmony to the brutal world of business. It is said that on one occasion he barely slept a wink for three whole nights when he was forced to make staff at a subsidiary redundant.

The meeting with Mayfair, Herz's company, proved less difficult for him. On Tuesday 20 March 2007, Pinault, Zeitz, Puma Supervisory Board member Thore Ohlsson and one of Herz's representatives met for the first time in Hamburg's luxury Hotel Vierjahreszeiten to begin talks. When they left, nothing whatsoever had been decided. Herz was keeping any thoughts about which way he would jump to himself and told the other parties that he would let them know his decision by no later than 12 noon on Easter Monday, 9 April. Twenty nerve-shredding days began, fluctuating between hope and fear. The patriarch wanted to be the only person to decide on the future of the company, regardless of what the other 73 percent of shareholders thought.

On Maundy Thursday, the first rumours that Puma was to have a new investor reached the market. The speculation was heightened by the fact that the group had called in 1.27 million shares, thereby reducing its share capital, to create more scope to buy up its own stock. In the afternoon of that day, the correspondent from the *Wall Street Journal* called Herzogenaurach and asked for comments on the results of his research, which were suggesting that PPR would be the new owner. He had spoken to managers of the French firm and was incredibly well informed. Puma's representatives said nothing. The next day, the *Wall Street Journal* reported that PPR would be taking a stake in Puma, and the floodgates opened. Puma's Head of Communications, Ulf Santjer, was not allowed to comment on the events. He would not have been able to in any case, as nobody in Herzogenaurach knew at that point whether Herz would accept or decline PPR's offer.

The media ran through all the possible scenarios. Hamburg's *Welt* newspaper reported: "The majority shareholder of sports equipment manufacturer Puma, equity investment company Mayfair, evidently does not plan to sell its shares to French luxury goods group PPR." The Franconians read these lines in horror, as they assumed that the journalists of the newspaper, run by the publishing house Springer, were well informed about the investor's plans. Zeitz, sitting at his desk at home in Nuremberg, was on standby every second of the day so that he could respond when necessary.

### The night of the decision

Easter Monday, the deadline for the decision, drew closer. When the clock struck midday, Herz had still not been in touch. Hour after hour passed, but the telephone resolutely refused to ring. It was not until precisely 2.22 am on the Tuesday morning that Zeitz received the call he was waiting for from Hamburg: Herz was selling to PPR. The price was 1.4 billion euros for a 27.1 percent stake, which meant that he had earned approximately 600 million euros in just under two years. Pinault wanted more, however. He also made an offer to the company's other shareholders of 330 euros per share. He wanted to pay 5.3 billion euros in total for Puma. The share price rocketed, far exceeding the 330 euro mark.

Zeitz was more than happy. As far as he was concerned there were only winners: Herz had realized a healthy profit in just two years, Puma's shareholders could be confident of receiving a princely premium and for the first time the company had a strategic investor. His closest confidants later described this as a masterstroke on his part. Having sharpened his intellectual powers in his youth by playing chess, he would probably describe it as the perfect game.

Zeitz immediately set the PR machine in motion. At 3.30 am the ad-hoc announcement of the intended sale ran across the ticker. Santjer notified employees across the globe via the intranet and woke key financial journalists from their slumbers with phone calls. After just an hour's sleep, he sent the official press release at 8.00 am: "The Board of Puma AG welcomes the acquisition of the shares of Mayfair Beteiligungsfondsgesellschaft by French luxury goods company Pinault-Printemps-Redoute (PPR), as well as the intended voluntary public offer to Puma's shareholders. With its phase-four expansion strategy in mind, this means that Puma is not only receiving the support of a financially powerful and leading international group, but is also benefiting simultaneously from its global orientation, strong portfolio of premium brands and know-how and experience in the area of retailing."

Würzburger Strasse has rarely seen as much activity as it did the day after the decision. Radio reporters stopped members of staff and asked them whether they feared for their jobs after the arrival of PPR. A never-ending stream of reporters rang or arrived in person to ask for interviews with Zeitz. He concentrated his efforts on just a few selected media, such as the television news programmes *Tagesschau* and *heute-journal*. To them, he confirmed that no job cuts or plant closures were planned. He then stepped in front of the microphone on the channels CNBC and n-tv and appeared directly from Nuremberg on the German morning news show *ZDF-Morgenmagazin*. His message got through. Almost all media and analysts followed his reasoning about the positive aspects of the change of shareholder. Only a few commentators reminded the public that PPR mainly knew about fashion and had no experience whatsoever in the area of sports products, which Zeitz wanted to push strongly in phase four, or mentioned how difficult it had been for Adidas-Salomon or aerospace group EADS to reconcile German and French corporate cultures.

The next day the General Meeting of Shareholders took place at the Puma Brand Center in Nuremberg. Never before had so many outside broadcasting units been clustered around the site. Zeitz chatted cheerfully in the foyer. You would never have guessed that for days on end he had been involved in a negotiation marathon. When Günter Herz and his Hamburg entourage approached, grim-faced, he quickly made his way to the podium: "Ah, the people from Hamburg are coming – I'd better get into the hall," an editor from *manager magazin* heard him say. During the meeting, Herz, as an ordinary member of the Supervisory Board, sat behind Zeitz. When Zeitz officially thanked him for having made the cooperation with PPR possible, Herz did not bat an eyelid. Exactly why Herz got out is a question that he only answered cryptically at the time: "My reasons are very complex. Ultimately I put the company's well-being first."

The real reason will probably remain a secret until one of the protagonists divulges exactly what happened during the negotiations. Zeitz remains silent and has never uttered a bad word about his former major shareholder. He stressed that Herz ultimately made a positive contribution by his investment in Puma, by buying the shares at a time when numerous investors were once again taking a critical view of the newly proposed phase four of the company's plans. Today he merely gives a mischievous smile when the subject of the Herz era and his departure is mentioned.

On the evening after the General Meeting, Pinault, together

with his fellow managers, disappeared into Nuremberg's traditional brewhouse "Barfüßer", where he polished off a knuckle of
pork and two portions of barbecued sausage. Zeitz flew to Vienna
to explain Puma's strategy for football's next European Championships in Austria and Switzerland to a gathering of international
sports retailers. For the first five minutes of his speech he put his
manuscript aside and spoke off the cuff about the opportunities
that he hoped the new strategic partnership with PPR would open
up. After only three hours' sleep, at 10.30 am the next day, Zeitz
opened the first joint press conference with Pinault. Puma
employees were able to follow the event all over the globe, as it
was broadcast live on the web. At the company's Franconian
headquarters people crouched in front of a big screen in the
"North America" room. Their collective relief at the departure of
the old shareholder and the arrival of the new one was almost
tangible.

### Captain Future

On 24 April 2007 it was unusually warm in Berlin. The thermom-
eter had already passed the 20 degrees Celsius mark just before
midday. Taxis were pulling up in front of the Hotel Maritim in
Stauffenbergstrasse practically every minute, dropping off young
people from all corners of the globe: Southern Europeans, Americans, Scandinavians, Asians, Africans.

None of them was sporting a smart black suit, as is usually the
case at this classy establishment. Instead, they were kitted out in
fashionable, sporty leisurewear – shirts, sneakers, baggy trousers
and, in some cases, pool shoes bearing the Puma logo. The Puma
non-conformist uniform. And rather than leather briefcases, they
were carrying mobile phones, sometimes more than one. From
their shoulders hung casual fabric bags, giving the impression that
they were going on holiday rather than attending a business conference. Never before had there been so many laptops inside the
Maritim at once.

Looking relaxed and constantly communicating is part of your
job at Puma. Especially on this particular Monday, the day that
would see the start of the international meeting "Go Live 2". Many
participants used the regular Puma strategy and order fair as an
opportunity to parade around in their own country's products.
This display of exhibitionism would bring a smile to the face of
many outsiders – for Puma's management, however, it is a symbol

of unity. If Puma employees, who are themselves a sub-set of the target group, desire the company's products and feel good in them, there is a good chance that they will be successful on the market.

In the foyer, beneath a huge chandelier, Puma staff were surfing the web. Others had formed little groups and were chatting – in English, of course. At the sides of the entrance hall hung four banners describing the most important product areas for 2008: "Puma Runway", the sports footwear and apparel division, "Urban Mobility", fashion products for hip city dwellers, "V-Speed", the football boot for the European Championships in Austria and Switzerland, and "The Black Label", clothing from the luxury sports collection.

To find out what Puma's developers around the globe had conjured up, delegates paid a visit to the "Berlin" room. There, lined up on dozens of partition walls, were all the shoes that national purchasers could include in their ranges. These had been arranged in groups with specific themes and names such as "Heritage", "Performance", "Training", "Golf" or "Sandals". In the hall opposite, the same had been done with apparel. One of the trends that Puma wanted to push on the market in 2008 was that of pop-art designs on footwear and clothing. Wearing Roy Lichtenstein on your feet may not be exactly new in the fashion world, but it is an old rule in the sector that "everything makes a comeback" – as long as the industry wants it to.

It was year number 15 under CEO Jochen Zeitz and everyone present radiated a willingness to continue the battle against the industry's big names, particularly Nike and Adidas, and overcome the drop in orders that was looming. On 7 May 2007 Zeitz had to issue a profit warning for the first time ever when presenting the company's quarterly figures: for the year in progress, he anticipated that the percentage growth in sales and profit would be in the lower single digits only. Previously, he had predicted a percentage rise in sales in the mid to high single digits, while profit was expected to increase by at least ten percent.

It was the American market in particular, where much depended on the success of the Foot Locker chain, that was – once again – giving Puma cause for concern. In the USA the order book had declined by almost 18 percent over the first quarter, following years of growth. Stock exchange operators and analysts racked their brains: was the industry's sprinter merely pausing for breath? Or was its winning streak gradually coming to an end? Perhaps the Franconians had even underplayed the company's position to keep

*Zeitz with Pinault (at right)*
*and Puma partners Lydia*
*Hearst and Rivaldo*

the share price down and thereby help new investor PPR with its offer of 330 euros to free floaters? Zeitz dismissed these last two points as "absurd".

It was a matter of scarcely two weeks before Puma had grounds for celebration again – on two counts: on 19 May 2007, the last day's play of the Bundesliga season, VfB Stuttgart won the "Meister-schale" – the Football Championship – and, one week later, became runners-up in the German Cup. The Puma logo was resplendent on the red shirts of the jubilant footballers on the news front pages. Puma had put the Swabians under contract in 2002. The "young maniacs" fitted perfectly into the portfolio and, just one year later, had made it into the Champions League. Against the advice of his managing director for Germany, Zeitz had extended the contract in 2005. It had been another example of the Puma boss following his gut instinct and his head.

The party continued but the questions remained: how long would Zeitz continue to do the job? Money alone was probably no longer enough to tempt him: in 2006 alone, he had received a salary of around 7.2 million euros – enough to finance a luxurious existence without having to work for the rest of his life. It was not even really possible for him to top his success as a manager: at the time of Pinault's arrival, he had almost always achieved two-digit growth in sales in 34 quarters in succession. Would he extend his employment contract with PPR, just so that he could still be head of the company for the football World Cup in South Africa in

*Friends for life?*

2010? Would he stay even if the French absorbed Puma entirely and removed it from the stock market? Would he be satisfied with the role of a managing director in the PPR Group? Or would he then start to take calls from a head-hunter or two after all, something that until now he had done his best to avoid?

It may be assumed that it was already pretty clear at this point what position had been envisaged for Zeitz at PPR. He was appointed as a member of the Executive Committee and a non-voting member of the Board of Directors of PPR later that year.

There was much shuffling of chairs as early as the summer of 2007, both in front of and behind the scenes. Pinault became the new Chairman of the Supervisory Board. Following the conclusion of the takeover bid, PPR held 62.1 percent of the voting rights in Puma. The management got down to re-organizing the Managing Board. As a successor to Martin Gänsler, Zeitz acquired Melody Harris-Jensbach. The American, who had lived in Germany for 22 years, had just turned 46 and came from Esprit. As of 2008, it was planned for her to take over the board remits of Product, Product Development, Design, Business Unit Management and Worldwide Sourcing – and to achieve new records.

It is impossible to foretell whether Puma will remain that breathtakingly successful company with headquarters in provincial Franconia or whether, one day, it will be assimilated further into the PPR Group. One thing is certain – the Puma story, which began on 20 June 1948 on Würzburger Strasse in the small

Franconian town of Herzogenaurach, will continue. Whether or not it is a success story will be decided by the managers of the future. They will find the right recipe for success in the words of the Danish philosopher Søren Kierkegaard: "Life can only be understood backwards; but it must be lived forwards."

**3**

# Chronology

| | |
|---|---|
| **1898** | Rudolf Dassler is born on 29 April. |
| **1923** | The Dasslers open their first factory. Year's sales: 3,357 reichsmarks. |
| **1924** | Concentration on sports shoes: Gebrüder Dassler Sportschuhfabrik Herzogenaurach is founded on 1 July. |
| **1931** | Annual sales rise to the healthy sum of 245,649 reichsmarks. |
| **1933** | Hitler seizes power on 30 January. |
| **1935** | The Dassler factory turns over almost 400,000 reichsmarks – 35 percent more than in the previous year. |
| **1936** | Jesse Owens, wearing Dassler shoes, wins four gold medals at the Olympic Games in Berlin. |
| **1940** | Pure production of sports footwear only is forbidden. Adolf Dassler is briefly called up to the army in December. |
| **1943** | Rudolf has to serve in the war. |
| **1945** | Rudolf flees before the advancing Russians. On 2 April, his father Christoph dies. |
| **1946** | Rudolf is released from Hammelburg internment camp where he has been held by the Americans. |
| **1948** | On 20 June, Sportschuhfabrik Rudolf Dassler is entered in the Commercial Register. The existing business assets are divided up. |
| **1952** | Son Armin Dassler joins the management and takes over distribution for the USA. |
| **1955** | Odour-blocking footwear is developed |
| **1956** | Puma outfits the US Olympic team. |
| **1957** | The factory building is extended. |
| **1958** | The Formstrip becomes the trademark. Rudolf's wife Friedl Dassler and sons Armin and Gerd become shareholders. |
| **1959** | The company is converted to a limited commercial partnership and becomes Puma-Sportschuhfabriken Rudolf Dassler KG. |
| **1960** | Puma invents the Lastic sole. |
| **1962** | Armin Dassler sets up his first branch factory in Salzburg. |
| **1963** | The Forth branch factory is set up for the manufacture of special footwear and running shoes |
| **1966** | A branch factory for training shoes is set up in Reckendorf, near Bamberg. |
| **1967** | Gerd Dassler sets up the Soufflenheim branch factory. The US business booms. |

**1968** The modern Puma logo is born.

**1970** Pelé wears the Puma "King".

**1974** On 26 October, Rudolf Dassler dies. He is succeeded by his son Armin.

**1975** Puma includes sports textiles in its assortment.

**1976** The world market for sports footwear grows to more than five billion dollars. Puma is the number four player.

**1977** In March, Armin Dassler announces that substantial portions of production will be transferred abroad in order to benefit from lower production and wage costs.

**1978** Puma's sales reach the 500 million mark point and the company employs around 5,000 workers.

**1979** Puma "discovers" Lothar Matthäus, the son of the janitor.

**1983** A new central warehouse is established in Oberreichenbach.

**1984** Tennis rackets are included in the product range.

**1985** The RS computerized running shoe with integrated sensor and mini computer is Puma's latest invention. Puma partner Boris Becker wins Wimbledon.

**1986** On 16 June, the company goes public. Issue price of the shares: 310 marks.

**1987** The Dassler brothers resign from management and move up to the Supervisory Board. After an intermezzo with Vinzenz Grothgar, Hans Woitschätzke becomes the new CEO.

**1988** Puma deteriorates into a cheap brand.

**1989** The Dassler heirs sell their shares to trading group Cosa Liebermann.

**1990** Jochen Zeitz joins the company. The Swedish group Aritmos becomes the new principal shareholder. Armin Dassler dies on 14 October. Puma's debts come to 180 million marks.

**1991** Stefan Jacobsson becomes the new CEO.

**1992** The Puma "disc" is launched.

**1993** Nils Stenhoj takes over briefly as CEO. Proventus becomes the new principal shareholder. On 1 May, Jochen Zeitz becomes CEO. The share price reaches an all-time low. Production in Herzogenaurach is discontinued. Restructuring begins. Zeitz introduces his phased economic plan.

**1994** Puma is back in profit. The bank pool is dissolved. The street soccer competition is held for the first time.

**1996** Previous licensee Puma North America, Inc. becomes a wholly owned subsidiary of the Group.

**1997** The US film production and distribution company Monarchy/Regency Enterprises becomes the major shareholder.

**1998** Phase two of the long-term corporate development begins. Cooperation with designer Jil Sander. Tennis star Serena Williams signs a promotion agreement. The brand appears for the first time in Hollywood films such as *City of Angels*.

**1999** The first "concept store" opens in Santa Monica, California. Serena Williams wins the US Open.

**2000** Collaboration with Christy Turlington. The Puma-backed national football team of Cameroon wins the African Cup of Nations.

**2001** Entry into Formula 1.

**2002** Four-year contract with the Italian national football team. Phase three of the long-term corporate development begins.

**2003** Monarchy/Regency sells up. Puma is left without a major shareholder. For the first time, sales come to more than one billion euros.

**2004** A one-piece kit for the Cameroon team leads to a row with FIFA. Designer Philippe Starck works for Puma. Michael Schumacher becomes a new sponsorship customer.

**2005** Mayfair Vermögensverwaltungsgesellschaft mbH, owned by Hamburg businessman Günter Herz, comes in as Puma's new major shareholder.

**2006** Start of phase four of the long-term corporate development. Start of cooperation with "United for Africa". The Puma footballers of the Italian national team win the football World Cup in Germany.

**2007** Mayfair sells its shares to French group Pinault-Printemps-Redoute (PPR). Puma starts sponsoring the "Volvo Ocean Race" sailing competition and announces that it is to participate in the Volvo Ocean Race 2008/2009. PPR acquires 62.1 percent of Puma shares. Puma and Peace One Day team up to support Global Peace Day. Groundbreaking ceremony for new headquarters at Puma Plaza in Herzogenaurach.

**2008**     Puma celebrates its 60th anniversary. At the Africa Cup in Ghana, Puma, with a portfolio of 9 out of 16 African teams, is the clear No. 1 sponsor in Africa. At Euro 2008, the host teams, Austria and Switzerland, are both sponsored by Puma. At the Olympic Games in Beijing, Puma sponsors 17 national teams including Jamaica, Sweden and Morocco. Puma enters the Volvo Ocean Race 2008/2009 with its own boat.